C T.

The New Atlas

Or, travels and voyages in Europe, Asia, Africa and America

C T.

The New Atlas

Or, travels and voyages in Europe, Asia, Africa and America

ISBN/EAN: 9783337318734

Printed in Europe, USA, Canada, Australia, Japan

Cover: Foto ©Andreas Hilbeck / pixelio.de

More available books at **www.hansebooks.com**

THE
NEW ATLAS:
OR,
Travels and Voyages
IN

Europe, Asia, Africa and *America*,
Thro' the most Renowned Parts of the

WORLD,
VIZ.

From *England* to the *Dardanelles*, thence to *Constantinople, Ægypt, Palestine,* or the Holy Land, *Syria, Mesopotamia, Chaldea, Persia, East-India, China, Tartary, Muscovy,* and by *Poland*; the *German Empire, Flanders* and *Holland,* to *Spain* and the *West-Indies*; with a brief Account of *Æthiopia,* and the Pilgrimages to *Mecha* and *Medina* in *Arabia,* containing what is Rare and Worthy of Remarks in those vast Countries; relating to Building, Antiquities, Religion, Manners, Customs, Princes, Courts, or Affairs Military and Civil, or whatever else of any kind is worthy of Note.

Performed by an *English* Gentleman, in Nine Years Travel and Voyages, more exact than Ever.

LONDON, Printed for *J. Cleave* in *Chancery-Lane* near *Serjeant's Inn,* and *A. Roper* at the *Black Boy* in *Fleet-street,* 1698.

TO THE

Ingenious Reader,

THE

PREFACE.

THE desire of Travel, and Voyaging to distant Lands, is so Natural to an Active Genious, that but few who have not had the opportunity of putting it in Action, have been no less desirable of such an improving undertaking. By what is visible in one's Native Country, there is no exalted Mind but must consequently tend to a higher elevation in Knowledge, to furnish it with a Completion of those wonderful things the scanty Globe Communicates to the Sight and Senses, so to enable one to give a true Judgment in difference of Countries, and

A 2 *what*

what is Rare and Remarkable in them. To this end, Princes have laid aside their Regal Ornaments, and the exuberant Pleasures of Thrones for a time, taking on them the Fateigue of long Journeys, through many dangers and difficulties, that so they might inform themselves of the certainty of things, and Affairs worthy to be entertained in the repositories of Royal Breasts, and to be the concern of Majesty. I need not enumerate Ancient Examples for this, one very Modern may suffice, to evidence Truth of what I Attest. It is well known how the Great and Powerful Czar of Muscovy, *in the midst of War shrouding Majesty in a mean disguise; left his Spacious Country and Armies Contesting with the mighty Nations of* Turks *and* Tartars, *making a tedious Journey to inform himself in those Matters; of which, at Home, he conceived he had but an imperfect Relation; also to pollish his pregnant Genious in the refined Courts of other Princes, and in all probability*
met

The Preface.

met with a *satisfaction* that made him conclude his *Time* and *Travel* well bestowed and undertaken.

I need not much enforce an Argument to perswade the Ingenious that Travel, renders a Man very much accomplished, and often raises his Fortune above the common level. It has been seen in Ancient and Modern *Ages*, whilst such as have supinely loytered away their Moments of Life, under the umbrage of their own Mansion, have made no figure in the World, whilst they remained in it; and when they dropt from the stage of Mortality were soon wrapped in Oblivion. But to come somewhat nearer to my purpose;

In this History of my Travels through many vast Countries, I have been very exact to set down nothing but what with much Care and Circumspection occurrred to me; where any thing is mentioned, as by Hear-say, which is but scanty. I had

The Preface.

had it in Conversing with those knowing, and, as I nearly conclude, of much Integrity, every thing bearing a probability and consonance to Truth. The whole Work is free from Impossibilities, or any thing that may carry the face of Romantick Stories or Fables, you may easily perceive in Reading, where I was an occular and aureal Witness, and where I had only informations from others, which contribute but a very little part of what I have Written. I have as much as possible affected Brevity, and must presume to say, that none who have gone before me, have in Large Volumes comprized so much material matter. I Writ it indeed at first for the refreshing my own memory, but my Friends, who on all occasions had been Dear to me, were impatient that it should rest in Silence, and swayed me even against my inclinations, to let it go abroad ; (for not without some Reluctancy) I submitted to their importunities, and the many reasons they urged to Frame or Mould me to a temper of complying.

The Preface.

plying. And now it is abroad, I am altogether perſwaded, it cannot but be gratefull to my ingenious Conntrymen, nay, even to Neighbouring Nations; for ſomething conſtrains me to imagin, it will not altogether be confined within the narrow compaſs of a ſingle Iſland, when it contains in it ſelf ſo great a ſhare of the World, and all that is worthy of Note in the Countries it mentions, and thoſe the moſt Famed in the Univerſe. I have digeſted it into a Method ſuitable for the underſtanding of all intelligent Capacities, and formed it in Chapters, that any thing deſired may be the ſooner found out, or turn'd to; yet the Contents mention not the Particulars at full, but only ſome as an Introduction to the reſt; for the matter being Conciſe and Compact, ſhould I bring every thing under the heads mentioned therein, they would ſwell too much, and perhaps be tedious to the Reader, ſeeing ſuch a method is a kind of doubling what is the ſubſequent, and an Anticipateing the the Readers Expectation.

To

The Preface.

To Conclude, I present you with Truth and Variety, and so resting on the ingenious Reader's good Nature, and Impartiality for a candid Construction of this Work, I take leave to subscribe my self,

Your Most Humble,

and Devoted Friend

to serve you,

T. C.

THE NEW ATLAS;
OR,
Travels *and* Voyages
In *Europe, Asia, Africa,* and *America.*

CHAP. I.

Motives that induced the Author to undertake these Travels; his first setting out for Constantinople, *and Voyage as far as the* Dardanelles; *the description of divers places he touched at in the way, and what else happened in that passage.*

INSPIRED by the Fame of distant Lands, by seeing what's rare and Worthy of Note nearer Home, I debated with my self whether the latter ought not to suffice my curiosity, and laboured very much to enforce it for many Reasons; but neither that, nor the Charge, Danger, and Hardships I was like to meet with in Voyaging tempestuous Seas, nor Travelling strange Countries,

Countries, had any such prevalent Effect upon me as to surmount the eager Inclination and restless Desire I had to be an Eye-witness of those things I had often heard, though imperfectly, in Relation to what they have since appear'd. This great Resolve labouring in my Mind, my Friends could not chuse but take notice of some great alteration in me, and their pressing desires to know the cause of unusual Emotions that were too evident, constrain'd me to open my self freely, which at first did not a little startle them; but perceiving I was fully bent on the undertaking, and that all their perswasions to the contrary were fruitless, they assisted me with a supply in a great measure to carry on my undertaking; and so having prepared every thing I then thought necessary, we parted with good Wishes, Prayers and Tears.

I sent my Cargo on Board a Merchant's Ship lying over-against *Eriffe*, in the River of *Thames*, on the 30th of *April* 1684, and travelling over-land, went on Board my self when she was fallen to the *Downs*. It will be needless to tell you what Agreement I made with the Master who was my Friend, and used me extream well during my Voyage, or how I spent my time e'er we quitted the Lands end; let it suffice we were driven back by stress of Weather, and forced to put in at several places with other Ships in our Company, before we had a fair Wind to carry us out to Sea; but at length Providence so ordered it, that the Wind came about as well as we could wish, and we lost no time to embrace so favourable an opportunity; but getting out of Harbour, where we had lain for Ten days Wind bound, in a few hours sailing *England* disappeared, but Night coming on, the Sun setting with a dusky Cloud a thwart it, and darting its Beams Pale to either Pole, the Mariners observed by that and some other Signs they have, that a Storm threatned us; nor were they deceived in their Conjecture, for the Wind arose by degrees, and about Midnight it was a full Storm, but with some difficulty
we

Europe, Asia, Africa *and* America.

we weather'd it, for about the rising of the Sun the Wind slackned and we kept on our way; yet this tossing a little indisposed me, so that all that day I kept my Cabin, but for the most part after this the Seas and Winds contended as it were to give us a favourable passage to *Constantinople*, whither this Ship was bound upon some particular occasions as well as that of Trade, which I do not conceive pertinent to this Relation of my own Travels, nor shall I describe, as some superfluously do, all the Coasts we made in our Sailing: Let it suffice then that we touched not till we came to *Messina* in *Sicily*, though in our passage I saw the Fires of the Mountain *Stromboli*, which in the night time looked dreadful, though at a great distance, and was informed that the People who live near it conceive a foolish opinion, that it is an entrance into Hell, because when the Fire makes its Irruptions they hear howlings as of the Damned, which is no more than the Winds breaking through the hollow Rockey Caverns in the Mountain, wasted by the long continuance of the burning, which makes a confused noise, that at a distance resembles howling.

Passing the Fare of *Messina*, we came before the Town, and dropt Anchor without the Port, where those that would had leave to go a-shore; I failed not to do it, and whilst the Sailers were employed in taking in some necessaries, I took a slight view of the place. It lies on that side the Island that looks to *Rhegio* in *Italy*, from which it is 60 miles distant, where the Ancient Town of *Zancle* stood: Nature has furnished it with a pleasant and safe Harbour, which for its compactness may be thought to have been made by Art. The Buildings that adorn the Port are Regular and Uniform, so that they give a pleasant prospect at the end of the Mole that shuts in the Port: There is a Tower well fortified to secure the entry, and about the middle of it is another Tower, on the top of it a great Light to guide Ships in the Night; The Streets of the Town are fair and large; The Cathedral

dral is very stately, and over the Door in large Characters is Written, *Gran-Mercy a Messine*. When the *French* became Masters of the Island, it was the first place that Surrendered, and *Sicily* caused and beheld the fatal Tragedy of the Intruders, for a design was secretly laid and carried on, so that on a set day, when the Bell rung to Evening Song, which was the Sign, the Inhabitants of the Island Massacred all the French Nation without sparing Women or Children, which is still called the Fatal *Sicilian* Vesper. Before the Church is a square Piazza, with a Theatre in the middle, where the Victory over the Turkish Naval Forces is represented in Brass, and in the same Metal stands the Statue of Don *John* of *Austria*, the Spanish Admiral, in that Expedition. The Country is very Fruitful, abounds in Sulphur Mines, and much subject to Earthquakes. The next Town of note is *Syracuse*, where the famous *Archimedes* made his Experiments, and fired the *Roman* Navy that besieged it with Burning-Glasses. There is a Castle built on the Rocks called *Scyla*, and the Water beating on these Rocks resembles the barking of Dogs. As for *Charibdis* it is opposite to the Port of *Messina*, and not dangerous, but when two contrary Eddies meet and make a kind of a whirlpool, so that sometimes Ships turn round and are sucked in, which gave occasion to Fable them two Sea Monsters set there to destroy Passengers, though there are Pilots always ready at the general Charge to guide Ships in and out. The Viceroy has his Residence here six Months, and as many at *Palermo*. Mount *Gibello*, anciently called *Ætna*, much infects this fruitful Island with its firey Irruptions. The Sicilians are very hauty, Proud, and exceeding Jealous of the Spaniards under whose Government they are.

From hence setting Sail, we directed our Course to *Maltha*, and having Coasted *Sicily*, there sprung up an East North East Wind, before which we drove a very swift Sailing, and soon made the Isle of *Maltha*, in the Port of which we came to an Anchor.

It

Europe, Asia, Africa, *and* America. 5

It lies in the *African* Sea, between *Sicily* and *Tripoly*, in the Latitude of 38 degrees, and in Longitude 34, extending from East to West 29 Miles, and is about 12 over; all the Earth is exceeding White; its Ancient Name was *Melita*. In the Year 1530 the Emperor *Charles* gave it, and the Isle of *Gozo*, to the Knights who were driven out of *Rhodes*, and they have ever since possessed it in spite of all the efforts the Turks have made. It seems to be a Rock with very little Earth on it, yet it bears Fruit and Corn, but they are mostly supplied from *Sicily*, it lying but 20 Leagues distant. Here St. Paul on his landing in his passage to *Rome* shook off the Viper; they show his Grott, and the Earth is dug there, and carried away for many Physical uses. The Natives wear Green Spectacles to prevent their Eyes from Dazling, by reason of the whiteness of the Earth. The Knights of the Order are under a great Master. They have many advantageous Ports well defended, and are formidable at Sea with their Galleys to the Moors of Barbary and Turks; for if they take them they make 'em Slaves. The Towns of *Maltha* are well scituate and defended; they have good Magazines, and always keep a good Provision of Arms and Naval Stores. They are very charitable to Travellers, especially the Sick, providing for them in their Hospitals while they stay, and pay the charges of their Voyage when they depart.

The Wind being again fair, we left *Maltha*, passing the Cape of *Metapan* and Isle of *Cerigo*, the Ancient Porphyrus and Citherea, where formerly stood a Magnificent Temple to *Venus*, the ruins of which, as I was told, are still to be seen near the Sea; and meeting with a storm, we were constrained to cast Anchor before the Island of *Zia*, which in Ancient times was called *Calle Ceos* or *Cea*; it is about 50 Miles in Circuit, shaped like a Horse-shoe; the Soil produces Wine, Corn, good Pasture, and many other useful things; the Harbour is stored with Fish, the Inhabitants are very civil to Strangers,

gers; the Women wear their Coats but to their Knees, and their Smocks about a Foot below that, with a Veil reaching their Breasts, which they turn aside as they think fit; when they will or will not Compliment any but lying in War's way, between the Turks and Venetians, they are much oppressed and impoverished, otherways the plenty of the Island would inrich them.

Sailing from hence we made the Isle of *Andra*: This is the Ancient *Andros* of the Greeks, but now Inhabited by People of several Nations, as *Albanians, Armenians, Turks, Jews, &c.* and these differ in Customs as well as Languages, very rude and unhospitable; the Chief Towns are *Arni* and *Amolacos*. The Greeks have several Churches in this Island, but the People are very Superstitious and odd in their Devotions, strowing Flowers, and rowling in them; but the Latins who have likewise Churches there, are more Civilized, and proceed Regular: The Island is very Fruitful, and here they make abundance of white wicker Baskets used all over the *Archipelago*.

Weighing Anchor, we got out to Sea, and stood to the Starboard, passing between this Island and *Negropont*, and having a South-west Wind, *Sciro*, and soon after *Ispi Cera*, and some other places appeared. In the Evening when we were pretty clear of Islands, the Wind turned East South East, and we soon made the Land where *Troy* stood, little of whose Ruins remain; for we had passed *Tenedos* in the Night, so passing the Mouths we entered the Channel of the *Helespont*, the place where the Turks passed from *Asia* into *Europe* to extend their Empire.

CHAP. II.

Of the Helefpont, *Dardanelles, Places about them, what is obfervable in* Conſtantinople *and its adjacents; Containing all that is Curious and Remarkable in thefe Parts.*

THE Gate, or Entrance, as it were, to *Conſtantinople* being by the *Helefpont* and *Dardanelles*, I think it here convenient to fay fomething of this fam'd Streight before I come a Land; It lies in 37 Degrees, 42 Minutes, North Latitude, and of Longitude about 55, not extending above 10 or 12 Leagues in length, and at the entrance it is a large League and an half broad; it divides the Country of *Thrace* from *Troas* a Province of *Afia*, that lies to the Eaft: To the North lies the *Propontis*, and to the South the *Ægean* Sea, and the *Archipelago* ; and in Sailing here one has a profpect of divers fine Towns, Villages, &c. and a curious Country on either Hand.

The Turks knowing the important advantage of this Streight, have Fortified the Paffage with two ftrong Caftles, one in *Europe*, and the other in *Afia* ; the Caftle built in *Afia*, called the *New Caftle*, is feated on a tongue of Land pointing out into the Sea on a fquare Platform, comprizing 4 large panes of Walls, flanked at the four Corners with Towers; thofe next the Sea, fquare with a fort of Redoubt only on one fide ; thofe toward the Land are round, and defend the Walls, but neither in thicknefs nor largenefs comparable to the other ; the Works wafhed by the Sea have Port-holes level with the furface of the Water, and I could number as I Sailed by,

about

about 40 Cannon mounted, to prevent any Ships from forcing their way into the Harbour; and to the South of this Castle stands a very fair Mosque.

The Castle on the European side, which the Turks call *Roumeli-inglu-issar*, is seated near to Cape *Greco*, and in form is irregular; within the compass of the Walls are Houses for the Aga, and other Officers, with a fair Mosque. There is a Platform on which many great Guns are planted, lying equal with the surface of the Water. Near the Castle lies a small Village noted for its Five stately Pilasters, that serve to underprop the Aquaducts bringing Water to the Fortress. But notwithstanding these Castles, whose Guns reach from Shore to Shore, the Venetians, and other Maritime Nations, have insulted the Harbour, for the Castles lie not directly opposite, least in firing they should batter each other. The Castles are appointed to examine Ships that pass and re-pass, and the Governors have Orders to sink such Ships as will not comply: Beyond these Castles that are of Modern building are two old Castles, one on each shore; that on the Asian side the Turks call *Natoli-jski-jfiar*; it is of square Building, flanked at the corners with Towers, and in the midst of it is a large square Tower, on which some Culverin is placed; and behind this Castle is a large Village of about 3000 Inhabitants, Christians, Turks, and Jews; These by us are called the Castles of the *Dardanelles*. That on the European side is of a Regular Fortification, and indeed we may esteem this narrow Passage well guarded by these Castles, and *Constantinople* so advantageously Scituated, that no great City in the World can boast of more Advantages; as will by and by appear.

Being examined at the Castles, and leave obtained to pass, we arrived at *Gallipoly*, about 35 Miles from them. This Town was anciently built by one *Callias*, Prince of the *Athenians*, and after his Name called *Caliipolis*, but now corruptly *Gallipoly*; it is thinly inhabited by Greeks, who mostly sell a
Liquor

Europe, Asia, Africa, *and* America. 9

Liquor called *Raki*, a kind of Brandy, and some Oyl. The Doors of their Houses are not above two Foot high, and so made to prevent the proud Turks Insults, who are hereby prevented riding in on Horseback. In this Town there is a square Castle, with a Tower joyned to it by the Pummel of a Wall; to the Seaward there is an Arsenal, where the old Galleys are laid up which the Turks affirm to have been taken from the Venetians when they took the Island of *Cyprus*; but in Truth they are a part of their own shatter'd Fleet that escaped from the Battle of *Lepanto*, and were by main strength carried over the Isthmus of *Corinth*, and put into the *Archipelago*, they not being able to bring them about by Sea, because the Christians had possessed all the Passes.

After having been a-shore, and pretty well refreshed in this place, we weighed Anchor, and with a West South West Wind passed the Isle of *Marmora*: At this place the Sea is wide, and this is properly the *Propontis*, though now called mostly *Mare de Marmora*; and here though we had a fair Wind, the Current setting strong against us, we could not make much way; however, Sailing on we in a little time came in sight of *Constantinople*, which is about 125 Miles from *Gallipoly*, and entering into the Streight of it we had a very fine Prospect of that Famous City; it is seated in *Thrace*, on *Europe* side, over-against the Scituation of Ancient *Chalcedon* on the Asian Shore.

Constantinople, by most that have seen it, is held to be the best Scituated of any City in the World for all manner of conveniency, *viz.* On a point of main Land, jutting out towards the *Thracian Bosphorus*, so little divided from *Asia*, that it requires but half an hours Sailing to pass thither; on the Right Hand is has the *Propontis*, or *White-Sea* ; on the Left the *Euxine* or *Black-Sea* and *Paulus Mæotis*, which receiving a great number of Rivers, and having on it many bordering People, this City is plentifully furnished with all necessaries; for let the Wind blow

blow as it will, the Channels of the White and Black Sea ferve it, becaufe, when it is contrary to the one it ftands fair for the other.

Between thefe Seas is the entry of the Port, which Nature without the help of Art has made exceeding ufeful, for it is always fo replennifhed with Water, that Ships of good burthen may lay their heads on the Keys, and one may ftep a-fhore without any difficulty.

It is held to be firft Founded by *Paufanias*, King of *Sparto*; who named it *Byzantium*; and upon his confulting the Oracle where to build a City, he gave no other Anfwer but this, *viz.* Over-againft the blind Men, intimating the *Calcidonians*, who had neglected the fair opportunity of a fight fo accommodated by Nature, and built *Chalcedon* in *Afia* oppofite to it. It was deftroyed by *Severus*, to punifh the Citizens for their Revolt, but reftored more Magnificent by *Conftantine* the Great, who named it *Conftantinople*, equalling it with *Rome* in her Ancient Glory, and removing the Seat of the Empire thither, as if it were defigned by the Nature of its Scituation, to bear Rule, and be the Miftrifs of Cities. There goes a Fame, that when *Conftantine* was about to meafure out ground to build an Imperial City in *Afia*, a ftooping Eagle catched up the Line, and carrying it over the Streight, dropt it in the place where the City now ftands, which was looked on as a fortunate Prefage, and prov'd a fufficient encouragement for erecting it. It was once taken by the *Latins* from the *Greeks*, Anno 1203, and re-taken by them *Anno* 1254; and laftly by *Mahomet* the Second Emperour of the Turks, *Anno* 1453, who fince made it the Seat of the Empire, and called it *Iftambol*, corruptly from the Greek Word Σταγπόλιν. The heat of the Air in Summer is cool, and much allayed by the Breezes that come from the Seas. It has been much fubject to Earthquakes, and is very often fo to the Plague.

Europe, Asia, Africa, *and* America. 11

Constantinople is in Figure Triangular, two sides of it are washed by the Sea, the one by the Propontis, or White Sea, and the other by the Port: the other side is towards the Land; the biggest of the three is that beaten by the Surges of the Propontis, reaching from the Seraglio to the seven Towers, and that towards the Port is the middlemost: The Seraglio being built on the point of the point of the Triangle, gives a curious Prospect, for it runs out between the Propontis and the Port: Its Gardens on the Shoar are very Charming, there being nothing that is scarce and rare but is found in them; and this is held to be the particular spot where the Ancient *Byzantium* stood. On the other Angle pointing to the Canal of the White Sea, are the seven Towers; they were built by the Christians, and are covered with Lead; the chief use they are now put to, is to keep the vast Treasure of the Empire, sent as Tribute from many Nations, though part of them are often made a Prison for Persons of Quality, and great Officers. At the third Angle which is at the bottom of the Port to the Land side, appear the Ruins of *Constantine*'s Pallace, by which it seems to have been very Magnificent.

This great City is encompassed by strong Walls, and to the Land side they are double; in some places the Walls are of rough Stone and Brick, in others of Smooth Freestoone; they are guarded by a good Ditch, Wharfed and Faced on both sides; the Walls are guarded by a great number of little Towers at an equal distance, and Guns planted commodiously, though I confess, I take it not to be very strong, compared with the Modern Fortified Towns and Cities: Some allow it to be 16 Miles in circuit, but I cannot well agree with them, for I, with another Person, walked and rowed it at a pretty moderate pace in three Hours, so that I guess it to be about 12 Miles in Circuit. It has 22 Gates, 6 towards the Land, 5 towards the Propontis, and 11 along the Port; those to the Water
answered

answered by Creeks, Landing places and Stairs. When I had made this obfervation I thought it convenient to enter the City, which I did on the fifth of *June* about nine in the Morning, I found the Streets moftly narrow, the Houfes generally built of Timber, and that is the reafon when Fires happen, which they often do, vaft numbers of Houfes are confumed before the raging Element can be overcome, and the Janifaries and others, appointed to extinguifh it, many times on a difguft, or for the fake of Plunder, encourage the progrefs of the Conflagration by hindering thofe that would affift them.

Going to the Befeftn which is a diftinct Canton of the City, enclofed with Gates and Walls, I found it to be very fine, for here the Merchants keep Shop, and the place is very Regular, the Houfes are covered above with Planks joyned upon Rafters, though there are holes left to let in the Light; and here the richeft Wares are vended, or at leaft Samples to be feen of fuch as they have in their Warehoufes; They are all ranked by themfelves, fo that bufinefs is quickly difpatched. At ten every Evening the Gates are fhut, and after that hour none can pafs without giving a fmall matter of Money to the Porter, and this is the place moft frequented; greateft part of the Streets though the City are very Populous, being eafie to pafs without Crouds at any time.

From this place I went to vifit the Hypyodrome, which fpacious place was built by the Emperor *Conftantine*, for Tilts, Tournaments, and other exercife on Horfeback, and the Turks at prefent call it the place of Horfes; It is 400 paces long, and about 200 broad; and at the end oppofite to the Seraglio, there are two Obilisks, the firft is 70 Foot high, and can be difcerned to confift of no more than one Stone; it is adorned with feveral Herogliphical Figures in Relief, placed on a fquare Marble Pedeftal; on one of the Faces of the Pedeftal is an old Latin Infcription fo defaced by time,

Europe, Asia, Africa, *and* America. 13

time, that no more can be gathered from it, than that it was built by the Emperor *Theodosius*; the Second has a like in Greek Characters; the Third is adorned with the Emperor's Effigies seated on a Throne, with his Officers of State about him; and on the Fourth is represented a Battle. The other Obelisk is of Free Stone, sharp pointed like a Piramid, and being much worn by time, has no Inscription on it to be discerned.

Near these stands a Brazen Piller of considerable heighth, commonly called the Serpentine Column, because it appears like three Serpents wreathed or twisted together, their Tails fastned to the ground, and at the top it has 3 gapeing Mouths; and it is the common opinion, that this Pillar was set up in remembrance of 3 Serpents, who in Ancient times wasted the confines of the City, till the Emperor *Leo Haurus* by Magick Art drew them into a great Ditch in the middle of the Hypyodrome, who were killed by filling up the Ditch with Stones and Earth. In this City there are two other Columns, one called the Historical, and the other the Burnt Column, the latter being defaced by Fire, but neither of them being much remarkable, I pass them over, yet adjoyning to them there is a Court where the Archers Exercise, and the Turks are very exact in shooting, for I see them stick their Arrows one after another in the circumference of half a Crown, at 100 Paces.

The next thing of Note my curiosity led me to visit was, *Sancta Sophia*, the principal Mosque in the City; it has several Doors that lead into a Portico that gives entrance into the Mosque, which is 120 Paces in Length, and 80 in breadth, having square Walls, but the Vault or Roof is round, so Artificially contrived, that the Frame is supported without Columns, though there are many rows of Columns, which only appear to support the weight of two Galleries, yet are placed so that they prove very Ornamental, being 30 on each side, about 16 Foot high, of hard pollished Stone; however, the

length

length of Time has made many Clefts and Chinks in them. The Vault of the Mosque retains much of its Ancient Beauty, as being adorned with curious Mosaick Work, consisting of small guilt Stones so neatly joyned, that they after so many Ages remain almost perfect; and at the four Corners where the Vault begins, in Mosaick Work, are the Figires of the four Beasts mentioned in the Apocalyps, yet Turks who pretend to abhor Images have somewhat defaced them, as they have the Figure of our Saviour, which is over the Principal Door: He is represented sitting on a Throne, giving Benedict to one that prostrates before him; the Figure of the Virgin *Mary* appears on the Right Hand; and in a Bass-Relief the Holy Ghost is represented in the Figure of a Dove, which they have not at all defaced.

There is to be seen the Tomb of the Renowned Emperor *Constantine* in this stately Structure, in former times a Christian Church; it is a Grey Stone, 8 Foot long, and 4 over, and the Turks hold it in remembrance of that worthy Emperor of great Esteem. This Mosque or Temple is paved with curious Marble covered with Mats, to abate the coldness of the Stone when they prostrate themselves, for the Turks are so devoutly superstitious, that they put of their Barbouches, or Shooes, when they enter their Mosques. There are also to be seen the ruins of other fine Paintings and Images, partly defaced by the Turks, and partly by Time.

Christians are not admitted here without Connivance or Bribery, and those only by the *Franks*; for if a Jew or Greek be found in the Mosque, he must either die, or turn Turk. It was built by *Justinian* the Emperor on recovery of his health, having vowed in his Sickness, if God spared him, to found one of the beautifulest Churches in the World, to the honour of the Soveraign Wisdom, for *Sophia* in the Greek signifies Wisdom, and this is the only Ancient Structure of this kind in *Constantinople*; for though there are many stately
Mosques,

Mosques in the City, they are of late building, Erected by the Sultans and Sultaneſſes, whoſe Names they bear; as that of *Solyman* the Magnificent, which is very Stately; of *Achmet Mohomet Selim*; with thoſe of *Chadaʒet* and *Valide*, new and very Beautiful, by the Idea of which laſt you may gueſs at the reſt; it was Founded by the Sultaneſs *Valide*, Mother to *Mahomet* the Fourth, ſeated in the middle of a large ſquare Court, reſembling a vaſt Cloiſter, by reaſon of the Arched Roof that environs it like a Portico, and under are divers Fountains with Cocks, where thoſe that are polluted waſh themſelves e'er they enter the Moſque; it has but one Gate, and that is ſurrounded by a Portico of extraordinary heighth, paved with white and black Marble, ſupported by 64 Pillars of Red Marble; the Platform is adorned with Painting and Figures after the Turkiſh manner. This Portico is covered with many little Domes, and a very large one in the middle higher than the reſt, the whole Structure being very curious Work covered with Lead; there are four Turrets at the four Corners of the Buidling, called Minarets, ſlender, but very high, with Balconies round them, ſtanding like Maypoles, with Creſſents on the Globes, and winding-Stairs, juſt enough for the Mueſans to creep up with their loud Bawlings to call the People to Prayers, for they have no Bells, where clapping their hands on their Ears, they go round the Turret in the Balconies, and when they cry their Voices are heard very far. They call in their own Language, which in Engliſh is to this Effect; *God is a great God, give Teſtimony that there is but one God, come yield your ſelves up to his Mercy, and Pray him to forgive you your Sins. God is a great God,* &c. This Moſque is Vaulted and Adorned with a great number of Lamps and Globes of Glaſs, and in the Globes are many curious Devices, as Galleys, the model of Moſques, Trees, Flowers, Cities, and the like. There is a Table at the upper end, where uſually the High Altar ſtands in the Romiſh Churches, and

to

to this they turn their Faces when they say their Prayers, over which is placed the Name of God, Written in Gold Arabick Characters, and over-against that are fixed two Brazen Candlesticks holding Wax Tapers of a vast bigness. The Sultans or Emperors lie Buried in their Mosques, their Tombs being covered with Rich Carpets, which have been laid on *Mahomet*'s Tomb at *Mecha*; for they conclude that sanctifies them, and keeps them from evil Spirits; their rich Turbans are placed at the Head, and if they have been Warlike, their Cimiters, and other Military Atchievements, are fix- on or near them: Divers Alcorans are chained to the Tombs, and there is always one or other that has a Pension left them by the deceased Emperor to Read the Alcoran to the People that come to visit the Tomb, and to Pray for his Soul. Sultan *Amurat* has two of his Wives placed at his Head, and eleven of his Children round him; and at the head of the Tomb or Coffin is a convenient place where his Prayer-Books are laid up, appearing through a Latten Grate, adorned with Gold and precious Stones. The Keepers of the Turbe, or little Chaple, in the Mosque where these Bodies lie, are obliged at certain hours of the day to Pray for the Souls of the deceased.

The Arsenal is at the end of the Port belonging to the City, being a very compact Building; it contains a considerable extent of Ground; the Galleys are laid up there under 120 Arches; the Christians are not permitted to come into it, but the Turks say, there are Arms for 60000 Men, besides Furniture for Shipping, and in the Baths many thousand Slaves are shut up who lead miserable Lives. The Captain Bassa, and all the Officers depending on the Admiralty, have their Apartments, and lodg in the Arsenal, that they may be ever ready to receive Orders about the Naval concerns.

In this City are many Hans and Kervanserais, which serve most for Warehouses, being strongly built, barred and guarded to prevent Imbezlement.

The

Europe, Asia, Africa, and America 17

The Hans consist of four sides of building, enclosing a square Court with a Fountain, the Roof consists of little Domes covered with Lead; and here Foreign Merchants, who bring their Goods to lay up, find entertainment; they only contain two Stories, divided into Rooms, that have no intercourse one with another, the lower Story consists of Warehouses for Goods, and the upper divided into little Chambers, where Strangers that are Travellers Lodge, but they must furnish themselves with all necessaries, or otherways they must want both Furniture and Provisions.

The Karvanserais are built after the same fashion, only the Stone work reaches but to the first Story, and the rest is Wood and Brick, whereas the Hans have entire Stone Walls of a good thickness for their better securities against Pilferers. They have each of them but one Gate, and in the latter indigent Persons are permitted to Lodg, from half a Crown to a Crown a Month.

The next thing of Note in the City is the Seraglio, which Christians and Jews are prohibited to enter, except Ambassadors, and some few Attendance when they have their Audience, and then some crowd in with them that are not concerned, or rather bribe their way, but it is very dangerous for them to pass any further than the Second Court, and further I could not gain access, though I profered liberally, and the Turks rarely refuse Money where they can oblige one for it, and therefore I shall give a description as far as I could observe, and something over according to the best information I could get.

The Seraglio is the Prince's Pallace, but of very irregular building; it is built on a point of Land that juts out into the Sea, as I have before mentioned, and surrounded with Walls of a greyish Stone, adorned at top with a Parapet and Battlement, suitable to the City Walls; it is near 4 miles in compass, but the greatest part is Gardens; the Building clusters together, like the ancient building of low

C   Castles,

Castles or Fortifications, so that on the out side they have nothing of Magnificence, except a few guilt Spires and Globes; the chief Entry is near *Sancta Sophia*, and the Gate is like that of the entrance into many Ancient Cities, without either beautiful Architecture, or Ornament; yet the Capigy keep their Court of Guards under it, and carefully watch the entrance.

Passing this Gate it leads into a large Court, where on the right Hand is the Apartment for such as fall sick in the Seraglio, with matted Sopha's along the Walls, so that they are no better lodged then in Hospitals; on the left Hand is a Magazine for furnishing 1000 Men, that the Grand Signior's Domesticks may, upon any sudden Insurrection in the City, defend the Palace, and the Person of their Emperor; though notwithstanding this precaution, several of them have been deposed by the Rabble and Soldery, and come by violent Deaths, as their Histories make mention at large.

There being little else remarkable in this Court, I passed into the Second, fronted with two large Porticoes; on one side are the Grand Signior's Kitchens, where they Dress for Him, his Women, and such as live at his Charge in the *Seraglio*; and on the other side are his Stables, where 100 Horses may conveniently stand, and many Apartments where the Officers Lodg; and this great Court is entered on Horseback by none but the Grand Signior, all others alight at the Gate: It is not so big as the first, but consists of a Square, extending 200 Paces every way; there is round it a Gallery in the Form of a Cloyster, supported by a great many Marble Pillars, and covered with Lead; and at the back of that there are Domes, ranging from one end of the Court to the other, covered with Lead, as the former, and on the right Hand, where the Kitchins are, the Stables I mentioned being towards the Sea. The Janisaries draw up in this Court to the right Hand, and the Horse to the Left; in the middle there is a delicate Fountain, shaded with Cypress, and Scycamore

Europe, Asia, Africa *and* America. 19

more Trees; and heretofore near this Fountain, the Grand Signiors caused the Heads of the Bassa's, and other great Men of the Court that displeased them, to be cut off, as a Terror to others; for the Government is Despotical, and the Lives of the Subjects are at the disposal of the Prince. On the left Hand, at the end of the Court, is a Hall, where the Divan or Council of State sits, and on the Right, a Door which gives entry into that, and is more properly called the *Seraglio*, and none but those who have particular Orders can pass it.

Very near this Seraglio, within the same enclosure is another building Founded by *Constantine* the Great, and intended a Pallace, but now it is called the *Old Seraglio*, having many additional Buildings, yet not fair on the out side, though these and the other have costly Gildings and Paintings within: the Turks in general having little regard what out side show their Houses make, so they appear Sumptuous and Magnificent within. It is surrounded with Walls of an unusual heighth, without any Windows on the out side, the better to prevent the Women from being seen; and here the Reigning Sultan shuts up the Wives of his Predecessors, whom he Sequesters from the World, except he likes any of them himself, or pleases to bestow them on the great Men of his Empire, for their signal Services; othewise this is a kind of a Nunnery for Life.

There is yet a Third Apartment, properly called a *Seraglio*, joyning close to that of the Grand Signior, so that he can pass to it by Galleries privately, when he has a mind to divert himself there. What more I could gather by sight at a distance is, that this place which is so much talked of, as the Pallace of the greatest Emperor in the World, especially as to largeness of Territories, gives but an inconsiderable Prospect; and one at a distance can form nothing regular in it, it looking like a confused Mass of Building, in Apartments and Domes.

The Grand Signior has here his Officers, who have a great many under them; most part of them are Eunuchs, Blacks of *Æthiopia*; and others, that are most comely of their kind; they formerly were only Gelt, but it is said, that Sultan *Solyman*, one day seeing a Gelding back a Mare, and perform, as he supposed, the office of a Stallion, came Home and caused them all to be smoothed by the Belly, to prevent their dabling with his Women, of which Wound a great number died, and now they make Water through a Silver Pipe, which they put into the orrifice of the Root of their Yard, to prevent polluting themselves, by scattering their Urine on their Vestments; for then, till they have Absolution, they think they are unclean, as I shall shew hereafter; and now they cut off the Genitals of Children they buy, or have as Tribute, upon the Borders of *Æthiopia*, and other Negro Countries; and though many die under this usage, for it is not done till they are 8 or 10 years old, that they may see whether they are Docil or Ingenious; yet they have enough to serve in all the Seraglio's in *Europe* and *Asia*; for there are others belonging to the Grand Signior, beside those at *Constantinople*; and many to the Bassa's, and Governors of Provinces in divers Countries; and these are so Jealous, or rather Envious, which makes them to watch over the Women so narrowly, that they are rarely too cunning for them; they are lodged in a separate Apartment, together; and the single Testimony of one of them, against the greatest Subject in the Empire, costs the party his Life; nay, a bare Sollicitation, or too near a View, without any Act, is sufficient for a Strangling; as for Example, Sultan *Amurat* used a Prospective Glass, to discover the Actions of those that were in the City, and by that means, espying a Man at a Window, with the like Prospective, taking a view of one of his Sultana's, walking in the Garden of the *Seraglio*; he thereupon sent a Capigi, with 4 Mutes, who entered the House, and immediately Strangled the over curious unfortunate.

These Eunuchs have, in a manner, the sole Government of the *Seraglio*, but particularly of the Women;

Women; and when the Sultana's take the Air in the Garden, the Boſtangis, or Gardeners, ſtand round the Walls, holding Staves with long and broad pieces of Cloth faſtned to them, which makes them as though they were Blind, and is much higher than the Garden Wall, to which their Backs are turned, it being Death to look, if any of the Eunuchs percieve it, and complain of it; and this Jealouſie proceeds ſo far, that no Boat is ſuffered to come within 400 Paces of the Garden-Wall, though it is very high, if the Sultana's be walking there; and if any preſume it, there are Sentinels advantageouſly placed, to Fire at them; ſo that thoſe who have buſineſs by Water, are conſtrained to fetch a great compaſs about. But, notwithſtanding this Jealouſie, which, in a great or leſs Degree reigns all over the Empire, the Turks eſteem Women as very inconſiderable Creatures, without Souls, denying that they go to Heaven; That they were only made to ſerve for the uſe of Man, and be obedient to him, and their main end was deſigned for Generation; otherwiſe, unleſs to ſatisfie their Luſts, they eſteem them ſcarce Rational, and little better then Beaſts: In a word, theſe of Quality are but ſplendid Slaves, and the meaner ſort miſerable ones.

The Eunuchs have the Charge of bringing up the Grand Signior's Pages, called *Ichnoglians*, who are the beautifuleſt Youths that can be got, and for the moſt part of Chriſtian Extraction, but taken ſo young from their Parents, that they eaſily Educate them in the Mahometan Superſtition with great care, till they are about 28 years of Age, and are taught ſuch Arts, and uſed to ſuch Exerciſe as their Inclination chiefly leads them to. If they are of good natural parts, and prompt in underſtanding, they uſually riſe to the greateſt preferments in the Ottoman Empire; if not, they are turned out, and entered into pay and employments of other natures, living but meanly; but whilſt they live in the *Seraglio*, the greateſt Preferment they can riſe to, is to be of the number of the Forty, who are neareſt

the

the Grand Signior's Person, and these the Eunuchs look narrowly after, least they slip among the Women, or defile one another by unnatural Lust, for these are not dif-membred; among the 40 mentioned, there are four in high Esteem, *viz.* the *Selihtar* or *Sword-bearer*; the *Tschoader*, who carries the Cock; the *Ibrictar*, who carries Water ready to pour on the Grand Signior's Hands when he requires it; and the *Kuptar*, who carries the Pot of Sorbet to give him when he calls for it. There are Seminaries of these *Ichnogleans*, as at *Peza*, &c. where they are Educated, and growing up, sent to *Constantinople*, to be entertained in the Grand *Seraglio*.

The next that make a considerable Figure in the *Seraglio*, are the Bostangis or Gardeners, over whom is a Bassa, called the *Bostangi* Bassa; he has his Lodging in the *Seraglio*, and the Priviledge of wearing his Beard, not any beside him and the Grand Signior doing it, the rest being Shaved in token of Servitude. He is very great with the Prince, and always steers his Barge when he goes to take the Air on the Sea, so that having his Ear, and liberty to Discourse with him, all the Grandees stand in fear of him, and much consider his Power, labouring to keep him their Friend: and when any considerable Person is put to Death in *Constantinople*, he is sent to fetch his Head.

There are in this City many little *Seraglioes* belonging to the great Men of the Court, but on the out-side, they look much like old decaying Buildings, and some hold, that they built them without external Beauty and Ornament, because the Grand Signior should not be Jealous of their Pride, as aspiring to too much greatness. but within it is otherways, for they have lovely Apartments, adorned with Gold and Azure; the Floors are covered with Rich Carpets, so that those who enter pull off their Shooes, to prevent any injury they may do them; the Walls of most of them are faced with polished Tiles, like *China* Ware; in their Halls, and Chambers, they have risings about a Foot, which

which they call Divans, covered with richer Carpets than the Floor, and Imbrodered Cushions placed in order on them. Here they Rest, receive Visits, and spend the best part of the Day, and the Womens Apartments in all these, are separated from those of the Lodgings; none but the Master of the House, and some Eunuchs, are suffered to enter where they are; the Women stir little abroad, having Baths in their Houses, with suitable Attendance, and other convenient Necessaries.

Thus having described all that is worthy of Note in *Constantinople*, I shall speak something of the Neighbouring places, which may properly be termed the Suburbs of this great City; and in the first place *Galata* is a very pleasant place, separated from the City only by the *Port*, which may be crossed in Caiques, or Wherries, who are always attending; however, taking a compass you may go by Land, and have a very fine Prospect of the Country. This Town is pretty Large, and formerly belonged to the *Genoese*, and then was more considerable, for it held out some time against the whole Power of the Ottoman's, after *Mahomet* the Second had taken *Constantinople*; the Houses are Fair, and well Built, mostly Inhabited by *Greeks*, though it is the usual Residence of *Franks*, and they have five Monasteries there, which much Beautifie the place; and near the Sea side, there is the finest Fish-Market that may be seen in any Country, for the Fishmonger's-shops are stocked with such numbers of various kinds of Fish, on Market days, that Strangers admire how they should procure them; the *Greeks* keep many Taverns here, so that there are frequent disorders, by reason of drunken People, though great care is taken to prevent it.

Pera, and *Tophana* are two other pleasant little Towns; the Former is appointed for the Residence of most Ambassadors; those of the Emperor of *Germany*, King of *Poland*, and Republick of *Ragousa*, having usually their Residence in *Constantinople*; the French Ambassador's House is here, very stately ly, having a curious Prospect of the *Seraglio*. The latter is the place where they cast their great Guns, and that in the Turkish Language seems to give it its Name; the Houses in both are very finely Built, rising and falling pleasantly, so that at a distance, they seem to represent a kind of an Amphitheatre.

To these I might add *Caffumpasha*, which lies first if one goes by Land, and appears like a great Village; her Galleys and Ships are Built and laid up with great conveniency, for it is accommodated with 120 Arched Docks, or Houses; in the way to this the Ocmeidan, or Field of Arrows, a very spacious place, where the Turks exercise shooting with the Bow; and many resort thither to pray for success on their Arms, and any thing they stand in need of.

One may go in a Caique from *Constantinople* to *Schudaret*, which the Turks call *Iscodar*, it being but a good Mile. In the way there is a Tower built on a Rock in the Sea pretty strong, the Guns command the Port, and the Mouths of the *White* and *Black-Sea*; the latter is so called, not because the Water is Black, as some imagine, but by reason of the many casualties that happen upon the rising of sudden Storms, that cast Vessels away, to the loss of many Lives; and beside, it not being very broad, there are several Currants caused by the *Danube*, *Boristenhes*, *Tunais*, and other smaller Rivers, that discharge their Waters into it, and occasion many Eddies that drive Ships on the Rocks, where they are lodged or split; but to return,

In the Tower I mentioned, is a fine Well of fresh Water, and some call it *Leander*'s Tower, but for what reason I know not. *Schudaret* is a pleasant Village on the *Asian* Shoar; The Grand Signior has a stately *Seraglio* in it, beautified with lovely Gardens; and a little lower, on the same side, stands *Chalcedon*, anciently very Famous, and Celebrated by the four General Councils held there; yet time has laid the Structures of Antiquity in Ruins, so that at present it is but an inconsiderable Village, which

which stands like the Ruins of *Troy*, as a Memorial there was once so famed a place. In another walk of four Hours from *Constantinople*, is the *Prince's* Isle, a very pleasant place to take the Air in, for though it is not great, it contains two little Towns, inhabited by *Greeks*. The Coast of the *Black Sea* is also a curious place to take the Air upon. This is the *Thracian Bosphorus*, which coming from the *Black Sea* to *Constantinople*, mingles its Waters with the *White Sea*, and is but a Mile over at the broadest place, no more than 12 Miles in length, and all about this Channel are a great many lovely Houses and Gardens, so that passing it, one would conclude it the loveliest Prospect in the World; the Fruits are here Plentiful, and very Excellent; on the *Asian* side there is a pretty Castle, where Sultan *Ibrahim* was hid 20 Years, when Sultan *Amurat* put his other Brothers to Death; and along the Shoar are other Villages, in which one may be furnished with what is needful.

In this Channel they take great quantities of good Fish of divers Sorts, and amongst them the *Sword Fish*, so called, because it has a long broad Bone on the Snout of it, like a Sword, or rather jaged like a Saw on the edges; there are store of Dolphins, usually playing about the Boats, as also many other curious varieties; so that I may conclude, *Constantinople*, and the Towns adjacent, to be exceeding pleasantly Scituated, which having thus sufficiently described, I now pass to other useful Observations, during my stay in the Chief City of the *Ottoman* Empire.

CHAP. II.

The Original of the Turks, *and Extent of the* Ottoman *Empire; The Officers, Civil, and Ecclesiastical; their Forces, and Order; with many things relating to their Religion, Customs, and divers other matters.*

THE *Turks* are held to be Originally a People of *Scythia*, though some will have them the Off-Spring of the Ten Jewish Tribes, carried into Captivity by *Salmenaser*; and the Jews to curry Favour, would have them believe however, that the first considerable Figure they made, was upon their coming out of *Turcomania*, under *Tangrolipix*, a petty Captain, to assist the *Persians*, and at length possessed themselves of that Kingdom, their Captain being made King in the Field, upon the Death of the *Persian* Sultan, who falling from his Horse, died there; and immediately setled the large Empire in *Asia*, but it was ruined by the *Tartars*, yet they renewed it again under *Akoman Gazi*, or the Warlike, about 346 Years after, building it on the Ruins of the *Persian, Babylonian, Grecian,* and *Roman* Monarchies, which till late years, they have continued to spread wider, so that it now consists of part of *Persia*, almost all *Greece*, the Kingdom of *Ægypt*, the greatest part or *Arabia*, the Islands of *Cyprus, Rhodes, Mitylene, Negropont, Chio* or *Scio, Candia*, and many other Islands. The Empire of *Treprezom*, the Kingdom of *Colchis*, now called *Mingrelia, Tunis, Algires, Dalmatia, Illizia, Tribalenia, Bulgaria, Valachia, Moldavia*, part of *Hunga-*
ry,

ry, &c. so that they hold all the Sea Coast, from the Confines of *Epidaurus* the utmost bounds of *Europe* Westward, to the Mouth of the River *Tanais*, now called *Don*, with all that lies between the City of *Belgrade* and *Constantinople*; and Southward, all the Sea Coast from *Velex* to *Belis*, the boundard of the Kingdom of *Fez*, unto the *Arabian* Gulf, or *Red-Sea*, and so proportionably every way; the greatness of which, may be the better Conjectured, by the vastness of part of it, for the *Mear* of *Mætis*, which is all at the Grand Signior's Command, is 1000 Miles in Compass, and the *Euxine* or *Black-Sea* in Circuit 2700 Miles; the *Mediterranean* Coast, which is subject to him, is in Compass about 8000 Miles; so that he may pass in his own Dominions, from *Tauris* to *Belgrade*, 3180 Miles, or thereabouts, and almost the like distance from *Derbent* to *Adena*, and from *Balsoza* in the *Persian* Gulf, to *Tremisena* in *Barbary*, may be reckoned little less than 4000 Miles; however, of late days the weakness of this vast Empire has very much appeared, which shows it is declining to a Period; their Naval strengths having been inconsiderable, ever since their total defeat in the Gulf of *Lepanto*, by the *Spaniards*, *Venetians*, &c. Their Land-Forces promise little better of late, as having been worsted in several Battles by the *Germans*, *Poles*, *Venetians*, &c. so that this once Terror of the World, seems to be dispised rather than feared; the vastness of the *Ottoman* Territories, causing such infinite expence of Treasure, that the many Millions yearly accruing by Customs, Impositions, and many other ways, are not a sufficient Supply to raise and bring any considerable Armies into the Field. Yet the Grand Signior will not abate any thing of his Grandeur, but boasts himself the mighty Emperor of the World, to do, and not to do whatever he pleases; alledging, that the strength of the Heavens and the Earth are given to him, and his Flatterers make him believe it; his Apartment in the *Seraglio* is hung with Cloth of Gold, gilded Skins and Tapestries, interwoven with Silk and Gold, wherein are lively represented the Wars of the *Ottoman* Emperors; the Chamber he lodges in is adorned with rich Painting, Gilding, and precious Stones, that cast a very glorious light in the Night: Six Pages do him Service in his Chamber by Night, watching his Person, two and two, by turns, with lighted Torches, the one sitting at the Head, and the other at the Feet of his Bed: When he attires himself, they put into his Pocket 1000 Aspers, and 20 Ducats of Gold, and all that remains not given away that day, they have, when he puts of his Cloaths, for their Fees, for he rarely puts on one Apparel twice; and when he goes a Hunting, or to divert himself, his Purse-Bearer carries great store of Treasure to distribute; and vast quantities of all sorts of Provisions follow him, though many times they are not made use of.

The Chief Officers of the Empire are, 1. The Grand Visier, who acts immediately under the Grand Signior, and by him he speaks to such as have important business; for no Ambassador is admitted to the Grand Signior's presence, but on his first Arrival, when he delivers his Letters of Credit, and Present, for particularly without the latter, none can have Audience; all other Audiences are had of the Visier, who is likewise called the *Capi-Aga*; he has power of Life and Death, is General of the Army when the Grand Signior is not in the Field, and all take their Directions from him. 2. The *Cafnader* Bassa is next in Rank, as to Secular Affairs; his Office is to take an Account of the Treasury. 3. The *Chilerpy* Bassa, or Cup-Bearer. 4. The *Seragli Agasi*, Steward, or Master of the Houshold. 5. The *Chiller Agasi*, or *Serinder* Bassa, overseer of the Seraglio of Women, who is always an Eunuch. 6. The *Bostangi* Bassa, or Chief Gardener, of who is already spoken. 7. The *Caimacan* of *Constantinople*.

The Grand Signior has always near him, six Mutes Men, very lusty in Body, that are born Deaf, and consequently are Dumb. These are very Bloody and Cruel, being the Ministers of his Vengeance,

Vengeance, to Strangle whom he pleases; and when any one is Strangled in the *Seraglio*, the Bodies are thrown out of a particular Window appointed for that purpose into the Sea, and as many Guns are fired, to give Notice, in terror to others, as there are Strangled Bodies thrown out. There are in all 40 of these Mutes, some of which he keeps as his Buffoons, to play with for his pastime.

He has 8 Lance-bearers, called *Mutafurach*, who attend him with Launces, when he goes abroad, and these are subject to no Command but his own. The Eunuchs of the *Seraglio*, I have mentioned elsewhere; the *Turks* call them *Hundurni*, and under their Care, there are constantly 500 Virgins, most of *Europe*, the choicest Beauties that can be procured; they are taken from their Parents under 8 Years, and are brought up to Work in the *Seraglio*, as in a Nunnery; and when the Grand Signior is desirous to enjoy any of them, the day before he gives notice to the Chief of the Eunuchs, who Commands the rest to set them in order in their best Attire; then the Grand Signior, attended by him, walks between them, as they stand in Rows on either hand, exposing all their Beauties and winning Allurements to tempt him, and where he likes, he drops his Handkerchief, of which he has choice hanging at his Girdle, which the Eunuch takes up, delivers to the Virgin, and immediately putting her into a Coach, carries her to Rich Lodgings, where she is gorgously attired, and so he does by all that are this way chosen, and there they remain till they are sent for in order, by the Grand Signior to his Bed, for he never Marries, but when one is brought to his Bed side; he gives her a Golden Head tire, and 10000 Aspers, causing her to live a part, and daily encreasing her Maintenance, and then she is called a Sultana or Sultaness, and the eldest Son, if he out-lives his Father succeeds to the Throne, and puts all his other Brothers (if they fall into his Hands) to Death, causing them to be Strangled with a Bow string; for it is held unlawful to shed

the

the Sacred *Ottoman* Blood, as they call it, on the Ground, though the Sultanas, and great Men of the Court hide some of them, till the Fury is over, and preserve their Lives, as it has three or four times happened ; and this cruel Policy they use, to prevent the dismembring the Empire by Civil broils, and the better to secure the Throne to themselves.

There are about 300 Persons called *Sollacchi*, who continually march near the Grand Signior's Person, and are as it were his Guard ; and these are under the Command of the Aga of the Janisaries. They are attired in Linnen Garments, hanging down beneath their Knees, and over them they ware quilted Wastcoats, with half Sleeves of Taffaty, Damask, or Sattin; and on their Heads a Cap and Feather, carrying Bows and Arrows. There are another kind of Footmen, called *Peichi*, exceeding swift in running, and these are employed in the nature of Lackeys, or Foot-Posts, and are attired in Cloth of Gold, with a Girdle of the same ; the Caps are in fashion of our Butter pots, with a Silver Pike standing out before in the nature of a Horn.

There are 4000 Porters that give attendance in the Court, the Chief of them is the *Capigi* Bassa.

The Judges they call *Cadis*, who are divided into all parts of the Empire, in Cities, or great Towns, to decide Controversies ; yet their Suits, especially between the Turks, are very few, and they make a quick dispatch of business; there being rarely Advocates allowed, to Procrastinate business ; nor do they admit of Evidence in Writing, always taking it by word of Mouth, so that Bills, Bonds, and other Contracts, are not significant in *Turkey*; yet there is much Bribery used, and he that can give the Judge most, usually carries the Cause. They punish Crimes with great severity, and so speedily, that rarely Thefts are committed by any private Turk, and the People in all Cities are careful to prevent Murthers, for if the Murtherer escape, a great sum of Money is required of the Person be-

fore

fore whose Door the Murthered Body is found, which is exacted with Rigor.

The Divan consists of the Grand Visier, and several other Visiers of the Bench, and there the important business of State is Controverted, and Causes heard; of all which the Grand Visier gives the Grand Signior an account; nor dares he dissemble, or hide any thing, as knowing the Grand Signior has a Window into it, before which hangs a thin Curtain, through which he can see and hear, but not be seen, and therefore the Visiers know not but he may be always there in the Divan time, which keeps such an awe over them, that they do better Justice than in other places, to prevent their Heads flying off, as it sometimes has happen'd, upon the least defect or partiality. Next to the Bassas, the Beglerbegs, or Lords of Lords, are in highest Authority in Temporal matters; they have Command over Provinces and Armies, and under them are divers *Zanzacks*, as their Deputies; but their Government is during the Prince's pleasure; and the Chief of these is the Beglerbeg of *Rormania* in *Greece*, under whose Command are 21 Zanzacks. These usually exercise and bring to the Field the Spahi and Tiraarcots, the *Turks* best Horsemen: These latter are certain Horsemen, usually on the Frontiers, that for Lands alotted them out of the Grands Signior's Conquests, are bound to give their attendance, and serve in the Wars upon Summons. The Spahi are most *Europeans*, trained up Young to manage a Horse, and exercise Cavalry, having Pay. There are also *Spachoglanians*, *Silictarians*, and *Olofagians*, who have Lands or Pensions assigned them to serve in the Wars; for none, as in other Countries, can purchase Lands for Inheritance, the whole Empire being in Fee-simple the Grand Signior's, and all things revokable at his pleasure.

The Horsemen march under a white Banner, mostly Armed with strong Coats, Bows, Arrows, Fire-Arms, Cimitars, Battle-Axes, &c. There are

are another sort of Horsemen, called *Caripices*, but not above 800: These are usually the Grand Signior's Guard, surrounding him in the middle of the Batallion of the Janisaries, and are Fellows so desperate, that they will venture on any Enterprise; being for the most part Sons of great Commanders, trained up from their Youth in this way.

The Janisaries are the *Turk's* best Footmen; and these at first are taken when Children from their Parents, mostly Christians, but brought up in the Mahometan Superstition; inured to all manner of hardship, and have Officers over them, to teach them the use of Arms; and these enclose the Grand Signior when he marches with the Army: They ware white Caps; their Arms are Harquibuses, and sharp cutting Cimitars; who since their first Institution, as a Nursery of Soldery, have been the chief support of the *Ottoman* Empire; they are commanded by an Aga, or Chief Commander, to whom nothing is so fatal as their Love and Respect, for that creats in the Grand Signior a Jealousie of his aspiring, and on this Account many of the Aga's have lost their Lives, but mostly they are put to Death privately, to prevent their being rescued; and if he be a Court Favourite, the Janisaries are distrustful of him, and sometimes on failure of their Pay, and other Occasions, Mutiny, and Murther him; so that on either hand he stands very ticklish in his high promotion.

The Janisaries in *Constantinople*, &c. have great Halls, or Apartments, where they Sleep together, their Beds being placed on either side; and all those of a Battallion usually Dine together, the younger being appointed to serve the elder, and if any one absent himself from his Lodging, unless upon leave, or some particular occasion, he is sure to be severely Cudgeled, yet obliged, by way of submission to his punishment, to Kiss the Hand that inflicts it.

In time of Peace their employs are different; some are appointed to wait on Ambassadors, others on Merchants, and Consuls, or such as Travel through the

Europe, Asia, Africa, *and* America 33

the *Turkish* Territories. They have power to Arrest Malefactors, and see good Orders kept, being in great Esteem with all Men: so that if they go into the Market to buy any thing, they will have it at their own price, the Vender not gain-saying; but this may be concluded to proceed rather from the effects of Fear than Love; and they carry such a Vogue, that no Grand Signior thinks his Throne setled, till they approve of him; so that to purchase their good Opinion, the new Sultan pays off their Arrears, distributes Money amongst them, and encreases their Stipends.

Though these are the Chief Strength of Foot, yet there others, but not so serviceable, *viz.* The *Acoujces*, which serve as a forlorn hope; these recieve no Pay, but have liberty to plunder in War time, allowing the Sultan a fifth part of the spoil. The *Asapi*, which are Rabble, raised as there is need for them, and serve as Pioneers, being of so small account, that they are set in the Front of the Battle to receive the first shock, and tire the Enemy with slaughtering them; and when a Town is Besieged, they are set first to scale the Walls, to amuse the Besieged, and their slain Bodies serve as a Rampart to mount on, or fill up the Ditch; and so little are these miserable Creatures esteemed, that a Spahi having taken five of them in a Civil War, offered them to a Butcher for a Sheep's Head, which he refusing, the Spahi swore if he would not make the exchange, he would cut of their Heads, and boyl them, and was preparing to do it; but the Butcher, though a Man of Blood, seeing him in earnest, gave him the Sheep's Head to save the poor Wretches Lives, and afterwards set them at liberty.

The Grand Signior has always 6000 Gunners in Pay, most of them Rhenegado Christians, turned Mahometans, many of them are *French* Men; and these are called *Topegi*; Twelve thousand others are in Pay, to look after his Ammunition; his Carriages are very numerous, and his Train of Artillery

lery large. There are 3000 attending the Grand Signior's pleasure, called *Chiaus*, or *Chiaux*, who act in the nature of Serjeants at Arms, and are in good Esteem, being often employed in Embassies; but their chief employ is to carry Letters, or Commendations from the Grand Signior, or Grand Visier, and are impowered to apprehend Mallefactors, yet go not to the Wars, unless the Grand Signior is there. These are Commanded by a Bassa of their own order, who is of such Credit, that when he is sent for any Man's Head, though he has no Warrant in Writing, his Authority is not disputed.

When the *Turkish* Armies March, it is with as great silence as may be; they are under a regular Discipline, and live very sparing in Diet; for the most part, on Rice, dried Fruits, Bread baked in the Ashes, and powdered Flesh dried in the Sun, rarely complaning as the Christians do of want, but patiently endure and wait till they can be supplied; no Women are found in their Armies, and the Servants attending on great Men are Listed, and do the Office of Soldiers in their March; they observe the beck of the Hand, or shew of the Countenance, as a Command, and understand to obey it; nor dare they in their March, enter into any Corn Field, nor plunder in any friendly Country, as other Soldiers do, under pain of Death, so that the People, as with us, are not concerned when great Armies march, as knowing they shall lose nothing if they look to it, that it be not privately stolen; and Theft is severely punished amongst them.

To support this, and other Charges in the Empire, the Grand Signior's Incoms are accounted 20 Millions a Year, most of it arising from Presents, Customs, and Confiscation; though in his Dominions, whole Kingdoms lie in a manner waste, by reason of the vast number of Men consumed in War, or rather, industry is discouraged; for should they get Wealth by their Labour, it is theirs but during the Prince's pleasure, and none are certain how soon he may strip them of all. As

Europe, Asia, Africa *and* America. 35

As for the Religion of the Turks, it is no Ancienter than *Mahomet*, an Impostor, Born in *Arabia*, who set it abroach about the Reign of *Heraclitus*, the Emperor, for taking his Tenents from the *Arian* and *Nestorian* Heresies, denying the Divinity of our Saviour, he drew a Multitude after him, and becoming Powerful, forced many to follow his Opinion; and since it has been carried on by the Sword to spread so wide. The *Jewish*, and *Christian* Religion being then most prevalent, after dilating with himself, he leaned to the first, and mixed his own wild Notions with what he took out of the Mosaick Law, and from the Custom of the *Jews*, as a distinction between Clean and Unclean Meats, Circumcision; but the latter not performed at the end of 8 Days, as the *Jews* Custom is, but at the end of 8 Years, when the Child is able to make a Confession of his Belief, and speak in the *Arabick* Tongue, *viz.* *There is but one God, and* Mahomet *is his Prophet, one God, and equal Prophets.* At the Circumcision, there is Feasting three Days, for all the Friends and Kinsfolks. The Female Children only speak the Words; yet the Moorish Mahometans, in some parts, use a kind of a Circumcision to their Females, cutting off a bit of the Nimphæ. If any Christian turn Turk, he is led about the Streets, as in Triumph, and receives Presents and Gifts as he passes, to encourage him to persevere in his new undertaking; but the Men, be they of what Age they will, that so renounce their Faith, must be Circumcised, yet the Turks afterward set Light by those that Renounce, and will rarely Trust or Prefer them, saying, *They are not worthy to be trusted that Renounce their Faith, be it what it will.*

Their Laws is contained in the *Alcoran*, wherein among other things, one God, the Maker of the World, and of all Things, is owned. Can the *Turks* Honour Christ as a great Prophet, but deny him to be the Son of God? They are forbidden by their Law to Worship Images, or to have any set up in their Mosques; but their *Alcoran* indulges them in

D 2 Sensuallity,

Senfuallity, and promifes them much of Worldly Felicity, or fuch like pleafures as we have here, in another World, but obtain'd and carried on with greater Eafe and Happinefs, for their Paradife confifts in the enjoyment of handfom Women, and fuch like Trifles, though here they look on them to have no Souls, and fcarcely Rational Creatures.

They hold their Sabbath on our Friday, and their Lent lafts 30 days, during which time they neither Eat nor drink in the Day, but take their repaft after Sun-fet; but not till they have Notice by the Voice of Men from the Minarets or Steeples; they alfo abftain from Women; Wine is forbidden in their Law, yet many times they Caroufe it fo luftily in private, that they get Drunk; this Lent they call *Ramadan.*

Their *Bairam*, or *Eafter*, is continued with great fhew three Days, but it begins not precifely at a time, becaufe it muft commence at the New of the Moon, yet not till fhe appears; and trufty Perfons are fent to watch on the Mountains, and high places, to fee her, and he that firft difcovers her has a Reward, and then it begins with Proclamation; they have other publick times, as the little *Bairam, &c.*

If during the reading of the Law they look Back, fcratch their Heads, or do any thing that is unfeemly, they think they have loft the benefit they were to have received at that time; and I muft confefs they feem to be very precife in their Devotions, though generally very Ignorant in Learning; yet of late, fome of the better fort put their Children to learn the *Arabick* Tongue, becaufe the *Alcoran* is Written in it.

By their Law they have leave to Marry as many Wives as they can maintain, and when any of them proves with Child, the Husband muft not Carnally know her till fhe is delivered. There is another kind of Marriage Contract during Pleafure, called *Kebin*, moftly practifed by Strangers, who, for a certain Sum, fignifying their intention to the *Cadi*, who notes down the Contract, may have a Wife

for

Europe, Asia, Africa, and America.

for as long as he pleases; but when he turns her away, he must give her what he bargained for, and keep the Children, if she has any by her. The *Turks* often Divorce their Wives with shewing little or no Cause, but the Wives have not that Priviledge. They must prove before the Judge, that their Husbands are not able to keep them, or that they have attempted to use them against the course of Nature, and the like. If a *Turk* debauch a *Christian* Woman, both of them, upon Conviction, must suffer Death, unless he can perswade her to change her Faith, and so it is with a Christian and a Turkish Woman, he must turn *Turk*, or be burnt, unless by largely Bribing the *Cadi*, he can get it off, which sometimes happens, if she be of mean Rank.

Notwithstanding this liberty to Marry, and take so many Wives, the *Turks* are great *Sodomites*, and the Bassa's, &c. are guilty of keeping handsome Youths, whom they purchase as Slaves, to satisfie their Brutal Lusts this way, yet they keep it as private as may be.

The Chief Interpreter of their Law is the Mufti, or Arch-Priest. The Grand Signior nominates and chuses him from among the Learned Men in their Law. He is greatly Reverenced by the *Turks*, and termed the Head of their Church, and the decider of all Controversies arising in matters of Religion. All the Bassa's are subject to his Directions, as a Rule to them in their Government. He abaseth himself not to set down in the Divan, only he passes very stately through it, when he is sent for by the Grand Signior, who rises at his approach to do him Honour, then places him by him on his Seat, and discourses familiarly with him about matters of Religion, State, or Previous Questions; and this Honour is allowed to no other.

Next to the Mufti, in this sort of Dignity, are the Cadile-Squires, Talismen, or two Doctors of the Law, whose business it is to examine the Cadi's, or Judges, dispersed in the Provinces of the Empire; and these for the most part are attendant on the

Grand Signior. One has Jurisdiction over the *European* Cadi's, and the other over the rest, and are Sovereign Judges within their own Jurisdiction, in all causes about matters of Religion, and are, as it were, Patriarchs. These are of great Authority, having places in the Divan, and in the Council of Bassa's, where they are consulted in the weighty Affairs of the Empire.

There are a degree of Churchmen not belonging to their Law, called *Mulli*, and these are instead of Bishops, but directed in their proceedings by the Mufti.

Another sort there are, called *Nuderisi*, who act in the Nature of Suffragans, and have under them several young Doctors of the Law, called *Naipi*, who are constituted, in the absence of the Cadi's, to hear and Redress grievances.

Next to the foregoing, are the *Hagi*, who write Books, and inferior to them are the *Caffii*, who Read to them as they Write. These are their several degrees of Churchmen and Lawyers, for the *Turks* are govern'd by a kind of an Ecclesiastical Law, according to their *Alcoran*. They have many Colleges, which they call *Medressa*'s, Scituate in *Constantinople*, and divers other Cities.

CHAP.

CHAP. IV.

The Belief of the Turks, *and many other things practised among them; as their Charity, Mourning at Funerals, Games, Just Observances,* &c.

THE *Turks* believe that after any Person is Dead and layed in the Grave, the Angels come to examine them, and that they have Angels to guard them in their Life time, every one being appointed to a particular Member; and when they take up any piece of Paper in the Street, least the Name of God should be writ on it, they will not take it along with them, for fear of putting it to prophane Uses, but stick it on the next Wall, so that the Cranies are often found stuck full of them; yet they will Swear by the Name of God, but it is to what is Truth, for otherways they are looked on as Ignominious, and Infidels. As to their Belief, they hold that divers Beasts go to Paradise, as the Camel of *Selch*: (one of their Prophets) the Ram of *Abraham*, offered up in Sacrifice; the Cow of *Moses*, whose Ashes was mingled with the Water of Purification, which seems to be the Golden Calf in *Horeb*; *Solomon*'s Ant; the Parrot of the Queen of *Sheba*. They also believe *Jonas's* Whale that cast him on dry Land, and *Mahomet*'s Ass shall be there likewise; four Sleepers, and a little Dog, who led them to a Cave in time of Persecution, where they slept 300 Years, which seemed to them but as one Night, for one of them going to buy Victuals when they awaked with Antiquated Money, the time was discovered by the Date of the Coin. They hold in *Paradise*, according to *Mahomet*'s promise, that they shall

shall enjoy Virgins, fresh Coloured, with large Black Eyes, and Beautiful Boys attending them; who at first shall be but Fifteen, and never exceed Thirty Years of Age, always in a Bloom or Spring of Beauty; and that God shall appear to them every Friday, which is their Sabbath; that there they shall have Rivers, pleasant Fields, Gardens, and the like. They say those in Hell shall Drink scalding Water, and Eat of the Fruit of a Tree called *Zacon*, which grows out of the bottom of Hell, and rises to a great heighth, the Branches of it being like the Heads of Devils; and if those that are in Hell have a little Faith, after they are purged by Fire, to consume their Sins, they shall be washed in a Water called *Selzaboul*, and then admitted into Paradise; but those that have not Faith when they are consumed to Ashes, shall be Created a new, and so prepared Eternally to endure the Torments; they hold a kind of Purgatory, but they say there are many back Doors, by which they may give the Devil the slip, if they are watchful and cunning. They Pray for the Dead, and invocate a sort of Saints of their own making.

 The *Turks* have many Fountains, and in washing they think they are free from Defilements, even after having lain with their Wives, Nocturnal Pollutions, their Urin dropping on their Garments, or touch a Dog, and indeed in any other matters that they conceive they are Polluted; and they are so Nice in it, that upon Travelling, they will go a great way to seek Water, and if they find none, to do it with Sand; and indeed they keep their Bodies in all parts extream cleanly, even to Superstition, in many Rights and Ceremonies they use, as the Abdest and Goust.

 The sober *Turks* are very Charitable to Men and Beasts, doing all they can to relieve them in their Necessities, so that they supply the Poor for the most part, without putting any to the Shame of appearing in the Streets to Beg; some of them when they die, leave Pensions to maintain Beasts, to keep them during

Europe, Asia, Africa, *and* America. 43
ring their Natural Lives; and in *Constantinople,* I
saw a Bitch who had got into a Corner to cast her
Whelps; the *Turks* no sooner saw it, but they made
a Wall with Bricks and Stones about her, and several run and fetched Victuals, and other Necessaries,
which in a wonderful manner shewed their compassion towards the poor Creature, nor did one or other leave attending her, till the Puppies were taken from her, and she capable of shifting for her
self.

Images, as I have already hinted, are prohibited
amongst the *Turks,* but they are very desirous of
curious Paintings, though they are not Artists at it.
There is a prohibition of Usury by their Alcoran,
though it is connivingly done by the *Turks,* and
the *Jews* practice it frequently. Swines Flesh is
counted unclean among them, and some *Turks*
would rather die than Eat it; nor dare the Shoomakers use Hog's Bristles in sowing their Shooes, if
it should be known, they would be punished. When
a *Turk* dies, there is great Mourning; the greater the
Quality, the more the Women fall a howling excessively, and those that cannot frame themselves to
it, hire those that are accustomed to it, and as often
as any Visitants come, the Lamentation is renewed;
and when the Corps is in the Grave, they go often
thither to Weep, the Widow expressing what good
things her deceased Husband has done for her ; they
often spread Carpets with Victuals, that those that
pass by may Eat it, and Pray for the Soul of the
deceased. They set at the Head of the Grave a
Stone, which they say, the Angel that is to examine
him sits on; and they bid the Dead Person answer him
stoutly, and not be afraid. They burn Incense about
the Graves, as they say, to scare away the Evil Spirits, and Pray to God to be merciful to the Party;
and according to his Quality, he has a Turban
placed at the Head of the Grave, or Tomb, by
which he is distinguished, as to his Rank.

As for the *Turks* in general, they are well proportioned, strong in Body; and the Women are mostly

Handsom, their Complexion Fair, because they seldom stir abroad, unless the Vulgar Sort. The Habit of Men and Women is very neat and commendable, keeping still in one Fashion. They are People of a Jolley temper, and much rely on Fatality, every one concluding there is a set time for all Accidents, and none believe they shall die before the appointed Hour, which in War makes them run upon desperate attempts, for they are verily perswaded, they may as well die in their Beds as in the Field at the same time; and if it is so decreed, their Fate is irresistable. They are in Passive Obedience to their Prince, and submit to his Decrees, without reasoning the Justice or Injustice of them; they play at divers Games, but never for Money, to avoid Quarrelling; and Duelling is a thing not known amongst them. However they are very Proud, and esteem all others inferiour to them, thinking themselves the Valiantest and Wisest Men on Earth; a conceited Vanity too much indulged amongst Christians; they are exceeding Superstitious, and their Ignorance is the Mother of their Devotion, for their Priests labour to keep them so, that they may not discern Truth from Fables.

As to Weight and Measure they are very Just, for one may send a Child to the Market, and they dare not in the least defraud it; for there are Persons who overlook those places, and if they discover a defraud, the Person who does it is Bastinado'd, and perhaps, unless he Compounds, severely fined; and although, as in all Nations, there are some Irregularities committed, yet here a great Caution is used to prevent it, though sometimes Broils happen in the Streets, when the *Turks* get Drunk, and Blood is shed.

After all this, they account *Christians* no better than Dogs, and as often, almost, as they see them in the Streets, put more or less Affront upon them, except such as are protected by Janisaries, or other Authority; they swear by their Beards, the Head of their Ancestors, and that of the Grand Signior, which

Europe, Asia, Africa, *and* America. 43
which they seldom break; for though none within the *Seraglio* but the Grand Signior, and the *Bostangi* Bassa, are allowed to ware their Beards, those without are not limitted.

CHAP. V.

Their Pilgrimages to Mecha *and* Medina; *the Birth, and Burial-places of* Mahomet *their Prophet; what they Observe; and a description of the House, Tomb, and what else is Curious and Admirable in this Undertaking.*

THE *Turks* are very Devout and Punctual in their Pilgrimages to *Mecha* in *Arabia*, to visit *Mahomet*'s Tomb, and every Year there goes a great Caravan from *Constantinople*, as well as from divers other places, which I shall mention at the conclusion of this Chapter, and they so time it, that they may be there at the time of their Carnaval. The Grand Signior sends Rich presents, as Velvet embroidered with Gold, and *Arabian* Characters in Gold and Silver, Pearl and Rich Stones, for Canopies, Carpets, Coverings for the Doors, &c. but these usually are sent from *Cair* in *Ægypt*, because it is much nearer to *Mecha* than *Constantinople*; and when the Holy Cammel, as they term it, who carries these Rich Ornaments passes by, there is great crouding to touch the Burthen, and those that do it, kiss their Fingers, and think themselves Blessed.

This Caravan amounts most times, to between 10 and 20000, and sometimes a far greater number. I shall not trouble the Reader with a Journal of the way, because I Travelled it not; however, it must
be

be very tedious, becaufe it is Long, and over Defarts, and rugged Mountains, which makes them take great ftore of Provifions with them, and Veffels to recruit them with Frefh Water, which in the Hot Countries they pafs, is rarely to be found; they moftly Encamp in the Fields and Defarts, being always conftrained to fet Watches, leaft Robbers fhould break in on the out skirts of their Camp, to kill and plunder, before the Alarum can be taken; nay, the wild Beafts near Forrefts affault them, and kill Men and Cattle, efpecially fuch as ftraggle too far from the main Body; but for the hardfhips they endure, fome Priviledges are allowed them, for whatever Crimes they commit lower than Treafon, if they efcape, and make this Pilgrimage, upon their return they are abfolved, and accounted as Honeft as if they had never Offended. They have a Guard of Janifaries, with many others who go Armed, and their number gathers by the way, like a Snow-ball rowled from a fteep Mountain; they appear all the way very devout, the number confifting of Men, Women, and Children; fome indeed, take the advantage of Trade and Commerce, carrying ftore of rich Wares with them; all the way, thofe in Pilgrimage Sing Verfes of their *Alcoran*, and beftow Charity according as they are able.

When they come within two days Journey of *Mecha*, they ftrip themfelves, only leaving their Privities covered with a Napkin, for it is a Capital Offence, either in Man or Woman, to let them be feen, and another Napkin about their Necks, alledging this kind of Franfey, to be out of refpect to the place where their Prophet had fo often Travelled; on their Feet they wear Scandals, faying, *The Ground is Holy, and we will not defile it with our naked Feet*: And in this State they continue 8 Days, during which term, it is not lawful to be Shaved, to Buy or Sell, kill any thing, or be angry with their Servants, nor fpeak any thing that is unfeemly; and if any one Trefpaffes, he is to attone by

Alms;

Alms; those that are Sick are dispensed from Striping, but they must in lieu of it give Alms.

When they come to *Mecha*, they stay there three Days, during which time they visit the several places of Devotion. This *Mecha* is an Ancient Town Scituate among the Mountains, built all of Stone and Mortar; and here they hold *Mahomet* was Born, prohibiting all but Musselmen to enter it on pain of Death. In the middle of it is the Kiaabe, or Square House; it is surrounded with a Wall to hinder approach; they go round it several times in Devotion, saying certain Prayers, an Imum, or Priest, goes before them, and what Antick Trick or Gestures soever he shews, they imitate him; first they walk softly and Mutter their Prayers, then, at certain Intervals, they Run and Skip, shruging and turning their Shoulders many ways; then they fall into a soft pace again, and so continue it by turns, till they have ended their Prayers. This House is covered with a Dome, and it has a Well of good Water, considering what other places afford about the City, they being mostly Brackish or Bitter; near to the Door, upon the entrance of this House or Temple, is a black Stone, as big as a Pumpion: This the *Turks* say, came down from Heaven, and was then White, but Man's Sins polluted it, and made it turn Black; and he that can first kifs it, when they have given one another the *Selam*, after the Prayer of *Koufchlouk*, on Friday, which falls within three Days that they sojourn there, is held a Saint, and every one strives to kifs his Feet; but this same proves Fatal to the Party, who is smoothered in the Croud. This House is never entered but four times a Year, and one of them is at the Ramadan, to wash it with Rose-Water, unless any one will give 100 Chequins of Gold for admittance. It is covered all round on the out-side with Stuffs sent by the Grand Signior, in whose Dominions it is, and other *Mahometan* Princes; and every Year the rich Covering is renewed; the old being cut out into Relicks, and sold by the Sultan *Scherif*, who

Commands,

Commands, to Pilgrims, at a good Rate, unless the *Little Bairam*, or *Easter* Sacrifice falls on a Friday, and then the Grand Signior has it, to send in pieces to the New Mosques, which being hung up there, serves instead of their Consecration.

When the Pilgrims have finished their three days at *Mecha*, they go to *Minnet*, where they are to arrive the Vigil of the *Little Bairam*, and on the day of *Bairam*, they Sacrifice Sheep, every one according to Ability, distributing part to the Poor; then they shave themselves, and put on their Clothes to visit Mount *Arafat*, and there they stay 3 days more; the first Day after they have said Prayers, they go to the Foot of the Hill, throw 7 Stones against the Mount, and stay there, the next Day they throw 14, and the Third 21: They say they throw these Stones to break the Devil's Head, who in that place tempted *Abraham*, when he was going to Sacrifice his Son *Ishmael*, for they will not allow it to be *Isaac*. Here they say, *Adam* and *Eve* fought one another for the space of 220 Years, after they were driven out of *Paradise*, the one going up the Mountain on one side, whilst the other went up on the other side, and so made it a Fruitless search, but at the end of this time met just on the top of it. Here the Sultan *Scherif* says some Prayers, and gives them his Benediction, and so this Work is concluded. He has abundance of ways, under the Umbrage of Devotion, to squeeze Money out of them, and is vastly Rich.

After this the Pilgrims go to *Medina*, to visit *Mahomet*'s Tomb, which according to Authentick Relations, does not hang in the Air by Virtue of Loadstones: It stands as other Tombs, and is indeed encompassed with Iron Grates, upon a suspition they once had, that 2 Christians, Habited like Deviles, intended to steal it away, and for that purpose had dug under it, to get the Body. *Medina* is 3 Days Journey from the *Red Sea*, its Port is called *Jambo*. This and *Mecha* are but indifferent Towns, though of such great Resort. About the middle of
Medina

Medina is a Mosque, and in a Corner of it stands *Mahomet*'s Tomb, covered as the Monuments of the *Turkish* Emperors at *Constantinople*. The Sepulchre is in a little round Building, or Tower, covered with a Dome, which the *Turks* call *Turbe*. The Building is quite open to the middle; up to the Dome, and all round there is a little Gallery, of which the out-side Wall has several Windows with Silver Grates to them, and the inside Wall of the little Tower adorned with a great number of precious Stones, being the place that answers to the Head of the Tomb; and this certainly is exceeding Rich, by the Gifts of many Princes, and others, as Diamonds, Gold, Rubies, Saphires, and other sorts of Jewels, that might, for their Value, purchase a petty Kingdom; and lower down, there is a half Moon of Gold of a vast Value, by reason of the precious Stones which enchase it.

The Turbe, wherein the Tomb is, is hung round with Hangings of Red and White Silk, like Damask, unless where the Jewels are, and there they are turned aside, that their Lustre may appear, and round the Hangings are Words in Characters of Gold, expressing the Names of GOD, and *Mahomet*, &c. The Door, by which one enters into the Gallery, is Silver, and so is that which goes out of the Gallery into the Turbe. The Pilgrims visit some other places hereabouts, but of no great Note, yet one thing more is confirmed on all Hands, to be very remarkable in those dry Countries, *viz.* The next Night after the Pilgrims are gone, so much Rain falls, that it seems like a Deluge, for a time, and much Fertelizes the Plains, washing away all the Blood and Filth of the Sacrifices, and this falls always the Third Night after the Sacrifice at their *Little Beiram*, or *Easter*, though this tide generally changes the Day, as with us our *Easter* does; and this they look upon as a Miracle, to confirm their Oblations are accepted; and indeed the wisest of Men may be puzzeled, to know, whether so exact a falling of Rain, in a Country, parched and dry,

for

for the moſt part, proceeds from a Natural, or Supernatural Cauſe.

Many times 100000 People meet at *Mecha* together, encamping on the Plains; as for their going to *Medina*, ſome refuſe it, becauſe they are not bound by their Law, to viſit *Mahomet*'s Tomb, but at Pleaſure, and then they muſt ſay a Prayer for his Soul. The other Caravans come from *Ægypt, Syria, Perſia, India*, and *Barbery*; ſo that the Concourſe, according to the Relation I had, is exceeding great.

CHAP. VI.

Travels and Voyages to Alexandria *in* Ægypt; *with many things remarkable in the way,* &c.

THUS having taken a view of *Conſtantinople*, with the places about it; the Religion, Manners, Cuſtoms, &c. of the *Turks*, I could not, however, reſt ſatisfied, my curioſity now abroad, leading me on to viſit remoter Countries; wherefore, I ſet forward for *Burſa*, the Ancient *Pruſea*, formerly the Capital City of the Turkiſh Empire, taken from the *Caramanian* King, by *Orcham*, or *Urcham*, Son of *Othoman*, in his Father's Life time. It was likewiſe the Ancient Seat of the Kings of *Bythinia*. In order to this, I went on Board at *Tophana*, and was tranſported to *Montagua*, but making no ſtay in ſuch an inconſiderable place, I took Horſe, and rid to *Burſa*, 13 Miles from it; this City is not above 10 Miles diſtant from Mount *Olimpus*: It is pleaſantly Scituated, and well Watered by Aquaducts; it conſiſts of many fair Buildings, and they reckon about 200 fine Moſques. There, in little Chapels covered with Domes, lie Buried the firſt *Turkiſh* Sultans,

Sultans, and *French* Sultana, in great State. The City is about half a French League in length, but not Walled in all parts; and upon a little Hill in the middle of it, is a little Castle, found to be built by a Maiden Princess, who was cured of a Leprosie by the Hot Waters; for as a wonder in Nature, there runs a Rivulet of Hot Water, almost scalding those that step into it at first; and there one sees the Tomb of *Roland*, or *Orland*, a very Valiant Man, who defended the City against all Assaults; his Sword, Mace, and other warlike Habiliaments hang by it; but this Tomb stands on a Hill, in a little Chapel, where usually a Turkish Hermit Lives.

From this place I set forward to *Smyrna*, and arrived there by several Stages, finding nothing in the way memorable. *Smyrna* is about 8 days Journey of a Caravan from *Burfa*; It is a noted Town of *Jonia*; they say it was first Founded by *Tantulus*, and since called *Smyrna*, by an Amazon of that Name, who Conquered it; it has been subject to Earthquakes, and felt the dire effects of them, by being reduced to a heap of Rubbish; and after that built by *Mark Anthony*, nearer to the Sea than at first it stood; the People boast that *Homer* was Born there; the *Turks* at present call it *Ismyr*. This City, Anciently one of the Seven Churches of *Asia*, to whom St. *John* was commanded to Write, is very well Peopled, and Defended by a Castle, but it is not strong; there is a huge Cistern cut out of a Rock, and the Amphitheatre, where St. *Policarp* suffered Martyrdom. There is another Castle nearer the Sea, and on the Gate, the Arms of the Church of *Rome*, supposed to be erected by the *Genoese*, who once were Masters of the City, and all the Coast. This Castle shuts the Port, which is but little, so that the Stranger Trading Ships ride at Anchor abroad, in the Road, which is good and spacious. There is another Castle at the Mouth of the Road, commanding the Ships that enter, and go out, for the Custom here is very considerable to the Grand Signior,

Signior, most *European* Traders having Consuls there. The Country about it is Spacious, Pleasant, and Fruitful; Oyl, and a pleasant sort of Wine, called *Smyrna* Wine, in abundance. The Air is Temperate, for in the Heat of Summer the Northern Breezes blow, and cool all the Region about it.

After I had tarried here 8 Days, I found a Vessel bound for *Alexandria* in *Ægypt*: I had read much of that anciently Famed Country, which enticed me to lay hold on the opportunity of being an Eye-Witness, of what had been almost every where spoke of it, so embarked with my Baggage, and in two Days came to an Anchor in the Port, or Road of *Chio*, a very fine Island, mostly inhabited by *Greeks*: There grows abundance of Mastick Trees, which yield the Owners great advantage; they grow crooked, like a Vine, and being cut, the Gum, called Mastick, at a certain Season, flows from them, and is the best that is to be found. The Christians, both *Greeks* and *Latins*, have their free Liberty to exercise their Religion, so that there are a great many Religious Houses, and they enjoy greater Priviledges, than any within the Turkish Dominions; for here they have Bells in some Monasteries, and elsewhere they are not allowed, particularly at *Niamoni*. The Villages stand here very thick, and the Inhabitants are numerous; but the Ship coming to Anchor here, only by reason of bad Weather, I had time to take but a slight View e'er I Sailed again; and passing many other Islands, as *Samas*, *Nicaria*, &c. in the former of these, in the Night, I saw a light near the Sea, rising and falling, as big as a large Candle, which the Patron of the Vessel, who was a *Greek*, told me, always appeared in the Ruins of a Christian Church, but as any Man approached it, it vanished, or removed further from them, which made me conclude, it was an *Ignis fatuis*, rising from the Unctuous Vapours, and kindled by Agitation. These Islands are now Poor, and of no great Note, though Anciently very

ry

ry Famous. I shall pass over others that appeared on Star, and Larboard, and sometimes a Head of us; we Sailed near some in great danger, by reason of the bad Weather, and Rocks that jutted out in the shallowness of the Sea near them, the Winds shifting, and the Waves running high; but after all, at Sun rising, a gentle Gale blowing from the South, we spread our Sails, and cleared our Vessel of a dangerous Streight, between some Rocks and Islands, that we were fallen in with; and about Evening, shifting to the North West, we stood away South and by East, so that next Morning we made the Island of *Rhodes*, and about Noon came to an Anchor in a good Harbour, to recruit our selves with Provisions, for the Storms we met with spoiled most we brought with us, the Waves frequently rowling over the wast of our small Vessel, during that Violence, so that a great deal of Water enter'd her, and all Hands were at the Pump Night and Day.

This noted Island has *Lycia* to the North, a Sea 20 Miles over, separating them. To the East, *Cyprus*; to the West, *Candie*; and to the South, *Ægypt*; it lies in a temperate Climate, and is in Circuit about 100 Miles; few Clouds are ever seen over it; it is very Fruitful, and the *Turks* strugled long before they could be entire Masters of it, which happened in the Reign of *Solyman the Magnificent*; for the City that gave the Name to this Island, was then taken, at the Expence of 150000 *Turks*, from the great Master, and Renowned Knights, Hospitallers, who Immortallized their Fame, in defending it to the last extremity. This City has two commodious Harbours, did not the great one lie so open to the East, and North-East Winds, that sometimes drive Ships from their Anchors, The *Turks* have built a strong new Tower in the place of the old one, to command the Entrance, and Centinels are placed in Turrets, to give Notice of the approach of Ships. It has a Bastion and Curtain, that reaches to the Town, so that it makes one side of the Port, and there is an Old Castle over-against it: Over this Port formerly stood a Huge Collossus of Brass, one of the Wonders of the World, for it stood stradling 50 Fathom, one Foot from another, and 70 Cubits high, so that Ships under Sail passed under it; it represented the Sun, and was cast by *Chares* the *Lydian*: In one Hand it held a Light-House, to direct Ships in, in dark Nights; but it was thrown down by an Earthquake, and being broken by the Sarasens, when they Conquered *Rhodes*; they sold it to a Jew, who loaded 900 Camels with the Metal for *Alexandria*, and now the Tower and Castle I mentioned, are built where the Feet of it stood. There are many Ancient Monuments remaining in this City; as the Statue of St. *Paul*, and divers others of Note. The Escutcheons of Christian Princes, and the Knights of the Order of St. *John* of *Jerusalem*. The Building is Regular, and the Streets pretty Fair. But now the Wind serving, I was constrained to end my Observation here, and return on Board; we set Sail with a North-west Wind, and soon left *Lindo* a-stern, being a little Rock at the point of the Island of *Rhodes*, 20 Leagues from the City, and on it there is a small Town, with a very good Fort. The next that appeared was *Scarpanto*, 17 Leagues distant from *Lindo*, leaving it to the Starboard, we enter'd the Gulf of *Satalia*, where, for a considerable time Sailing, we had a Rowling Sea, the Current there setting with Eddies, and it is many times dangerous passing, for Ships are often cast away there; and here we were encompassed with many flashes of Lightning, that glancing on the Waters, made the Sea seem as on Fire, looking very terrible; and I plainly perceived the Master of the Ship was at a loss to stand in with the Coast, so that it growing somewhat Calm, we made little way that Night.

The Morning proving Fair, the Man sent up to discover, could, however, see no Land, but the whiteishness of the Water made the Sailors conclude, we must be near the Land of *Ægypt*, which is the only Mark at a great diftance, that can be obferved, the Land lying fo low, that it is not made till a Ship is in a manner upon it.

This whiteneſs is occaſioned by the River *Nile*, that carries it a great way into the Sea, and at this diftance from the Coaft, we had many Flurreys, accompanied with great Showers of Rain, but they were in a little time over, and the Wind coming about North-weft, we tacked, and fent up again to difcover, but no Land appearing, we kept failing South and South-weft; but fearing to loſe the Windward of *Alexandria*, we ſtood Eaſt and by South, but finding that a miftake, we tacked about that we might get nearer to the Land, from which we knew we could not be far diftant, and held on the ſame Courſe, till we found our ſelves obliged to Tack, and bear away South-weft; here we ſaw the Moon riſe Eccliṕſed, half an hour after Sun ſet, which was not viſible in *England*, *Holland*, *France*, &c. becauſe there, according to the Almanacks, the Ecclips, was to happen at 3 in the Afternoon, Feb. 11. and the next Day we percieved the Sea very white about us, and the Man that looked out cryed Land; ſome thought it to be *Damiette*, and others *Bouquer*; but in the mean time, that we might not Sail to Leeward, we continued our Courſe South-weft, and in a few Hours we Tacked and ſtood North eaſt; and about a quarter of an hour after the Wind turning North-weft, we bore away South and South-weft, and in concluſion we made the *Bouquer*, and a little after the *Farillon*, or Light-Houſe of *Alexandria*, and at 3 of the Clock in the Afternoon the ſame day, we entered the Haven by the South. One thing I found remarkable in approaching Land, from *Damiette* to *Roſſetto*, between the two Branches of the *Nile*, that from 40 Fathom Water, it leſſens every Mile till you come to Land. *Ægypt* is bounded on the Eaſt with the *Red Sea*, on the South with *Aſia*, on the Weſt with *Cyrene*, and on the North with the *Mediterranean Sea*.

CHAP. VII.

The Author's Arrival at Alexandria, *and what is observable there; and his passing from thence to* Caire.

BEING now at Land, and recovered from my Sea fatigue, by suitable Refreshments, my curiosity lead me to take a view of this once so Renowned City, Founded by *Alexander* the Great, when, after his *Persian* Expedition, he brought Ægypt under his Subjection, though it is not comparable to what it has been in its flourishing time, as may appear by the Ruins about it, and within its Circumference, and the Venerable remains of Antiquity.

This Town is called by the *Turks*, who possess all *Ægypt*, *Skenderia*. There are in it several Fondicks, or large Houses, where the *English*, *French*, *Dutch*, and other *Europeans*, have their appointed Residence, paying no House Rent, but on the contrary, the Consuls receive Money of the Grand Signior Annually to keep them in suitable Repair, they being every Evening shut up, and the Keys carried to the Aga of the Castle, who sends them back every Morning; they are likewise shut up, as is the Water-gate, every *Friday*, during Noon Prayer; and this arises from an old Prophesie, that the *Franks*, for so they call all Christian *Europeans*, shall become Masters of that place, during Noon Prayer, on a *Friday*.

Scarce any thing of the Ancient Town remains unruinated but the Walls, and some Buildings towards the French Fondick, which are almost ruined; it being easie to distinguish the Ancient from the Later Buildings, for the latter are low, and ill-contrived.

This

Europe, Asia, Africa *and* America. 55

This once Famous Town has three Ports, one called the Old Harbour; it is pretty large, but the entrance difficult, so that but few Vessels put in there ; the other two are separated by a little Island, and higher up, the Island was anciently called *Pharos*, and is joyned to the main Land by a Stone Bridge, and in the middle of it is a square Tower, where the Powder is kept, and at the end, another Castle, called *Farillon*, standing where the Ancient Watch-Tower of *Pharos* stood, which was accounted one of the Seven Wonders of the World. The first of these Ports is a Harbour for the Galleys, and is on one side defended by the *Farillon,* and on the other by a slighter Castle ; but these Ports are encumbered with Stones and Rocks, requiring a skilful Pilot to guide in Vessels of any considerable Burthen. The Custom-house here is Farmed by a *Turk,* and has a *Jew* for his Deputy, and indeed the Receipt of Custom mostly passes through the *Jew*'s Hands, who can pleasure, or displeasure many that Trade there: There is also an Old Custom house, but of little Note.

In *Alexandria* there is a Mount made of Ancient Ruins, on which stands a square Tower, and a Sentinel, who puts out a Flag so soon as he descrys a Sail, and every Vessel coming into the Port pays him something. All Officers here depend on the Bassa of *Ægypt*, who places and displaces them at his pleasure.

The Walls of this Town have Fals, Brays, and are flanked with great square Towers, about 200 Paces distant one from another, and a little Tower between every two of them; in each of the great Tower there is a large square Hall, the Vault of it supported by Pillars of *Thebaick* Stone, and a great many Chambers above, and over these a large Platform, of 30 Foot Square, and each of these anciently were able to maintain 200 Men; the Walls are very thick, and every where Port-holes in them; these Castles have Cisterns, replenished with Water, but most part of those that encompassed the

E 4 ancient

ancient *Alexandria*, as it was in its former Extent and Lustre, are ruined by the length of Time, and neglect of Repair; but if the *Turkish* Officers catch an *European* Christian in these Towers, they presently charge him as a Spy, come to view the strength of the Town, and then nothing but Money will release him from Punishment.

Near this Town is the famous Pillar of *Pompey*, so much celebrated by Historians; it stands about 200 Paces distant, upon a little rising, placed on a square Pedestal, about 7 or 8 Foot high, that resting on a square Basis, about 20 Foot broad, and 2 Foot high, made up of several large Stones; the Body of the Pillar is an entire piece of Garnet, about 6 Fathom in Compass, having on the Top a very curious Capital: and it must create Admiration, by what strong Engines so vast a Stone could be brought thither, which makes some believe it was cast, and made of a certain Cement on the place, which Art was usual with the Ancients, though now, for any thing that appears, it is lost.

In this place appears the remains of *Cæsar*'s Pallace, but all that can be called entire of it, are some Porphery Pillars, and a Frontispiece, which looks very curious. There is a *Kibalis*, or *Canal*, cut from the *Nile*, which brings Water to this place, and is the only good Water they have; this fills their Cisterns that are Magnificently made, and placed under in Vaults, the whole Town being hollow underneath, and supported by fair Marble Pillars, and some say, there are fair Streets under Ground, wherein there are Shops to be seen still; but the *Turks*, for some Reasons, will not discover them, nor suffer any to go down in the Vaults that lead to them. All along, the Gardens border on the *Kabalis*, planted with Lemon, Orange, and other curious Trees, as Caffa, and Corab Trees, and the like.

Here stands St. *Catharine*'s Church, kept by the *Greeks*, where they show a hollow Pillar, on which they say her Head was cut off, and would make

Travellers believe, that the Blood and Fat it is smeered with, remained ever since her Decolation. There is a pretty neat Church built to St. *Mark*, where he received his Martyrdome, and the Picture of St. *Michael*, said to be drawn by St. *Luke*; there are to be seen in some ruinous places, Pillars of Porphyrian Marble, and Obelisks of Garnet, with Hierogliphicks upon them, yet but one of them standing on a Pedestal.

Many other things are here to be seen, but not to be tedious, I shall omit the describing of all the Statues and Figures mostly encumbered with Ruins, which are very numerous, and rather demonstrate the former Magnificence of the place, than what it now is; and having setled my Affairs here, I hired a Janisary for my greater security to pass on with me to *Caire*, the Principal place of *Ægypt*; but before I went thither, I visited *Rossetto*, about 60 miles from *Alexandria*, there being but one place to bait at by the way, called *Maudie*, or the Passage, because you Ferry over a Lock there, full of Fish, though there is a Castle nearer called *Bouquier*, to defend the Road, the rest, or the greatest part, being Desart Sands; on the other side of the Water is a Kervanserai, or Inn, where you may be welcome to Eat and Drink such as you bring with you for nothing; most part of this Journey you Travel along the Sea-side: You may see where the *Nile* discharges it self into the Sea, which is a very dangerous Passage, there being Saiques and Barks usually cast away in venturing, especially when the Sea is rough, for then it occasions an Eddy in the Water of the River, which turning the Vessels round casts them on Shoar. *Rossetto* is the ancient *Canopus*. Lying in a Branch of the *Nile*, falling into the Sea five Miles below the Town; and this is accounted the neatest Town in *Ægypt* for its Piazza's and Hans, being a Town of good Trade, encompassed by five Gardens, the Houses high and well built; Provisions plenty, and at a very cheap Rate. From hence taking Water on the *Nile*, I pass'd with
many

many others to *Boulac*, a Port of *Caire*. This is a long narrow Town, built on the side of the *Nile*, and has about it many pleasant Gardens and Country Houses; and here by Custom, you must, being a *Frank*, pay at your first coming to *Caire* a Piastre, which is received by *Jews*, Authorized for that purpose. At this place we hired Asses to go to *Caire*, which the *Moors* kept ready sadled, on purpose to wait for Travellers, and accommodate them, and you have the Ass, and the Master's Attendance for a small Charge; the latter running after and driving the Ass on, and crying, *look to it*, which the Ass hearing, is very cautious of stumbling.

CHAP. VIII.

A View of Caire, *and what is Remarkable in it,* &c.

*C*AIRE is the Capital City of *Ægypt*, and with it runs the fortune of the whole Country; when it was wrested from the *Mamalukes* by Sultan *Selim*, Emperor of the *Turks*, *Anno* 1571, who caused *Thomambey*, the *Mamaluke* Sultan, to be hanged on a Hook, under one of the Gates, and exterminating the whole Race of those Men; setled the *Turkish* Government under a Bassa, as his Viceroy. This City is Scituate at the Foot of a Hill, on which a Castle is built to Command it, which renders it unhealthful, insomuch, that the Pestilence often rages there, and sweeps away a multitude of People, for the Wind intercepts the free passage of the Wind and Air, and occasions a stifling Heat; and the good Water they have is brought on Camels Backs from *Boulac* in *Bourachios*, which is half a League from the City, and this Water is sold very dear. This

Europe, Asia, Africa, *and* America. 59

This City is exceeding large, and full of People, being in the form of a Crescent, yet is narrow, and may be compassed in two Hours and a quarters Walking: It is surrounded with many stateley Pallaces of the Beys, and other great Men of the Country; the Houses are little, but full of People, so that when the Plague sweeps away 200000, it is hardly perceived, especially in a little time after. The Walls have handsom Battlements and Towers, at less than 100 Paces interval, able to hold many Soldiers; they appear to have been very Stately, but at present mostly ruinous. The Castle likewise is much decayed, the *Turks* being Supine, make little account of repairing them; near the Walls are large Church Yards, full of Sepulchers, adorned with fair Stone, that gives a pleasant Prospect, and all agree, that in this City there are 23000 Precincts, and as many Mosques, there being one in a Precinct at least. A Precinct is a set part, and in some of them there are several Streets; and each Precinct is watched by two Men Chained together, to prevent them from separating, and they demand certain dues of the Inhabitaints and Strangers; the Sons-Bassa keeps the Keys of the Padlocks that lock up their Chains. The Streets here are short and narrow, except the Street of *Bazar* and the *Khalis*, which is dry but 3 Months in the Year, and few People frequent it; the rest are little, turning and winding, which makes me believe the Houses were first built without any design of compacting them into a City, every one placing his House on the ground he liked best to build on, without considering whether they stopped the Street or not. Some Mosques are very Magnificent, with curious Frontispieces and Gates, with very high Minarets; but the greatest part are little and inconsiderable; The fairest is called *Degemiel Azem*. The Houses are high, with flat Tarass-Roofs, where they take the fresh Air when the Sun is down, and lie on Carpets there in the heat of Summer.

On the out-side the Houses make little show, but within, they are Richly adorned with Gold and Azure, especially those of Quality, and their Halls have an open round hole in the Roofs, to let in the cool Breathings of the Air, and commonly there is a Cupulo, or Lanthorn, over the hole, to keep out blustering Winds.

CHAP. IX.

Of the Piramids of Ægypt, and other Buildings and memorable Antiquities; of the Catacombs, *where the* Munices *are. The River* Nile, *and the Creatures found therein*, &c.

HAving taken a view of *Caire*, I was desirous to see those Wonders of the World so much every where discoursed of, *viz.* The Piramids of *Ægppt.* These are seated on a Sandy Plain; two of them are shut, but the third, which is biggest is open, and seated very near the other, two or three Leagues from New *Caire.* This is a vast Artificial Monument, built mostly of Stones of a Prodigious bigness, though they differ in that, for in Reason, we cannot suppose, that so many Stones of an equal bigness should be found for the supplying so stupendious a Work; yet the smallest are a Foot thick, and 2 Foot in length; some 3 Foot thick, 6 long, and 4 broad: The highth of the greatest of these is 520 Foot, and each Face in breadth 682 Foot.

The Ascent consists of between 200 and 210 Steps; the Top, to those that are below, appears like the point of a Spire, though on the top there is a Platform of 24 Foot square, and is paved only

with

Europe, Asia, Africa, *and* America. 61

with 12 Stones, some of which are broken, or rather worn out by time; and from thence you have a Prospect of *Old Caire*, *Boulack*, the Ruins of the Ancient famed *Memphis*, the Mountains and Desarts of *Ægypt*; but it requires a strong Head to look down to the bottom, where Men and Cattle seem no bigger than Crows, and a good Arm cannot throw a Stone beyond the Foundation, for it will light upon some part of the Work; there were formerly Steps on every side, but Time, the Consumer of all things, has wasted and crumbled several of the Stones, so that in some parts there are dreadful Precipices, therefore Strangers take with them a Guide, who is used to Ascend, and it is their safest way: They as it were clamber up the Steps, being of that heighth, that they are forced to use their Hands and Knees, some 3 Foot, and others less; there is a Room by the way to rest and refresh one, in which are divers Images, Sculptures, and other Contrivances, according to the manner of the Ancients, and near the bottom you enter into a descending Alley 20 Paces long, and 3 Foot high, so that one must stoop very low; at the end of this there is a place to creep through like a little Wicket, which is even with the Ground; and this brings you into another little Alley like the former, only in this you must ascend, and this Alley ends in two others; that on the right Hand has no inclination, and leads to a vaulted Chamber 18 Foot long, and 12 broad; at the entrance into this Alley is a very deep Well, or Pit, though destitute of Water, in which are divers Caves, entering at the bottom, by the sides, and into this one must be let with Ropes, having a lighted Torch or Tapour, for it is exceeding Dark, which you must take care to secure, by reason of the great number of Bats that are bred, and flutter about that dark aboad; wherefore the more Prudent carry Tinder-boxes along with them, to re-kindle the extinguish'd Light: Opposite to the last Alley, there is another that begins so high in the Wall, that we were constrained to climb up

to

to it, but to make amends, we found it much higher and broader than the reſt; and having walked 70
Paces, ſtill aſcending, a ſpacious Room diſcloſed it
ſelf, which was 33 Foot long, and 16 broad, paved with 9 entire Stones, the length of them equal to
the breadth of the Room; the Walls are of a curious Porphery, and at one end there is an empty
Tomb of a very hard Stone, between 7 and 8 Foot
long, and between 3 and 4 Foot broad, but broken
about the Edges by ſuch as viſited the place, to carry with them as a Token. This Tomb is held to
be made for the ſame *Pharaoh* that was over-whelmed in the *Red-Sea*, purſuing the *Iſraelites*.

The Piramid ſtanding neareſt to this is little, in
compariſon of it, being only 150 Foot, and each
of the Sides or Faces 200 Foot broad: The common opinion is, that it was built by a beautiful
Woman, called *Rhodope*, who was *Æſop*'s fellow
Slave in *Ægypt*, with whom the King became Enamour'd, and ſhe got ſo much Money by her Love
Intrigues, as defrayed the Charges of building it.
The third is little inferiour to the firſt, for it is 510
Foot in heighth, and the breadth of each Face is
630 Foot, being a manner a Quadrilatrial Figure,
as are the reſt.

There is to be obſerved the Ruins of an Ancient
Temple, before each of them, and a huge Idol of
Stone ſtanding very near thoſe ruinated Structures,
about 26 Foot high, and in all, proportionable,
where they ſay, Oracles were delivered of old; but
the Cheat now appears plain, for in the Head of it
there is a deep hole, wherein a Man may eaſily hide
himſelf; and here, no doubt, the Prieſt was placed
who gave the Oracle to delude the People, his Noiſe
coming through holes made in the Noſtrils of the
Idol; and ſo we may conclude of the reſt, who with
Ambiguous Anſwers, abuſed thoſe that came to en-
quire future Events, or to be reſolved in doubtful
Matters. This *Coloſſus* is cut in a Rock, repreſent-
ing a Woman.

From

From hence we Travelled to a large Village, called *Sacara*, the Burying-place of the Ancient *Ægyptians*, in which there are Catacombs, or Sepulcheral Vaults. These are distinct Subteraneous Chambers built of square Stone; and in these are the Bodies that are called the *Mummies* of *Ægypt*, where a Moor is the Master of them, to open them for such as will give him Money, the entrance otherways being covered with Sand; the opening is above, through which one must go, and so down by a Ladder, or with a Rope; they were heretofore full of Bodies of the Ancient *Ægyptians*, so skilfully Embalmed, that they were, perhaps, preserved 3 or 4000 Years, with their Epitaphs in Letters of Gold on Cloth; their Coffins were enriched with Hierogliphicks, and the Figures of the Deceased in Relievo, and many Images, much Gold, and Jewels, were found with the Bodies; but the covetousness of the *Moors* and *Turks*, and the curiosity of the *Franks*, who purchase them of the former at a dear Rate, have almost exhausted them, though 'tis believed there are some that were never opened, and that the *Moors* conceal them out of Avarice, to take out what is precious, and raise the price of such Rarities to a higher Rate: Being let down in one of these Vaults, I saw many parts of Bodies, but little entire, they being much broken and mangled by such as had, out of Curiosity, carried away pieces of them.

This place is full of Piramids, but most of them very small, unless one that never was finished, which, if compleated, had been near in bigness, to the largest I have mentioned, proportionable to the Basis; there are in it, Ascending and Descending Alleys, at the end of which are 3 Rooms; but it not being finished as the rest, as to what it might have been is but Conjecture; some hold that this mighty Work ceased when *Alexander* the Great seized on *Ægypt*, and the *Greeks* wrested the Kingdom from the Race of the Ancient *Ægyptian* Kings.

On

On the other side of the *Nile*, opposite to this place, are to be seen the Ruins of the Ancient *Memphis*, where the *Ægyptian* Kings held their Court; but Time, and the spoiling Hand of War, has made it as *Troy*, a heap of Ruins: It seems to have been exceeding large, and extended along the River, till you come over-against *Old Caire*, so that although I spent many Hours in viewing these Ruins, I could find nothing of Note, but pieces of Pillars, and Images, the low Foundations of what seem to have been Ancient Temples, and little else Remarkable.

Returning towards *Caire*, I came to *Maltherea*, 3 Miles distant from the City, where are a great many curious shading Orange-Trees, and a delicious Spring of Water, which is said to have been the abiding place of the Blessed Virgin, when she fled with our Saviour into *Egypt*: There are likewise Mirtle, and Lemon-Trees, that render the place very pleasant. This Spring and *Joseph's* Well in *Caire*, are all the Springs of Water I could see or hear of in *Egypt*. That Well is of a prodigious Depth, cut in a solid Rock 106 Foot deep, yet so broad and winding are the Steps, that two Oxen may go down to the bottom, where, in a Hole, is a very curious Spring, and that Water is held precious; near it are some remains of *Pharaoh's* Pallace, and a Room called *Joseph's* Hall, adorned with Gold and Azure, and many Pillars, also his Steward's House, remarkable for 12 Columns of *Thebaick* Marble. Near to this there is a dreadful Prison, in which, it is held, that Patriarch was cast, upon the false Accusation of his Mistress; this consists of several Dungeons cut of the Rock, and if Tradition be true, his case in that place could not but be lamentable, for it appears very Dismal and Loathsome.

The common received opinion that it Rains not in *Ægypt* is groundless; the Showers fall seldomer, and less violently than in other places, so that a great part of the Country is dry and barren Sand; the

the chief Fertility is occasioned by the melting of the Snow from the Mountains, and the overflowing the River *Nile*, of which famous River, I come now to speak more particularly.

This River has its source near the Mountains of the Moon, or Jews Mountains in *Æthiopia*, where it is very small, but gathers many Rivers in long running, which makes it swell much; it runs through the length of *Egypt*, having its course from South to North, discharging it self into the *Mediterranean* Sea, by two Mouths, making a Triangular Isle, by the *Greeks* called *Delta*, because it resembles the Greek Δ; these Mouths are Navigable for large Vessels; for though it has others, they are less, and can properly be called no other than Rivulets: It is broader than the *Seine*, and for the most part glides smoothly, unless where its Cataracts make it rage and foam, by its falling from a great heighth; when it overflows it appears like a little Sea, the Water is naturally thick and muddy, but they have a way to Clarifie it, by running it through Vessels, filled with white Earth, and then it is very wholesome. Most of the Cities, Towns, and Villages, are Scituate on its Banks, or very near it, for the conveniency of Water, which is precious in that Country, for there are so many Villages, that you have scarce passed one, but you come at another. This River abounds not much with Fish, and there is but one good sort found at *Cairo*, called a *Varicle*, but there are a vast number of *Crocodiles* in it, who, no doubt, devour the Fish; this is an Amphibeous Creature, living at pleasure in the Water, or on Land; the Head of it is flat above and below, and the Eyes of it indifferently big, and very darkish; they have a long sharp Snout, with long sharp Teeth, but no Tongue to be perceived; the Body large, and all of a bigness; the Back covered with high Scales, like the Heads of large Nails, of a greenish colour, so hard, that they are Proof against a Halbert; their Tailes are very long, covered over with Scales, but the Belly is white, and pretty tender;

der; it has four short Legs, with five Claws on the foremost Feet, and but four on the hinder. It grows as long as it Lives, and some are about 20 Foot from Head to Tail; these great ones many times snap young Children at Land, and sometimes put up their Noses, and pull People out of their Boats in the River; so that many go with Spikes to prevent their putting up their Noses; and it is dangerous to swim, where their haunts are: But that they Weep when they have taken their Prey, is, for what I could find, a Fable.

To take these Creatures, they make a great many Pits by the River side, and cover them with rotten Sticks, so that passing over, the Sticks give way, and they fall in; then Men let down a Rope with a running Nooze, to muzzle their Snouts, and so they draw them up, and kill them for their Skins, which they sell to Strangers at good Rates: None but the *Moors* will Eat of their Flesh.

There is also in the River a Hyppopotamuses, or Sea-Horse, and is of a tawney Colour, the hinder part like a Bouffler, though its Legs are short, yet very thick; it has the muzzle of an Ox, and some are about the bigness of a Camel: its Head resembles that of a Horse, and is very great, but the Eyes are small: the Ears little; the Neck thick; the Tail like an Elephant's; in the lower Jaw it has four Teeth half a Foot long, two of them are crooked, and as big as the Horn of an Ox in circumference.

This famous River mainly fertilises *Ægypt*, and without it, it would be desolate; nay, if it should fail but one Year to overflow, there would be a Famine in the Land, which some hold it did for seven Years, when the mighty Famine happen'd in *Joseph's* time, restrained by an Almighty Power; but seeing that Famine extended to others Land., this may be but Conjectural; when it Ebbs it leaves a fat nitreous Slime, that greatly enriches the Land, and makes it produce plentifully. They have few Fruit-Trees, and no Wine; for the small quantity of **Grapes** found, are thick rhined, producing little

Europe, Asia, Africa *and* America. 67

tle Juyce. The chief Trees are, the Fig-Trees of *Pharo*, the true Sycamore, Cassa, Papyrus, Colocasse, Orange, Lemon and Myrtle Trees, but these three last are mostly brought thither; they have great store of Onions, and other Roots; also plenty of Corn, and divers sorts of fine Fowls, as Yellow Birds, wild Turtles, Pidgeons, and Larks; and indeed *Ægypt* may be rightly termed an Earthly Paradise, did not the Oppression of their Governors much abate the Peoples pleasure, but that is very great, as in other parts of the *Ottoman* Empire.

At the cutting of the Khalis, or Sluyce of the *Nile*, there is a great Festival held, and triumphant Shows by Land and Water, with much rejoycing for many Days, and whereas the Ancient *Ægyptians* used to Sacrifice a Boy and a Girl taken by lot, to their fancied God of the River; but the *Turks* abolished that ill Custom, and instead thereof, place on each side, in the Night, the resemblance of a Man and a Woman in Fire, by fixing Lamps very dexterously to represent their Figures.

Ægypt, as other Countries under the Turkish Government, consists of a mixed People, of divers Nations, as *Turks, Jews, Arabs, Franks, Armenians, Greeks, Moors*, and the Ancient Inhabitants, who have liberty to exercise their Religion as they please, but have Mulcts set upon them, for the *Turks* care not what they do in that nature, so they can screw Money out of them, they being, next to the *Jews*, the most covetous of all People. The Chief Government under the Grand Signior is in the Hands of a Bassa, who has his Sub-Bassa's: The great Men of the Country are called Beys, who often bring his Head into danger, if he displeases them, by their sending complaints to the *Ottoman* Port: And thus having given you an account of the most considerable rarities of *Ægypt*, as to what I saw there, &c. I shall further entertain you with my Travels to *Palestine*, or the *Holy-Land*.

F 2 CHAP.

CHAP. X.

Travels in Paleſtine, *or the* Holy Land, *and all the remarkable Things and Places to be ſeen in it, more exact than ever yet deſcribed;* Of Mount Libanus, *and places Adjacent.*

BEING deſirous to viſit the *Holy Land,* ſo much Famed throughout the World, for the many Wonders God wrought there, and the many Memorable and Venerable Antiquities yet to be ſeen. I provided my ſelf of ſuch Neceſſaries, as my Reaſon dictated, and as I was told I ſhould ſtand in need of. Upon Notice that a Caravan was ready to part, I went and enter'd my ſelf one of the Company; ſo every one having Notice, and being in a readineſs, we ſet forward, but the Wind blowing hard, we had like to have been over-whelmed with Clouds of Sand raiſed by it, which flying about our Ears, ſpoiled ſome of our Proviſion; however, the Storm being over in 3 or 4 Hours, we kept on our way, with Timbrels Sounding, to chear the Cammels, that they might purſue their Journey with more Alacrity. The firſt place that offered it ſelf to us, was *Ithanque*, a little Town, where the Caravan of *Jeruſalem* makes its firſt Stage; the next was *Balveys*, and from thence we proceeded, the next Day to *Salabia*, where are the pleaſant Woods of *Tamariſk*, and there we lay in Tents, ſetting Guards, for fear of a ſurprize from Robbers, lurking in thoſe Woods: Our Caravan conſiſting of above 100 Camels, beſides Mules, and Horſes, with a conſiderable ſtrength of Men, but no attempt was made;

and

and the next Evening we reached *Elbir Devedar*, and encamped near some dirty Wells of Water, that our Beasts might be the better refreshed; and then marched to *Catice*, where we had a Guard of *Turks* Armed, to conduct us to *Riche*, for now we were come within danger of the *Arabs*, and there I saw a long Pit, of fine white Salt, which the People affirmed was made only of Rain Water. We parted from thence, and went to *Birlab*, and having rested there, we journied to *Bir Acat*, a place in the Desart destitute of Water, yet full of Quick-sands; however, we were forced to lie there; but the next Day travelling on, we found a Well, called *Sibile-El-Bar-Acat*, made by an Aga, who passed that way in his Journey to *Constantinople*; it is covered with a Dome, supported by Pillars. This Water very much refreshed us, and our Cattle; but going from hence we entered again into the Quick-sands, which reach as far as *Riche*, and well it was we got to that place, for about a quarter of an Hour after a Storm arose, which lasted about 30 Hours. This Village is not far from the Sea, and has a Castle built of little Rock Stones, as is likewise all the Houses of the Village; and here I observed they had so much Marble, that their Wells were made of that Stone, and their Burying-places are full of them. Having refreshed our selves, we departed for *Cauniows*, with a Guard of 8 *Turks*, and from thence we Travelled through Quick-sands, though it Rained, Thundered, and blew hard, to *Zaka*, a place where no Houses are, for that Name was only given it from three Wells of Brackish Water we found there, but passing on, we came to Wells of pleasant Water, and now we begun to have a prospect of a fine Country, where some Corn-Land appeared, which much encouraged us; there we found many pleasant Trees, and good Meadows, so that now we concluded we were on the Borders of the *Land of Promise*, and indeed we soon reached the City of *Gaza*, which stands about two Miles from the Sea, and was anciently very Stately and Famous for Trade;

Trade; many of the Ancient Pillars are yet remaining, there being almoſt every where Marble Pillars to be ſeen; it was one of the five Lordſhips of the *Philiſtins*, the Gates of which *Sampſon* carried away on his Shoulders, and left them on a little Hill a Mile diſtant. Near the City there is a Caſtle, with 4 corner Towers, and the Gates are of Iron: Hard by this are found lumps of ruined Walls, that cannot be broke with a Hammer, being the Ruins of a Caſtle, built by the Ancient *Romans*; near the Caſtle, behind the Burying-place, where we encamped, ſtood the Houſe that *Sampſon* pulled down, when he by that means deſtroyed ſo many *Philiſtines*, and many other things of Note, which I had not time to obſerve, by reaſon the Caravan was in haſte to depart.

From *Gaza* we paſſed to a Village, called *Megdel*, and ſo to *Ithanſedoud*; all the way there are pleaſant Plains, full of Trees and Corn, and in the Seaſon theſe Plains are Embroidered with Tulips and Emonies, that grow without planting; ſo paſſing a Village called *Yebna*, at the end of it we croſſed over a Bridge, and from thence proceeded over lovely Plains to *Rama*, and encamped in a Plain over-againſt it; however, I went with a few others, to viſit ſome Merchants that reſided there: This Town depends on the Baſſa of *Gaza*. Here is the Houſe of *Nicodemus*, now inhabited by French Merchants; there is alſo a pretty Church: The Church of the Forty Martyrs is in this Town. The Doors of the Houſes are not above 3 Foot high, and they make them ſo, on purpoſe to prevent the Inſolent *Arabs*, that Border on them, from entring their Houſes on Horſeback: there is likewiſe a Church Dedicated to the Honour of St. *George*.

Decamping from hence at 6 a Clock in the Morning, we ſaw, about 9, on our right Hand, the Village of *Good Thief*, called in *Arabick*, *Bethlakij*. After that we paid the Caffaire, or Cuſtom, and ſo had a Guard allowed us to *Jeruſalem*; but being led about to avoid another Caffaire, we were entangled

tangled among the Mountains, and obliged to encamp there, in a place close by a ruinous old Building, which had been a Convent of *Franciscan* Friars. Some Arches of the Ruins are yet standing above, and many others under Ground, where the *Arabs* keep a few Cows; a Spring of pleasant Water issuing out of a Rock near it.

The next day, we passed on towards *Jerusalem*, once exceeding Famous, but now contracted into a small compass; we left *Degib*, a small Village, so called in *Arabick*, and was once the Town of *Samuel* the Prophet; it stands upon an Eminence, there is a Mosque covered with a Dome, they say *Samuel* is Buried there, and the *Jews* visit it out of Devotion; and soon after we discovered the City of *Jerusalem*, which the *Turks* call *Coudscherif*, and came before it, but being *Franks*, as they call the Latin Christians, we could not be admitted till the Religious sent for us; and when we had waited about an Hour, at that which is called the Gate of *Damascus*, we were introduced by the Trucheman of the Convent, who came with an Officer belonging to the *Basha* of the Province, who visited the Bagage, and then we were conducted to the Convent of St. *Saviour*, who Entertained us Charitably, and shewed us to an Apartment were we might rest our selves, and a Monk came and washed our Feet, and the Religious were very Industrious to shew us the places of Note, and to begin our visits of the Holy Places. First we passed near to the *Judgment Hall*, from whence our Saviour went out bearing his Cross; it is so called, because, those that were Condemned to die, went out of the City by it: At present within the City, advanced a few steps, proceeding on our way, we pass under an Arch, where is a Stone on which they say, *Pilate* set our Saviour, when he said, *Ecce Homo, Behold the Man*. This is a large Arch reaching from one side of the Street to the other, and has two Windows looking into the Street, only separated by a little Marble Piller, and under this Window is an Inscription, *viz. Tolle Tolle Cru-*

cifice eum; Take and Crucifie him. A little further is the Palace of *Herod*, from whence our Saviour was sent back to *Pilate*, and although these two were at variance before, yet the Prince of Peace passing between them, they soon, even that very day, were at Agreement: And indeed, there are many of the Antient Structures remaining, though this famous City has undergone so many Revolutions, yet it is Conjectur'd, that many new Works have been added to the Old Ruins, and they much repaired in many places. The *Sheep Gate* still remains entire, and over the place where our Saviour was Scourged, there is a pretty Chaple Erected; the Front and some other parts of *Solomon*'s Temple are yet remaining, and there are several Arches that make a lovely Porch before the Door of the Temple; nor is the Tower of *David* quite defeated, there remaining many Ruins to shew the Strength and Magnificence of it There are abundance of Chaples in this City, some belonging to the *Latin Christians*, others to the *Greeks*, and some to *Armenians Abasines*, &c. and these were raised on several Religious occasions, where the passages in Holy Scripture are recited to have hapned; but they pay the *Turks* a large tribute for possessing them, yet they get much Money by the visits that are made in Pilgrimages, the *Turks* often choping and changing with those that will give most Money, and they who are the richest, commonly possess those that are most in Veneration, and consequently most frequented; but above all the rest that are very numerous, the Church of the Holy Sepulcher is in the highest Veneration, therefore I shall briefly describe it.

All *Franks* that enter it at first, are taxed 24 Piasters a piece, and the Religious pay only 12; but when you have once paid that Tax, and Entered it, you may go in as often as you will when it is open, giving a Mudine to the *Turk*, who keeps the Door.

Before you enter into the Church, you pass a kind of a large Court that is before it, laid with Freestone; and on this, the *Jews* do not, or, as some say, dare

Europe, Asia, Africa, *and* America. 73

dare not tread: Then the Steeple appears, which is on the left side corner of the Front of the Church; it is square on all sides, has three stories of Windows, two in front, supported and separated by two Marble Pillars, and heretofore is said to have 18 Bells in it. The Door of this Church is very Magnificent, and over it are many Figures in Brass Relicks, being the Representations of several Sacred Histories; the Door is sealed with the Seal of the *Basha*, and when any enter, it is immediately shut again. In this Church, there is the Chaple of Apparition, so called; because it is held, our Lord appeared in that place to the Blessed Virgin, immediately after his Resurrection; and from thence we went down to the Chaple of St. *Helena*, Inventrix of the Cross, and having viewed some others, we passed through the said Chaple, where it was told the Women, that Christ was risen in this Chaple. There is a little Altar, and three Windows to give light before the Door, a Lamp, and seven Lamps within it, and there lies a Stone said to be rowled from the mouth of our Saviour's Sepulcher, on which the Angel set, when his Brightness appeared so transparent.

On the right hand as you enter, is the place where the Body of our Lord was laid in, cut out of the Rock, in which there is a Table of the same Rock raised about two Foot from the Ground, or somewhat more. This takes up one half of the Breadth, and the whole length of the Chaple; it has been faced with white Marble to prevent its being broken, for the *Christians* who came to visit it, strove eagerly to have little Bits of it, to place in Rings and other Gold Ornaments as a precious Relick. And now it serves for an Alter, where the Latin Priests celebrate Mass, none being permitted to do the like; and in the Roof of it are three Holes to evaporate the Smoak of the Lamps, there being 44 of them in it of Silver and Gold, sent by the Kings of *France*, *Spain*, and other Princes. The inside of this place is faced with White Marble, and

environed

environed on the out-side with 10 curious Pillars of the same Stone, and the Lamps are round about it. It is covered with a Plat-form in the middle, whereof just over the Holes that Evaporate the Smoak, there is a Dome about 6 Foot in Height, covered with Lead, which stands upon 12 little Porphery coloured Pillars, two and two on the Plat-form, which makes six Arches, and under every one of them hangs 3 Lamps; though when it runs, the Water falls through the Aizie in the Dome of the Church, on the little Dome, from whence it is conveyed by a Pipe into a hole.

Before the Door of the Sepulcher, at an equal distance from it, and the Door of the Quire, is a prodigeous Lump of Silver; they say, that two Men can hardly Fathom it, it was sent by *Philip* III. of *Spain*, whose Arms are on it in several places with this Motto: *Philipus* III. *Rex Hispaniorum me donavit.*

The Quire and the Body of the Church is of curious Work; it is said to be placed in the middle of the World, because in *Psalm* 74. its said, *God wrought Salvation in the midst of the Earth*, but not to be too tedious in this matter, I must cut short and proceed to other places. We went soon after to visit the Mount of *Olives*, the place where our Lord wept over *Jerusalem*, and foretold its Destruction; and from thence indeed there is a curious prospect of the City. On the top of this Mount is the place of the Ascension, where is a Chaple with 8 Fronts, and a little Dome covered with Lead, supported by 8 Pillars of White Marble; in this Chaple is the print of a Foot on a piece of Rock, which they say, our Saviour left when he Ascended; and that there was an other of them which the *Turks* have cut away and kept to shew to such as will give Money to see it in the Temple of *Solomon*. Then we visited the G*z*ot, in which it is held the Apostles made the Creed, and the Sepulchers of *Absalon* and *Jehosaphat*; the Valley wherein they stand is no other now, than a great Ditch, that conveys the Water from

from *Jerusalem*, but the chief *Jews* hire their Burying Places here of the *Turks*, superstitiously fancying, that Judgment will first begin here at the general Resurrection, and therefore they who are Buried in it, shall be first dispatched. About *Absalon*'s Tomb is a great heap of Stones, for every one that passes by, is obliged to throw a Stone at it, in detestation of his Rebellion against his Father.

Near this, there is the Tomb of *Zacharias*, and the Brook *Kedron*; this Brook has over it a Stone-Bridge, but many times it is dry, as it hapned at this time, so that we passed over without wetting our Feet, though not near the Bridg.

As for the Garden of *Olives*, it is a very small place, and few Trees remaining in it; it is inclosed with a very inconsiderable Wall, and into it is taken the Garden of *Bethsemany*, where our Saviour was in his Agony, and near it is the Sepulcher of of the Blessed Virgin *Mary*, which is a Church almost under ground, of it, nothing but the Front can be seen, and hereabouts are several other Sepulchers to be seen, as those of *Joachin* and *Anna*, and the place where St. *Stephen* was Stoned; so entering by St. *Stephen*'s Gate, we came to the *Sheep-pool*, which is near to *Solomon*'s Temple; and here are yet to be seen the Sepulchers of *Godfrey* of *Bulloin*, the first *Christian* King of *Jerusalem*; that of his Brother *Balwin*, and others that succeeded him, though time has much defaced some of them. From hence I went to Mount *Calvery*, where is a Hole half a foot Diameter, and 2 foot Deep, in which the *Christians* there say, the Cross stood when our Saviour was Crucified; they shewed a Rock, with a cleft in it, that they say rent at his giving up the Ghost.

My curiosity now led me to visit the Burying Places of the Kings of *Jerusalem*, which is of great Antiquity; and to this you go out of the City by the Gates of *Damascus*, and when I came there, I entered into a great Court, cut out and made even in a Rock, and the Rock serves to it as a Wall; and on the left hand there is a Gallery cut out of the same
Rock,

Rock, with several Pillars beautified with Stone, Embelished with curious Figures, and Engravenings on Stone; and there is a little open place at one end of this Gallery, through which I crept on my Hands and Knees, and then found a large square Room cut out of the Rock; and further there are other Rooms, and curious square Tombs cut out of the Rock also, so that it seem'd a Palace rather than a Burying place, though here many of the Antient Kings of *Jerusalem* lye Interr'd; and returning from this Magnificent Palace of the Dead, I went to visit the Cave, where, it is held, the Prophet *Jeremiah* composed his Lamentations. It is a large lightsome *Grot*, the Roof of it supported by a Pillar that stands in the midst of it, being very near the Burying Place of the Kings.

Having been curious in making these Observations, I had a desire to see the famous River *Jordan*, so renowned in Holy Writ; and so taking Provision for the way, and Company also to guard us against the insults of the *Arabs*, who watch all opportunities to rob Strangers and *Turks*; We set forward with a great many more that had the same desire, and joyning with us in our way, lay almost all along among the Mountains, the Road being very Stony from *Jerusalem* to the Plains of *Jerico*; before the latter, our Caravan, as we may Term it, Encamped, having passed *Bithany*, and the Fountain of the Apostles. Here we refreshed our selves, and though *Jerico* was once a famous City, it now consists of a few Brick Houses, inhabited by *Arabs*, who live a miserable poor life; near to this is the House of *Zacheus*, and here we found the so much talked of Roses of *Jerico*; these Blow not unless they are put into Water, and then they Blow in all Seasons, contrary to the Opinions of those who say they blow not but on *Christmas Day*, and others on all the Festivals of our Lady.

Travelling by many places of little Note, at length we came to *Jordan*, and Encamped near it: On the Banks there are many Almond, and other pleasant

Europe, Asia, Africa, *and* America.   77

pleasant Trees; it is not broader than the *Thames*, but very deep in most places, it has its beginning from 2 small Springs, called *Jor*, and *Dan*, towards Mount *Libanus*, and from them, put together, it takes its Name. The Water of this River, they say, will not corrupt by length of time, though it appears not very clear: It runs from *East* to *South*, and passing through the Sea of *Tiberius*, loses its Waters in the *Asphaltian* Lake, or *Dead Sea*, which sprung up in the Plains, when the Cities of *Sodom* and *Gomorah* were sunk in Flames; in the Sylvian places, on the Bank of this River, the warbling of Birds is very Harmonious, especially of Nightingals, who are there in great numbers. At this River many paid their Devotions, in remembrance of the Wonders that had been done there ; as the Children of *Israel*'s passing it dry shod ; *Elisha*'s dividing it with his Mantle ; and our Saviour's being Baptized.

As for the Dead Sea, it is a great standing Lake of Salt and Bitter Water; all the Plains that border on it are Bitter, and they say there are Trees growing on the brink of it, that bear Apples with a Scarlet and Golden Rhine, fair to the Eye to delude Travellers, but as a Curse on the Place, they are within, Ashes and Smoke. Some hold, that a living thing will not sink in this Water, but the fumes arising from it were so extream it being hot Weather, that I thought it convenient not to approach too near it. I was informed that this Sea, or rather Lake, was 100 Miles in length, and 25 over, but that no Fish can live in it. In our return, I saw the Mount where our Saviour Fasted Forty Days, and was Tempted ; on the top of it there is a Grot, wherein is an Altar : This Grot is said to be the place of his Residence, during that time, and there the Monks say Mass on publick occasions ; and coming down again, I saw the Prophet *Elisha*'s Well, where he made the Bitter Water Sweet, by casting Salt into it; and now the Water is of an excellent pleasant Tast; This Well is about a quarter of an Hours Travel from the Foot of the Mountain.

Going

Going now to *Bethlehem*, they shewed us by the way the House of St. *Simeon*, and the place where *Elias* was Born; also the House of *Jacob*, *Rachel*'s Sepulcher, and *David*'s Cestern.

Bethlehem was anciently a Town of the Tribe of *Judah*, and has been, as appears by the Ruins, a very fair place, but now greatly reduced: There is in it a Convent of Monks; and the place where St. *Jerom* resided, and taught the People, is a pretty compact Church, dedicated to the Honour of St. *Catherine*: There is also the Sepulcher of the *Innocents*, where many of them that *Herod* caused to be Slain were Buried: The Oratory of St. *Jerom*, and his Tomb: The place where our Saviour was laid in the Mainger, is to be seen. There is an Altar where the three Kings adored him, and made their precious Offerings; and all these places are adorned with pleasant Structures and Ornaments, Lamps burning in most of them, and Sculptures resembling the Histories; in one of which, the Virgin *Mary* is represented, kneeling before our Saviour, who has 2 Crowns of Silver on his Head, which things are the only Ornament of the place; near it is the Sealed Well, and the 3 Fish-Ponds of *Solomon*; the Well is a pleasant little hole, but deep, with 3 Springs bubling up; at the end, Aquaducts convey the Water to *Jerusalem*; the Fish-Ponds seem to be cut out of a Rock, being smooth Stone at bottom, with Springs, one at the end of another, lowering by degrees, so that they communicate their Water; and Travelling on, there is the Garden of *Solomon*, shut in between 2 Hills, which serve for a Wall on either side; also the Cave where *David* cut off the lap of *Saul*'s Garment; and passing the Town of *Sanacarib*, we came in with the Mountains of *Judea*: the Town is called so, because *Sanacarib*'s Army Encamping there, was cut off by the Angel: The Fountain is likewise in the way, where the *Æthiopian* Eunuch was Baptized by St. *Philip*, and is a pleasant Spring of Sweet Water; and by bad way passing the Village of *Battir*, we came to the Desert of

Europe, Asia, Africa, *and* America. 79

St. *John* Baptist, and upon an Ascent are seen the Ruins of an Old Monastery; under this is a Grot, where they say he lay, and in it, the form of a Bed cut in the Rock. There are many things to be seen, in the Mountains of *Judea*, more than here mentioned; but being tedious ways, Rockey and Stoney, I declined to Travel further in them, they being composed of many Risings and Fallings, some very Craggy, others Smooth, with pleasant shading Trees on them, as Olives, Palms, *&c.*

Having rested a little after this Journey, and escaped some Ambushcades of the *Arabs*, I, as well as many more of my Companions, being desirous to see other memorable places before we left the *Holy-Land*, our curiosity lead us to pass through the Gate of *Bethlehem*, which we did, pretty early in the Morning, and the first thing of Note that saluted our Eyes, was the Foot of Mount *Sion*, on the Right Hand, and the two Fish-Ponds of *Bersheba*, in one of which, *David* beheld her bathing from his Pallace in Mount *Sion*, when he fell enamour'd with her, and committed that grievous Sin, which made not only him but all *Israel* Mourn. Then we passed to the Field which is called *Acaldema*, or *the Field of Blood*, and here the *Armenian* Strangers find a Burying-place: so going forward, we saw the Grot where 8 of the Apostles hid themselves, when our Lord was made a Prisoner; it is now a pleasant cool place for shelter, and in it are to be seen the Pictures of the Apostles. Near this there is a Burying-place for the *Greeks*, and Strangers, and a Pit, where tis said, the *Jews* hid the Fire of the Altar, by the Command of the Prophet *Jeremiah*, when they were carried away Captive by *Nabuchadnezzar* into *Babylon*; close by it there is a Mosque, with a Reservatory of pleasant Water to refresh Travellers.

But going on, we came to the Pool of *Shilo*, where the Blind Man washed, and had his sight restored him, and passing on, saw where the Prophet *Isaiah* was sawn asunder with a wooden Saw, by the command of *Manasses*. Then we journied by the Fountain

tain of the Bleſſed Virgin, to the Mount of *Scandall*, near which *Judas* hanged himſelf, after he had betrayed his Lord ; it is ſo called, becauſe the Concubins perverted his wife Heart, and made him commit Folly, in offering Sacrifice to *Moloch*, and the Idol of *Chamos*; and ſo we came to *Bethany*: There we ſaw the Ruins of the Houſe of *Simeon* the *Lepar*, where *Mary Magdalen* anointed our Saviour with the precious Oynement; alſo the Ruins of the Caſtle of *Lazarus* on a little Aſcent, and at the Foot of it is the Sepulchre out of which he was raiſed; it is a little Grot, and in a Table of Stone, where the Prieſts on Solemn Days ſay Maſs, they ſhow there the Stone that our Saviour ſat on, when he bewailed him, and called him forth; and places where the Houſe of *Martha* ſtood; as alſo the Fig-Tree that withered when Chriſt Curſed it; and that where the Aſs ſtood, which he ſent for and Rod in Triumph to *Jeruſalem*: Then we went to the Grot where St. *Peter* Wept bitterly after, he had denied his Maſter; and from hence we turned to Mount *Sion*, where our Lord celebrated the Holy Supper with his Apoſtles, and inſtituted the Bleſſed Sacrament. Here is the Room he entred when the Doors were ſhut, and the Holy Ghoſt deſcended on the Day of Penticoſt.

Not far from hence we beheld the Sepulchers of *David*, and *Solomon*. This Mountain was formerly within the compaſs of the Walls of *Jeruſalem*; but *Selim* the *Turkiſh* Sultan rebuilding them, it was excluded, and the City much ſtreightned. We ſaw many other things hereabouts, as the Iron Gate, the Houſe of *Zebedee*, and that of the High Prieſt, *Annas*; the place where St. *James* was beheaded; the Houſes of St. *Thomas*, and *Mark*; the Priſon of St. *Peter*, whence he was delivered by the Angel, &c.

And now returning a little again to *Jeruſalem*, I ſhall give ſomewhat more of its Deſcription than hitherto I have done.

This Famous City is ſeated on a Barren Mountanous Ground for the moſt part, it produces no
Food;

Europe, Asia, Africa, *and* America   81

Food, but at a distance the Land is exceeding Fertile. The Streets are narrow and crooked, the Building but indifferent, all the Ancient Magnificence being in a manner laid in Rubbish; it has 6 Gates, *viz*. That of *Ephraim*, the Gates of *Bethlehem*, *Jaffa*, *Damascus*, *Zion*, and the *Dungate*, and one that is walled up, called the *Golden-Gate*, because our Saviour entered in Triumph at it; the *Sheep-Gate* is not reckoned, as being much ruined. The *Turks* keep them all shut at Noon-Prayer, because they have a Prophecy, that at that time, the Christians shall surprize *Jerusalem*, and particularly on a Friday, on which Day they are very apprehensive it will happen; not far from the *Golden-Gate* there is a Pillar bearing out of the Wall like a Cannon, and on this the *Turks* have a foolish Opinion, that *Mahomet* shall sit at the Day, to see whether *Christ* Judges the *Christians* Uprightly, and if he does, *Mahomet* will give him his Sister in Marriage, with a great Portion; and then changing himself into a great Sheep, he shall fly up in the Air a vast heighth, with the *Mahometans* entangled in his Wool, and there shake himself terribly, and such as can hold fast shall go with him into Paradise, but such as fall off shall drop into Hell. The Walls of this City are fair and strong.

Again, leaving *Jerusalem*, I went with a considerable Company to visit *Emans*, and *Jaffa*; the first of these is but 2 Leagues and an half from *Jerusalem*; by the way stands the Well where our Lord appeared to the two Disciples, after his Resurrection; a little further is the Castle where our Lord was known to them in breaking Bread, which is now very ruinous, and the Village is of little account, there being very few Houses, and those inconsiderable, which made us keep on by the way of *Ramah* to *Jaffa*, which is 4 Leagues beyond it: This *Jaffa* was Anciently called *Joppa*. It is built on the Top of a Rock, and is altogether Ruinous, there remaining no more than some Towers, and the Port at the Foot of the Rock; and to a crag of

G   this

this Rock it is Fabled, *Andromeda* was tied, when *Perseus* the Son of *Jupiter*, and *Danae* delivered her from the Sea Monster. Here the Prophet *Inah* embarked when he fled from the Face of God. Here St. *Peter* raised *Tabitha*, *Acts* 9. and saw the Sheet let down from Heaven, *Acts* 10. There are Grots by the Sea-side for Pilgrims to rest in; there is also a little Castle, with two Towers, one round the other, square, and a great Tower separated from it on one side, but no Houses by the Sea. The Port has but little Water in it, and none but small Barks can come up with the Fortresses. Mount *Carmell* being but a little distance from hence, by Water, I agreed with others, to take small Vessels to visit it, but we met with a Storm by the way, that much endangered us; but at length we arrived safely there, and lodged in the Village of *Cayplias*, which, by the Ruins appears to have been formerly a considerable Town, it is at the Foot of the Mountain, and the next Morning we ascended the Mountain, where we found a Convent of bare-footed Fryars, called *Carmelites*; these observe a very strict Rule, neither eating Flesh nor drinking Wine, totally Sequestring themselves from the World, nor will they suffer others to do it in their Convent. This is the place where the Prophet *Elias* lived; and there is in this Mount, as they say, a Garden of Stone Mellons, which happened on this wise; the Prophet asking the Man to give him some of that he was gathering, he to put him off, told him they were Stones, when immediately they proved so indeed, by turning into Stone; they shewed us one of these, but would not shew us the place where they grew, least we should covet to carry them away; however, they feasted us with Fruits, boiled Roots, and gave us Water to Drink; for though the Hill is Rockey, ye by their industry, they have raised many Fruit-Trees, and have variety of good Flowers. Then we saw the Well *Elias* made to spring out of the Ground, and another little Well by it; we saw a little distant from these, the Grot, or Cave of *Elias*

and

and *Elisha*; it is cut very smooth in the Rock, above and below, near 20 Paces in length, and 15 in breadth, and very high: The *Turks* have built a little Mosque by it. This Mountain, and the Country about, it is commanded by an *Emir*, or Prince, who pays the Grand Signior a Tribute of Twelve Horses.

I forgot to tell you of Mount *Libanus*, so famed for its tall Cedars, but such wast has been made of them, that I could number great and small but 23: There is a Church and Monastery in it; there is a Patriarch belonging to it, that lives at a Village beneath, called *Cannobin*. Thus much for the *Holy Land*, whose Fame has over-spread the World.

CHAP. IX.

Travels through Syria, *and divers other Countries towards the Kingdom of* Perfia, *with many remarkable Things occuring in fo long and hazardous a Journey by Land, and Water.*

HAving heard many Famous Things reported of *Perfia,* too many here to enumerate; and being recruited with Bills of Exchange, and other Advantages for Travelling, it being a curiofity I was enclined too from my tender Years, I found an opportunity to go in good Company for *Damafcus.* This City is ftill in good Reputation, and has fix Gates, *viz.* the *Eaft Gate,* the *Sphaies,* or *Seraglio Gate,* the *Shoo Gate,* the Gate of *Paradife,* the Gate of *Peace,* and St. *Thomas's Gate*: This City is an Hour and a quarters walk round it; but the Suburbs are as big again as the Town. It has in it many ftately Buildings, fome New, others of great Antiquity, having been Anciently the Capital City of *Syria*; but being on a Journey, I had not much leafure to view it, or few other Towns or Cities on the way, therefore I fhall but lightly touch on them in my Paflage.

From hence we parted for *Aleppo,* which is one of the moft confiderable Cities of the *Ottoman* Empire in *Afia,* by reafon of the great Trade Merchants drive there; it is as large as *Damafcus,* and has a fruitful Country lying about it. The Walls are ftrong and well fortified; it has ten Gates, and many curious Buildings in it. This and the former are govern'd by Baffa's, who have large dependencies.

There

Europe, Asia, Africa, *and* America. 85

There is a Court of Wells, with a Canal full of good Fish, but the *Turks*, on some superstitious account or other, forbid any to take them, alledging, for excuse, that those who Eat them will fall Sick and Die. There are in this City People of all curious Trades, and were not the oppression of the *Turks*, as it is indeed all over the *Ottoman* Empire, very great, Riches would flow here in abundance.

From this place our Road lay to *Mosul* by the way of *Bir*, and *Orfa* the Ancient *Edessa*, but before we came to *Bir* we passed *Euphrates* in great Boats. This is a little Town in *Mesopotamia*, on the side of the River, and passing by small Towns, and the Ruins of some great ones, we came to *Orfa*; The Walls are about two Hours Walk in Circumference, and pretty entire, but the Town within, though it has been Fair and Stately, lies now mostly in Ruins. We refreshed our selves here, and passed on by *Codgtafar*, in the Country of *Meredin* and *Nisibia*; we saw in our way many Villages, some Towns, and other things of Note, as *Job*'s Tomb, Fields of Mellons, Cucumbers, *&c.* Our way was sometimes over Mountains, then into Valleys, and now and then in Plains, seeing but few, except some few wandering People, who move from place to place, feeding Cattle, and carrying their Tents with them; and after a weary Journey, we came to *Mosul*, and entered it by *Bagdad Capisi*, that looks towards the South, where we paid a Paistre to the Janisary that kept the Gate.

This City, Anciently called *Aasour*, stands on the side of the *Tigris*, which runs to the East of it. It is encompassed with strong Stone Walls, plaistered over; and these have little pointed Battlements on the top, 2 Fingers thick, and 4 or 5 broad. There is a Castle in the Water of an Oval Form, and pretty strong, which keeps the Pass of the River. Many of the Houses are fairly built with Freestone, and the City is about an Hours walk in compass: It has five Gates, beside that I mentioned. On the other side of the River is the place where once stood

stood the Famous City of *Nineveh*, and some of the Ruins are to be seen, and not far distant, a Tomb, wherein *Jonah* is said to be Buried. In Summer it is extream Hot, insomuch, that the People keep in Vaults in the heat of the Day, and some in Stone Troughs of cold Water.

Having recruited our Provisions here, it being *July*, to prevent the danger of the *Semiel*, or infectious Wind, which arises about this time, kills many that Travel by Land. I, and some of the Company, passed by Water on a Keleck, or a kind of a Float, fastned on a great many Leather Baggs, filled full of Wind; but they would not suffer us to carry any Wine on Board, foolishly fancying, that it would sink their Boat; and in this we did wisely, for we afterwards heard of many that passed by Land, who were not accustomed to that Wind, died, being stifled or Poysoned with the infectious Air. In our Passage we saw many Towns and Villages; and Men, Women, and Cattle were swiming their Passage over the River. In the Night we heard the Lions Roar on either Hand, which made us keep from the Shoar, least they should leap into our Kelechs, though the Natives would perswade us, they were afraid of a Man, and that the *Arabs* usually pursued and killed them with a Staff; but we thought fit not to lay too much stress upon this, for I had heard in *Mosul*, that many who had stragled from the Caravans, had been snaped by them, for they rove in great numbers, and Fire-Arms are the best defence against them; besides, we were forced to stand on our Guard, for fear of the Thieveish *Arabs*, who often get aboard by swiming, and surprise these Kelechs, nor did they fail to Alarum us, but when we espied them, they Dived, and got to Shoar, and by that means escaped our Shot we made at them: But to be Brief, at last we came to *Bagdad*. This is a long Town, lying on the River: The first thing that appears is the Castle, to the side of the River, on the left Hand, and seems to be very well Fortified. It is built of
curious

curious white Stone, though the generality of the Houses in the Town are low and inconsiderable; it is very strong on the Land-side, and in circuit Large, requiring at least two Hours to compass it, at a moderate pace on Foot; there are lovely Bagnios, and fair Bazars in it. It was Founded by the *Persians*, but taken from them by the *Turks*, and has a Bassa for their Governor. It stands advantageous enough on the *Tygris*, but is thinly Peopled, by reason of the Licentiousness of the Soldiers, who are scarcely under any Command.

It is extream Hot in this place in the Summer time, as in all others of the same Latitude. There are but few Fruit-Trees hereabouts, but every where store of Licorice. They generally use Oyl of *Naphta* in their Lamps, it being plentiful in their Borders. They often send their Expresses from place to place by Carrier Pidgeons, fastning the Note about their Necks, which they exactly perform, unless they are killed by the way, which rarely happens.

I found here a Caravan, mostly consisting of *Persians*, bound for *Hamaden* in *Persia*; this opportunity I and others embraced, though we found the Retinue did not exceed sixty, slenderly Armed, and mostly without Tents, appearing resolute and hardy; and passing*Caranluocapi*, leaving on the left the *Persian* Tower*Adgdadom Coulasu*, we came near *Lockman Hakin*, and encamped there all Day, where the *Chakales* entertained us with Musick: From thence we Marched, and Lodged in a Village, called *Aacube*, under the pleasant Shade of divers spreading Palm-Trees, and so proceeded Eastward to *Harounia*, where are many pleasant Gardens, and passing by *Adiga* and *Immanisker*, and many other Villages, we were informed the *Arabs* lay in wait for us in the narrow Passes, which caused us to get 15 Janisaries well Armed; but we needed them not, meeting with no opposition, for we safely arrived at *Mendeli*, the utmost bounds of the *Turks*, on the Frontiers of *Persia*: It is a little Town and Castle among

among Palm-Trees, made with Mud and Clay, and here we refted fome time.

CHAP. VII.

Travels into Perfia, *and a particular Account of the Places, and what occured in the way to* Ifpahan, *the Metropolis of the Kingdom.*

THE famous Kingdom of *Perfia,* fo much Renowned in Hiftory, is the Ancienteft Monarchy now known in the World, having, for the moft part, had an interrupted Succeffion of Kings, who have Govern'd that vaft Region Valliantly, in wife Conduct, and much Glory.

It is bounded on the Eaft with the great River *Indus,* on the South with the main Ocean, on the North with the *Cafpian-Sea,* and on the Weft with the *Tygris* and *Perfian-Gulf,* and is divided into 11 Provinces, *viz. Perfis,* now called *Far, Sufiana, Caramania, Gedroffo, Drangiania, Irica, Arachoffa, Parapomifus, Seccha, Hircania,* and *Ormus;* all very large, and moft of them Fertile.

On the confines of this Kingdom, we found Men Armed with Bows and Quivers, who ftopped us, becaufe we were advanced before the Caravan, but being certified that we belonged to it, they let us pafs. Thefe are the King's Officers, fet on the Roads to examine Strangers, thereby to prevent Spys and Robbers entring into the Country, and are upon moft Roads, having a pretty good Sallary out of the Treafury for their diligence; and they get much Money of Paffengers.

Having paffed thefe Men, we Travelled fometimes over Plains, then Hills, and then into Plains again,

Europe, Asia, Africa, *and* America. 89
again, and through many narrow Passages, seeing on either Hand a very fruitful Country, and the *Persian*'s Houses, many of them being made of Cane, and built straglingly here and there; we often changed the Point, sometimes North, or East, or South-East, as the way led us, till we came by a Village of *Cures*, called *Nian*; the Hills about it were covered with Turpentine, and wild Chesnut-Trees; the Waters bordered with *Agnus Castus*, and Rose-Laurels. Here the Weather altered, for it was very Cold in comparison of the Hot Countries we had passed before. From hence we passed to a Village, called *Chegiafer*, it is composed of stragling Houses, of rough Stone, Earth, Cane, and Reeds, covered with green Branches; the former are their Summer-Houses, and the latter their Winter-Houses. Their Mosques in this place are built of rough Stone and Earth, and on the way there are many Kervanserais commodious to Inn at, very fine for the most part, being beautified with a kind of black Stone, some pollished and some rough; but passing on through a vast track of Country, we came to *Hamadan*, to which place the Caravan was bound.

Hamadan is a large Town, but in many places of it void spaces, there being many Gardens and Ploughed Fields within the Walls; the Houses are Stately, yet built of Brick baked in the Sun: It has one fair Street, where they sell Stuffs and Cloaths ready made; it has many Shops in it, and lies near the *Bezestein* which is little, but well compacted; and indeed it is a Town of a pretty Trade, many Caravans coming thither out of *Turkey*, and other parts, to buy and sell Merchandize, though the Air and Water are unwholsome, and no Wine to be found, so that I was very ill there, which made me hasten to be gone to a more agreeable Air. It is Commanded by a Cham, under the King of *Persia*, who is the same there, as a Bassa in *Turkey*. The *Armenians* have a Church here, but keep it in no good Order: To this and other Chams the King every Year sends a Rich Vest, who go out of the
Gate

Gate to receive it, and return with it on, without any other Ceremony, then being attended by the chief Men of the place on Horseback, and this is usually Cloth of Gold.

From hence we took Mules with our Lading, for five Abasis a piece, and one of these will carry 600 weight, if need requires it; and so taking leave of those of the Caravan that staid to negotiate their Affairs, we set forward for *Ispahan*, the Regal City of *Persia*, and Metropolis of the Kingdom, in a very strong Troop; for though such care has been taken, that Robberies are less frequented in *Persia* than in *Turkey*, yet it is prudence, however, to be armed against Danger, and passing early in the Morning through the King's Gate, so called, because it looks towards the Royal City: We Travelled over Hills and Downs, the way often altering, from good to bad, till we came to the Town of *Nischar*, where we refreshed our selves in a ruinous Kervanserai, on the Ground, where Carpets were spread, and drank Water out of a leathern Jugg, called there a Matera: From thence we Marched along the River side, and came to lodg at another Village called *Bouloufch Kifar*, and the next Day encamped under Trees near *Haran*, another Village, where we were warned by our Muliters, to keep a good Guard in the Night time, for they told us, Spys had been amongst us that Day, to visit our Arms, and see how we were provided; but whether they liked them not, or stood in fear, I know not; but certain it is, we had there no disturbance.

Early in the Morning we marched again, and passed by several pleasant Villages and Gardens, and foarding the little River *Dizava*, we came to a Town of that Name, lying amongst Gardens, in a spacious Plain, and here we had a plentiful shower of Rain, which was the first, except a little mizling in our way, since my departure from *Aleppo*; and so by a long Journey, taking in our way *Sari, Debile, Mouchafaba, Machat, Scheber-Gird, Angovan, Agatch*, or *Farfang, Nichova, Fagafun, Ithua, Ghulpaigan,*

Europe, Asia, Africa, *and* America. 91

paigan, *Arbane*, *Deba*, little Villages, and Towns of no great Note, and passing by divers Kervanserais, we came to *Ispahan*, having seen by the way, several Antelopes, a great Beast, between a Deer and a Goat, very swift in running and climbing the Mountains.

CHAP. XIII.

A Description of Ispahan, *in what is curious and worthy of Remark in it.*

Ispahan, as I told you, is the Principality, and stands in the Province of *Iraca*, part of the Ancient *Parthia*: Here the Air is Dry, Pleasant, and more wholsome than in many other parts, which is one main Reason the King usually keeps his Court here. This City was Anciently called, *Hecatompolis*, being Recorded to have had 100 Gates. It is beautified with Walls of a great heighth, built of a red kind of a Marble; and though the Houses are very Stately, they are built with Brick baked in the Sun, daubed over with a fine Clay, mingled with Straw, and white cast over with a very fine Plaister, which is made of a Stone got out of the Neighbouring Mountains and burned to that whiteness, this Plaister is the third part of the Charge of building a House; they burn their Tiles indeed in a Kiln, but they are not so lasting as ours. There is in this City many very stately Mosques, curiously adorned; also sundry Pallaces, Seraglios, and Buildings of great Antiquity, but many of the most Ancient are Ruinous. The *Persians* take great delight in their Houses, keeping them very neat, and adorning them with curious Paintings, Carpets, and Tapestry; for in these, and their Gardens, seem to consist

sist their greatest Pride. The Walls of this City will take 5 or 6 Hours, at a pretty round pace, on Foot, to compass them; because, within them there are spacious Gardens, adorned with pleasant Flowers, and delicious Fruit-Trees, served by Aquaducts that run there in Chanels, watering and Fructifying the several quarters; and in those Gardens are artificial Mounts, bedded with Flowers and pleasant Summer-houses on the top of them, shaded with Trees, besides many stately Pallaces; and the quarter where these are, is called the New Town. The Suburbs of this City are very large, and the Nobles have Pallaces in it, especially in *Golfa*, lying beyond the River *Sendera*, which is mostly inhabited by *Armenians*, transplanted by *Sheba Abba*, a *Persian* Sultan, when he utterly razed their Town of that Name in *Armenia*. About this great City are cantoned People of divers other Nations; and there is hardly any Country in *Europe*, *Asia*, or *Africa*, but there are Natives of them to be found here.

In this City there are many Squares, which render it lovely; the greatest of which, is that of *Meidan*; it has regular Piazza's, and is about 700 common Paces in length, and near 300 in breadth; it is built round, and the Houses are all in the form of Porticoes; over them is a second range of Arches, more backward, and these serve for Galleries and Passages, the Houses being all of an equal heighth, give a curious Prospect: There is a pleasant Canal near it, bordered with Palm-Trees, and fed by a Spring, at the end of which is a Bell, said to be taken out of a Nunnery in *Ormus*, with this Inscription, *Ave Maria Gratia plena*. Hail Mary *full of Grace*. Hither the Musicians resort, there being a Gallery, and found several Instruments to divert the People, especially in the Night time, and amongst others, a Trumpet of Copper, which is 8 Foot long, making a strong hoars sound, and may be heard in a still Night all over the City, being almost in proportion, like a speaking Trumpet.

Passing

Passing on to the Right, or West side, is the Gate of *Aly*, their great Prophet; on the Threshold of it, which is a round Stone, the *Persians*, out of a Veneration for the place, will not tread on; and if Malefactors can escape into the Court beyond it, or in the King's Stables, or Kitchin, they are in a Sanctuary, none daring to remove them from thence. This Gate is plain, and guarded by Sofies-men of great account there, and many *Persians* out of Devotion, kneel and kiss the Threeshold e'er they pass over it.

The Street of *Techebarbag*, or the four Gardens, is very large, near 100 Paces broad, and about 2 *Itallion* Miles in length: There is a by way into it from the King's Pallace, through narrow Passages as it were a Curtain; its watered with a Canal, and adorned with shadowing Plan-Trees, being divided by the River *Senderu*, over which is a curious Bridge of Stone, with a Gallery, covered and raised above the Level for Foot Passengers; its about 300 Paces long, and 20 broad, founded on many Arches, some Brick, edged with Free-Stone, and others all of Stone. Over the Gallery there is a Platform, giving a fine Prospect of the River, and other places, the Gallery serves likewise for a Horse-way in the Winter, for then the overflowing of the River fills up the middle of the Bridge, and renders it a kind of a Canal. The Gates of the King's Pallace, and the Front of it, gives a good Prospect, as do the Mosques, being adorned with Domes, and other Beautifyings; but the Christians are forbidden to enter, under the Penalty of gross affronts, if not a good Cudgeling, though some of them out of curiosity do it in *Persian* Habits, mingling themselves with the rest, and so pass undistinguished, amongst which I took my Lot, and saw their curious Cielings, Paintings, Mosaick-Work, fine Marble, and many other curious things. As for their Burying-places they are without the City, and so they are in all the Cities of *Persia*.

They have a curious way to secure the hot Air in sultry Weather, *viz.* They have on the tops of their Houses a Wall about 2 Fathom high, and as much in breadth, to which, at the intervals of other Walls of about a Foot broad, and as high as the first, are joyned in right Angels, and these are covered with a Roof, so that let the Wind blow which way it will, the Air being pressed between 2 Walls, is driven through a hole in the Roof of the House, and diffuses cool breathings, but in Winter this hole is stopped.

This City is full of Artists, and each Company pays the King a certain Sum, which they raise again upon all the Crafts, and they are very dextrous in their several Handicrafts, in which, principally, consists the riches of the Kingdom.

In the King's Court the *Turkish* Language is mostly spoke, but much differing from what is spoke at *Constantinople*; this distinguishes the Courtiers from the rest of the People, and gives them certain Authorities and Preeminencies they affect, for they covet Honour above all things, and are profuse in their Diet, Habit, Houses, and Equipages, which renders many Noble Families Poor. Their Equipage in Travelling is extraordinary. They smoak much Tobacco, and usually do it through a Vessel of Water. Their Games are chiefly Chess, and Draughts, which they use in their Visits. There are amongst them a great many Mathematicians, and Astrologers, and the King maintains many hundreds of them liberally, though most of them appear to be very ignorant: However, these are their chief Studies. They have also Dreamers among them, who pretend to see and foretel things that way.

If a Man has killed another, the Widow, or next Relation, demands the satisfaction of his Blood, and if it be not made up for Money, the Murtherer, if taken, is delivered to the Prosecutor, who puts him to Death with great Torments, especially if he falls into the Hands of a Woman, for they

are

are more cruel here than the Men; and though they often compound, yet the Relations that are not confenting to it, will privately revenge the Blood of their Friend, concluding, their Honour fuffers if the Murtherer efcapes unpunifhed.

If any one has been Robbed, he muft make a prefent to the *Deroga*, who is the fame in Office, with the Sons, or Sub-Baffa, in the Turkifh Government. He fends his Men abroad to take up fufpected Perfons, and puts them to the Rack to make them confefs, and if the Goods be recovered, he takes a tenth, and fometimes a fixth part; but he feems to be kinder to the *Franks*, taking only a prefent of them, though may times by concealing the difcovery, he cheats them of all.

As for the Habits of the *Perfians*, they are more gaudy than fubftantial or lafting, generally waring flower'd Silks, or Callicoes, quilted Coats, and the like, having a flowing loofe Garment over a clofe Coat, or Waftcoat, with a Girdle; their Drawers down to their Heels, their Stockings are of Cloth, wide and big; their Shoos are like Womens Slippers, with high Heels, peaked at the Toes with a bit of Iron, but fo fhort, that moft part of the Heel hangs over, though they ftick clofe, and are covered with Shagreen. They ware Turbans very large, and of divers colours, except the Moulla's, who are Priviledged to wear them white, though the *Perfians* ware Caps with little Turbans about them, and the better fort have them embroidered with Gold and Silver. They take a Pride to have every piece of their Apparrel of a different colour, and affect neatnefs. As for Rings, the Men, nay, the King himfelf wears Silver ones, but the Women thofe of Gold, though they cannot give any reafon for this diftinction. They paint their Hands, &c. with a Dye, called Hanna, and will not fuffer their Beards to grow long, as the *Turks* do, for they clip them to a quarter of an Inch, and take care to have large Muftachoes.

The

The Women go vailed all to their Eyes, and the Bridegoom never fees his Bride bare-faced till the Wedding Night. They wear Gold Rings in their Nofes, their Noftrils being boared for that purpofe, which is a mark of Servitude, though they take it for a Pride. When they ride, they are placed on a Cammel, in Cafchave, where they are as eafie as in a Chair. They fit at their Banquets, and otherways, as the Men do, crofs-legged, on Carpets fpread on the Ground, or on Cufhions, and lie on Quilts in their Smocks and Drawers, but have curious fine painted Coverlids over them.

They eat but fparingly, and wonder the *Franks* can eat Meat twice a Day, they doing it but once, and then they moftly Boyl or Bake their Meats, not much approving of Roaftmeat; nor indeed they do not eat much Flefh, living moftly on Rice-broth, Herbs, and Fruits. They burn Oyl of *Napta* in their Lampts, and in Winter have Stoves in their Houfes, which keeps them very warm. They Drink Wine, though they are prohibited it, and many times do it over plentifully; which makes them, as other Drunkards, quarrelfom. They have a great many Ice-Houfes curioufly Vaulted, and deep under ground to keep their Ice in, to cool their Liquors in the hot Seafons. Many of the *Perfians* take Opium, which intoxicates them in a kind of Drunkennefs, and they carry it about with them, for having once habituated themfelves to it, they dare not leave it of, for if they do, they have moft commonly dangerous Sickneffes, and Death is frequently the attendant.

As for the *Perfian* way of Mourning, it is expreffed by a Girdle, hanging down with 2 ends before, and croffing them; but on the Death of a near Relation, the Men rend their Caba, or Vefts, in fign of Grief, and for the fpace of 7 Days give Alms; but the Women make doleful howlings or lamentings for fix, and fometimes twelve Months, and keep themfelves clofe, unlefs when they go to vifit the Graves, rehearfing to fuch as vifit them, the

Praifes

Praises of the Dead, who, with their forced Lamentations, for it is mostly no other, disturb their Neighbours rest, and disorder themselves.

CHAP. XIV.

The King of Persia an Absolute Monarch; of the Great Officers of his Court, and other Matters.

THE King of *Persia* has an Absolute or Despotical Power over his Subjects, and anciently, the Kings were in a manner adored by their People: He meddles in matters of Religion, as well as in Secular Affairs, and they begin not their Festivals till they have obtained his leave to keep them; and sometimes, though the Moon has appeared, he sets them back, notwithstanding it is their great Feast of *Ramadan*. His Subjects give him great Reverence and Respect, and scarcely look upon him but with Trembling, paying an implicit Obedience to his Orders. If they swear by his Head, the Oath is more binding to them, than when they swear by the Deity; and without consulting the Law, he is the Arbitrary Judge of their Lives and Fortunes, appointing such Rewards and Punishments as he shall think fit, without controul: And if the greatest Officer of the Court falls under the King's displeasure, all his Friends forsake him, none daring to own him, or subsist him with necessaries, so that he puts to Death whom he pleases, and the nearest Relations of the party are constrained to seem pleased with his Injustice; nay, sometimes the Sons are commanded to cut off their Fathers Noses, or to kill them, which order they readily obey. These Kings are so jealous of being deposed, by reason of their great Tyranny, that they cause the Males of all
their

their Female Kindred, to be shut up in a Stone Trough, as soon as Born, and there starved to Death. So soon as a King comes to the Crown, he puts out the Eyes of all his Male Relations, except Sons. He sometimes changes Wives with his Nobles, giving them his instead of theirs, and it is not murmured at, especially in publick; and if he likes not his Bargain, will exchange again at pleasure.

He has a Seraglio of very beautiful Women, who are kept mighty strict, for he is exceeding jealous of them, and it is Death with extream tortures, for any Man, except Eunuches, to be seen there; nay, they are prohibited to look on them, though they are Vailed; and when he takes any of them into the Country with him, no Men dare be in the way; and in the Town where he lodges in his Progress, all the Men are obliged to leave their Houses, till the Harum, or Lady is departed; the Eunuches to give them Notice, by crying the Courouk, and if any stay after, they are severely punished: Sometimes there is a Courouk for Provision, and then none dares sell any therein mentioned, but for the King's use, and this frequently lasts not above a Week or two. Many times the King lays aside the stifness of Majesty, and is familiar with his Subjects, and Strangers, Drinking and Eating with them in private, but it is dangerous speaking amiss, least he falls into a Passion to the Party's destruction, and therefore the least said proves always the best; for many have been put to Death for their prating and advifeing him, which the *Franks* getting Drunk will often attempt to do, when they see him so familiar with them.

The King gives Audience to Ambassadors, but transacts no business with them, for that is left to the Ministers of State, and is well pleased if they drink lustily with him, and he has a Remembrancer to tell him the next Day, all that he says or does when he is Drunk, for then, many times, he gives away Prodigally, as his Rings from his Fingers, and large possessions, but if he finds it an over-sight, or
too

too great a value for the Perſon, he recalls it again, and requites the Perſon with ſome little Preſent. He has an Eatmad-Doulet to tranſact for him, as his chief Miniſter, who uſually attends his Perſon. He has always great ſtore of Gold in Plate, and a vaſt Treaſure in Jewels; for the Nobles preſent him in their Order, every Spring, with one rich thing or other, and he poſſeſſes the Treaſures and Eſtates of thoſe he puts to Death, unleſs he pleaſes to give it to their Relations; beſides, the Silks are a Royal Manufactury, and he has great Incomes from them.

The Forces of the Kingdom conſiſts in three Bands, or Bodies of Men, *viz*. the *Corſchi*, the *Goulams*, and the *Teufencgi*, the firſt of theſe are deſcended of *Turks*, and Inhabit the Country, living in Tents, for the moſt part, and are able to make a great Body; there are about 25000 of them conſtantly in the King's Pay, having from ten to fifteen Tomans a Year; their General muſt be of their Body, and is called *Corſchi*-Baſſa, who executes the King's Commands in putting any great Man to Death, for they will not ſuffer the Native *Perſians* to do it. Their chief Riches conſiſt in Cattle, which they drive from place to place, and feed in the vaſt Plains and Mountains.

The ſecond Rank of Soldiers are Slaves of many Nations, but chiefly *Georgians*, and about 14000 of them are in the King's Pay, and have from 5 to 8 Tomans a Year; their General is called Kouller Agaſi.

Thoſe of the third Rank are ſuch as are raiſed in the Villages, moſtly *Armenian* Renegadoes, and are about 8000, having equal Pay with the laſt mentioned; theſe are of little regard though they March on Horſeback, for in the Battle they alight and Fight on Foot; the other two Bodies Fight on Horſeback, with Bows, Arrows and Harquibuſes.

Beſides theſe, there is a new Militia of Guards that bear Muskets, but theſe rarely go into the Field, unleſs the King be there in Perſon. As for the Court-Officers,

Travels and Voyages in

The *Eatmad Doulet* is as the Vifier *Bafha* in *Turkey*; next to him is the *Sedre*, who manages matters of Religion, and has divers under him; thefe makes all Contracts, Teftaments, and other publick Deeds, Judges of Divorces, &c. As for the *Sedre*, he is the High Prieft of their Law; there are particularly under him a Scheick of the Law, and a Cidi, or Judge, and thefe are Eftablifhed in the Principal Towns of *Perfia*, and are nominated by the King, and only depend upon him.

The *Pichnamaz* is an Officer in every Mofque, and in the King's Houfhold he directs the Prayers, and makes the People fay as he does, and ufe the fame Jeftures, always ftanding before them, that they may not fee him; there are as many of thefe in *Perfia* as there are Mofques, and they bear a confiderable Authority. The *Mulas* are of the fame Tribe, living on the Ecclefiaftical Revenues, and their Bufinefs is to Teach the Sciences and Law, being properly the *Perfian* Doctors, wearing relute Turbans. The *Nuzar* is the Wardrobe Keeper, and Mafter of the Jewels, and is a kind of a Treafurer. The *Melitar* is the chief Gentleman of the King's Bed-Chamber, and carrys a Pouch by his fide full of Hancarchiefs, which he prefents to him as often as he requires them.

The *Deroga* is Judge of Criminal Matters, of the fecond degree, as Robbery, Quarels, and the like; and under him are the *Aatas*, or Conftables: There are a great number of other Officers of lefler Note, whofe Names and Offices, for Brevities fake, I am conftrained to pafs over.

They Hunt the Antelopes with Panthers, brought up to that purpofe; this Beaft creeps on its Belly till it comes near the Game, then runs with main force and leaps at it; but if the Panther miffes at two or three leaps, he purfues no further, but returns creeping back as afhamed of his being Baffled. They Hawk much in this Country, and the Faulcons brought from *Mufcovy* are of great Value; they bring them up to fly at the Antelope, by feeding them

Europe, Asia, Africa, *and* America.

them on the Nose of a dead Antelope; then flying at the living ones, they fasten on his Nose, and pierce him with their Beaks and Tallents, fluttering so with their Wings, that blinding his sight, he stops, and the Dogs coming up easily, takes him. The King keeps for his Pleasure a great many Lyons, Elephants, Leopards and Tygars.

To Encourage Christians to turn *Mahometans*, they have a Law that gives them the Estates of their Christian Kindred when they dye, though they be in the first Degree of Kindred, and the Deceased leaves Children; but the Judges for Money have found out a way to invade it, by causing them to make it over to some *Mahometan* Friend by Testament, who possess it in trust for the Widow and Children.

They have an odd way to make Women confess their Crimes, *viz.* they tye their hands behind them, and then put large live Rats into their Drawers next their Flesh, which runing up and down, and pinching them, extort Confessions from them; for of all Creatures in the World, the Rat is most terrible and frightful to them. As for the Men to bring them to a Confession of their Guilt, their flesh is pulled off with Pinchers from their Legs, Arms and Thighs.

When the Sun is Eclipsed, they run to their Mosques, and say a Prayer made for that purpose, imploring God to avert heavy Judgments from them, and not to leave them in Darkness; at the Eclips of the Moon, they beat their Kettle and Brass Pans, making a Hedious din, perswading themselves, they help her so in her Labour to expell the Darkness, which upon the going off of the Eclipse, her motion makes her seem to strugle with.

When a House is on Fire, they let it burn out, saving however what Goods they can, saying, *Providence will stop it of it self when it sees fit*; yet they freely permit others, who are not of their Religion, to endeavour the Extinction of the Flames.

They

They hold Chriftians fo impure, that if they have touched any Food in the Market, and they know it, they will not buy it; and if one comes into a Bagnio, the Mafter of it is obliged to wafh it again before the *Perfians* will enter; yet they own Chrift fhall come at the laft Day, and be *Mahomet*'s Lieutenant, and then all fhall embrace the *Mahometan* Profeffion, for then *Mahomet* will take a Wife, and have a numerous Iffue. They hold Marriage in fo great Veneration, that they blame him becaufe he never was Married. They keep their Feafts a Day before the *Turks*, for the *Turks* begin not their *Bairam*, or *Eafter*, till they fee the Moon, and the *Perfians* do it according to the Moon's courfe, being more knowing in the Celeftial Sciences. The *Perfian* Kings are the more Reverenc'd, becaufe they are held to be of the Race of *Aly*, *Mahomet*'s Succeffor. The *Perfians* are divided into two Sects, one called *Schiai*, the other *Sunni*; the firft think it enough to follow the Commands of the Law; but the other do that, and likewife obferve Councils.

At their *Little Bairam* they Sacrifice a Camel in *Ifpahan*, the King firft ftrikes it with a Javellin, and then the People from the four Quarters of the City Affemble in a tumultuous manner, and hew the poor Beaft to pieces, with Swords, Axes, Glaves, and the like, every one ftriving to get a part of him, fo that it often comes to a quarrel, and many are killed; the pieces they get they broil and Eat, accounting it Sacred Meat. In other Cities they kill an Ox in like manner, and in their Houfes many Sheep, which they diftribute to the Poor.

In their Creed they have an odd imagination concerning Man's dying: They hold that every one muft come and die in the place where the Angel took the Earth on which he has been formed, imagining that one of the Celeftial Spirits has the care committed to him, of forming the Human Creature, by mingling a little Duft with the Seed of the Parents.

They

Europe, Asia, Africa *and* America. 103

They allow liberty of Conscience to all Strangers, and there are at *Ispahan*, a great many *Jews*, *Banians*, *Guebres*, and *Armenians*, who pursue their several Tenents. They have a great many Horses, Mules, and Camels, at all Seasons, and though these things are here set down, many of the Particulars may serve in General for all *Persia*; and therefore, having been detained in this City too long, I fear, from the intended Travels, I now take my leave of it, to proceed on my Journey.

CHAP. XV.

Travels from Ispahan *to* Ormus *and* Bassaru, *in the* Persian *Gulf; with an Observation of many Places and Things by the way, of* Persia *in General,* &c.

HAving stayed about 4 Months at *Ispahan*, I resolved to visit *Schiras*, and took the opportunity of a Caravan then setting out; we parted early in the Morning and journied South-east, meeting in our way with large Plains very barren ; some of these produced pieces of Salt Earth, made by the Salive part of the Ground, and the working of the Rain on it, and this being refined makes good Salt ; leaving these Plains, we encountered with Hills, very difficult to pass, because, though not high, they were Rockey, and very Slippery. so that many of the Mules cast their Burthens, which proved very troublesome to us, and took up much time to reload them; but having passed these Hills, we came to *Mayar*, a ruined Village, which is the beginning, or entrance into the Country of *Fars*, the real Ancient *Persia*, and there we lodged in a Kervanserai, and

going

going from thence, had, for a good way, a pleasant Country on either side of us, fruitful in Trees and Corn Ground; but meeting with a Chan, and his Harams, or Women, we were forced to fetch a compass to give free Passage, for these great Governors in their Provinces, are as Absolute as a King, and will have their Commands as strictly obeyed.

It will be in a manner endless, to tell you all the Villages, Hills, Plains, Valleys, and Rivers by their Names, that we passed in this long and tedious Journey, therefore, for brevity sake, in a tired condition, I hasten as fast as I can to *Schirars*.

This City is the Metropolis of the Ancient *Persia*; some will have it to be the Ancient *Cyropolis*; the Gates we enter'd at were very Fair and Stately, leading to a broad Street, bordered with Gardens, and at the end of it is a large Stone Bason full of Water to refresh Travellers; further there is a Bridge with 5 Arches, under which runs a small River, and a little beyond a covered Bazar; and though this Street is very fair and long, it is accounted only the Suburb to the City. It lies in a pleasant fertile Plain at the East of it, where is a little Hill covered with Orange and Lemon Trees, intermixed with Cypresses: It lies from North to South, and is about two Hours walk in Circumference. It has many fair Mosques, and a Colledge in it: There are Sallaries allowed to divers Learned Men in the latter, to teach Theology, Philosophy, and Physick, and sometimes there are 4 or 500 Students in the it: The Gates are laid over with blue Earth varnished, shining like Saphires.

The Gardens are exceeding pleasant, adorned with Fruits, Flowers, Canals, Fountains, and Summer-Houses, on little raised Mounts, but many of the Houses are ruinous, for the *Persians* are very Supine in repairing decayed Fabricks.

This is a City of great Trade, in comparison of many others, by reason the *Indian* Merchants bring the rich Commodities of that Country hither. There is a Well of a vast depth and circumference, into
which

which they throw Women convicted of Adultery, and there suffer them miserably to Perish; it is cut all out of a hard Rock. A little distant there is a stately Mosque, and in it the Tomb of *Scheik Sadi*, an excellent *Persian* Poet, whom they Honour as a Saint: There is a Well not far from this, and a Stream running under it, full of Fish, which none may take on pain of Death, unless the Dervish who looks after it, connive at them, which he will do for a little present, and keep off all Spies, by pretending there are Women in the Wells, and then the Men run away as from some fearful Monster. One goes down to it by a pair of Stairs.

There is much Glass made in this City; they make a Glass Bottle, called a *Caraba*, that will hold near 30 Quarts, covering them with Cane, or Straw; and here is to be found the best Wine in the Kingdom; they have abundance of Capers, plenty of Rose-Water, and preserve Grapes for the whole Year. A Vizar Governs here as the King's Farmer, and pays yearly 1000 Tomans, amounting to 15000 Crowns.

We stayed here but 2 Days, and then set out for *Lar*, in our way to *Bender*, and passing over Plains, Hills, and Rivers, meeting by the way whole Families of *Arabs* driving their Cattle, we arrived there. This Town is small, and seated on a Rock; it is Commanded by a Chan, who has a stately House, with a Divan; it has a fine Market-place, a Bazars, and a Castle; the last is very strong, and built all of Stone. There are a great many *Jews* inhabit, and drive a considerable Trade here; all the Country about *Lar* is full of Tamarisks that are very large here, and in most parts of *Persia*; the Sparrows being in great numbers, destroy and waste the Fruits of the Earth exceedingly.

Taking a good refreshment in this Town, we took our way through a Country much like the former we had passed, since our leaving *Ispahan*, and by tiresome Journeys came to *Bender-Abassi*, where we no sooner entred but were carried to the Custom-House,

House and had our Goods searched; in our way I should have told you, grew poysonous Plants, of which a strange story goes, *viz.* That if any Man comes near them in *June* or *July*, when South Winds from the Sea blows upon them, they send forth such a poysonous Vapour, which drawn in with the breath, causes the Body all over, to be in a burning heat, and immediately the Party dies, so that in those Months the way is little frequented. The *Persians* affirm this for Truth, and call the plants *Kherzchreb*; but this infection is rather concluded by the Judicious to be in that Wind they call the Burying-Wind.

This Town is very little, govern'd by a Chan, and is of a prodigious Traffick, as being commodiously Scituated for Trade; the *Schah Bender* is the chief Custom-House Officer, part of which Customs belong by right to the *English*, by a Contract, when they assisted the *Persian* King in taking *Ormus*, but they have been much defrauded, and reap little benefit. It has only one publick Gate, a Bazar, and a Fort to the Sea-side, which is a square Platform of about 4 Fathom each Face, and 2 in heighth, there not being above 5 or 6 Port-holes for great Guns; the *English* and *Dutch* have their Houses by the Sea-side, and the proper Flags of the Nations fixed on Poles on the Tarrasses, to direct Ships thither.

About 2 Leagues from the main Land is the *Glory of Islands*, so termed, *viz.* the famed *Ormus*, at the Mouth of the *Persian* Gulf; it is Southward from the main Land, the Gulf reaching from thence to *Bassora*, which is in the bottom of it. *Ormus* lies in 27 degrees North Latitude, 180 Leagues from *Bassora*; it has a Fort that was built by the *Portuguese*, but taken from them by the great *Schah Abbas*, King of *Persia*, assisted by the *English*: The Island is no more than 3 Leagues in circumference, and mostly Rockey, but it has gotten its Fame from the Riches that flowed thither, from *India* and *Persia*, as being a considerable Mart, especially when the *Portuguese* held

held it. As for the Water and Provisions, they are moſtly brought from the main Land, and becauſe there is a deficiency of Springs, they keep rain Water in Ciſterns, and little more now is Inhabited beſide the Fort, round which the *Perſians* have cut a Trench, and let the Sea into it by a Canal, for it ſtands on the point of the Iſland, and is the laſt Province of *Perſia* this way. There are great ſtore of Oyſters about it, about the bigneſs of ours, but much harder to open. A League to the South-weſt is the Iſland of *Lareca*, it is bigger then *Ormus*, but very Barren, the Ground conſiſting of a burning Sand; it reaches in length from North-weſt to South-eaſt: There is little in it except a Fort, which was begun by the *Dutch*, but the *Perſians* fearing they would prove ill Neighbours if they fortified it, took it out of their Hands, and finiſhed it.

As for *Perſia* in General, it is environed with Mountains and Barren Deſarts, which are main Bulworks againſt the attempts of powerful Enemies. Their is a ſcarcity of Money, which is one main reaſon they cannot ſet a great Army on Foot in ſo vaſt a Country : and this, I think, proceeds from the ſmallneſs of Trade, for the *Perſians* are not very induſtrious, all of them ſtanding much on points of Honour. There are few or no Fruit-Trees to be found but in Gardens; and in moſt places the Water is bad, and Wood exceeding ſcarce in almoſt all the Provinces. Their chief Manufacture is Silk, and ſome Stuffs. There is abundance of Liquorice growing almoſt every where, but little of it ſet. The Country abounds in Brooks, which render the ways very bad to Travel in Winter, and ſome Rivers, moſt of which are in *Mazandara*; whoſe chief is *Eſchref*, and moſt of theſe Rivers fall into the *Caſpian* Sea.

Here is the greateſt ſtore of Wood in the whole Country of *Perſia*, but there are a vaſt number of Serpents and Scorpions, who dying in multitudes, during the hot Seaſon, corrupt and infect the Air, rendering it unwholeſome; ſo that in fine, *Perſia* is

ſaid

said to be a large Kervanserai, that serves for a Passage for the Money and Goods that go out of *Asia*, *Turkey*, and *Europe* to the *Indies*, and to the Stuffs and Spices returning, of which they have a small Profit.

Designing, now I was thus near to visit the *Indies*, I found some of my Company willing to embrace the opportunity of leaving *Ormus*, and embarking for *Bassora*, at the bottom of the Gulf; and accordingly, with all our Baggage, we safely Arrived and Landed there.

CHAP. XVI.

A Brief Account of Æthiopia, *as I received from Mounsieur* du Pau, *who resided many Years in that Court.*

BEING now at *Bassora*, preparing for a Voyage to the *Indies*, it will not be amiss to entertain you with a brief Relation of *Æthiopia*, or the Country of *Abyssins*, which I had of a *French* Gentleman I found here, who had Travelled in that vast Country, and lived some time in the Court; and this I the rather set down, because I know not whether I shall ever Travel into that famed Country, yet I shall be as Brief as may be.

He told me it was bounded on the East by the Red Sea, and *Zanguebar*, on the South by *Avousa*, *Ziela*, *Narea*, &c. on the West with *Nubia*, and the Country of *Negros*; on the North with part of *Nubia*, and *Bugia*, and is about 7 Months Travel in Circuit. The King has four Kings Tributary to him, *viz.* The King of *Sennar*, who pays him Tribute in Horses, and lives in an excessive hot Country; the King of *Naria*, who pays him Tribute in dust Gold; the Kings of *Bugia*, and *Dangala*, who
sends

Europe, Asia, Africa, *and* America. 109
sends their Tribute in Stuffs and Slaves. In this Country are Mines, out of which Gold is gotten, and sent to the Coasts of *Saffala* and *Guinea*, and these Mines are shallower than in other Countries. They have likewise a great deal of Civet, which is scraped from the Testacles, or rather from an opening slit between or near the Cods of a Civet Cat; this Beast is almost as big as a midling Grey-hound, with a sharp Nose and Head like a Fox; they have Feet, Tail, and Whiskers like a Cat.

When the People of the Country fall out, they go before their Scheiks, who do the good Office to make them Friends again. They anoint their Heads with a strong Oyl, extracted from the Root of an Herb, to keep them from swarming with Lice, which they are very subject to. The Provinces of *Æthiopia* are, *Gouyan* (where the King has a Viceroy) *Beghandir*, *Amara*, *Dambia*, all very Mountainous; *Damoud*, *Tygre*, and *Barnegas*; also other Provinces depending on it, Governed by Princes who are his Vassals. The Air is in some places temperate, but in *Senner* very hot. In this Kingdom are 24 Tambours, or Viceroys. The Capital City is *Gonthar* in the Province of *Dambia*. The King has 100 Wives, and yet so little Jealous, contrary to the *Persians*, and *Turks*, that he keeps no Eunuchs to look after them, it being counted a Sin in that Country to geld a Man; He is of easie access, so that the poorest have freedom to make their complaints to him, or speak to him what they are minded: He keeps the numerous Children he has by his many Wives, on a Mountain, called *Ouohhni*, 2 days journy from *Gonthar*. On the top of the Mountain there is a pleasant Cave, where they keep them a Nights, and in the Day time when they are big enough, their Guardians let them play about the Mountains. When the King dies, they chuse one of the wittiest and likeliest of them, and Crown him, not regarding Birth-right; then are the Brothers removed a distant place to be kept Prisoners, and his Children as he gets them, sent to the forementioned Mountain. The

The Burying-place of the Kings is called *Ayefus*, and is a Grot cut out square in a Rock, there the Aged are laid on one side, and the Younger on the other side: and near it stood a very pretty Church built by the Jesuits, but they diving into Politicks, and State Matters, gave such suspition to the King, that they intended to undermine his Throne, as made him banish them, and demolish their Church and Houses, puting some to Death that lingred behind, as also divers Capuchins, setting a bag of dust-Gold on their Heads, which made the *Abyssins* hunt out, and cut off divers of them, which they sent to the King, and received their promised Reward; so that the poor Fathers were forced to pack up and be gone; however, in the place where the Church stood, there is a place erected which contains a curious Library, stored with Books of divers kinds of Learning, in various Languages. This Country produces very good Wheat and Barley, and is pretty Fruitful in most places where the Desarts are not, for there are very great ones in it, of 3 or 4 Days Journey, which are Wavey, like the Sea, when the Wind blows strong from the South, or South-west, insomuch, that Men and Cattle are buried under Mountains of loose Sand, if they be in the way, where the Desarts lie most exposed to those Hurricanes.

The King in his Progress, always lodges in Tents, the Houses of their chief Nobles being very mean, in respect of those in *Europe*; and the Walls of those of the meaner sort are of Mud and Slime. There are almost Men of all Trades in this Country; they have no Camels here, but store of Mules, Horses, Asses, and Oxen. The People have an ill custom in eating raw Flesh, except the King, who has it dressed, and drinks Wine of the Grape; the rest drink a Liquor made of Millet, or Sarasin-Wheat, and they have a Spirit made of it as strong as Brandy. They have Cloths, Stuffs, and Velvets, Imported by the way of the *Red Sea*, and are Habited like the *Franks* or *Europeans*.

The

The King has a Guard of Harquibusiers. As for their Money, it is pieces of Cloth cut out, going by weight, and little pieces of Salt they cut out on the side of the *Red Sea*. The places where they make it is called *Arbo*. There is amongst them the Nation of the *Gauls*, who have no Fire-Arms, but use in War Sphears and Targets, and often make War with the *Æthiopians*; their Riches consisting in Cattle, and as this Gentleman informed me, there are a great number of different Languages spoken in this Country; and discoursing him about the River *Nile*, which has its rise there, he told me, he had seen the source of it, and that the Spring rises in, and issues out of a Well in a large Plain, shadowed with many Trees, and that well or Spring is called O-*vembromina*.

It rises in the Province, or Little Country of *Ago*, and is a very pleasant Water there; from the Spring it runs Northward, through a long tract of Land, and having passed several Cataracts, or falls, which are very high places, with a terrible roaring, it passes on smoothly till it enters *Egypt*, and is, as I have elsewhere said, the main support of that Country; for should the *Æthiopian* King turn the Current, *Egypt* would be little better than a Desart, which the Grand Signior, as many have guessed, fearing, is the cause he molests not the *Æthiopians* with War; and the reason of its over-flowing in *Egypt*, may be supposed to proceed from the great Rains that fall in *Æthiopia* about that time; for when it is Summer in one place, it is Winter in another. There are but 2 Mountains any thing near the Spring of *Nile*, and those are called the *Jews* Mountains, because they once inhabited them, but growing powerful, were driven out for fear they should Rebel, and compelled to live in the Plains. These Mountains are exceeding high, for in that hot Country they have always Snow on their Tops or Spires.

There is a Generation of *Portuguese* among the *Æthiopians*, for anciently the Moorish King of *Zeila* forcing a King of *Æthiopia* to fly into the Mountains,

tains, he implored aid of the *Portuguese*, to restore him to his Throne, who, with their Fire-Arms flew the Moorish King, and so terrified his Army, that they left the Country; and for this, their Traders on the Coast, were put into Offices, and had rich Possessions bestowed on them, when setling and Marrying with the Native Women, their progeny encreased.

The King, and all his People, are a kind of Christians of the Cophlish Religion, and believe, but one Nature in *Jesus Christ*; at the end of 8 Days they Circumcise their Males, and Baptise them 14 Days after, their Patriarch depends on him of *Alexandria*. They say Mass as the *Cophites* do, but their Books are in their own Language. When their Patriarch dies, they send to *Alexandria*, and that Patriarch sends them a fit Person.

CHAP. XVII.

The Author's Voyage from Bassra, *in the* Persian *Gulf, to* East-India, *and Things remarkable in the dangerous Passage, particularly Water-Spouts rising from the Sea, and remarks on them.*

STaying at *Bassora* for a fair Passage to *East-India*, in a little time it happen'd, as I could wish; I found an *Armenian* Ship there of 28 Guns, and most of the Mariners were *Banians* of *India*, the rest *Armenians*, except the Master and two more, who were *European* Christians; the Master an *Itallian*, and the two Mariners *Greeks*: This Ship was *English* built, and very stench, but how it came into their Hands

they

Europe, Asia, Africa *and* America. 113

they declined to tell me, though I afterward understood, they had bought it for 16000 Roupies when it was in a bad condition, and repairing it they put up *Armenian* Colours, and had 3 Pasports to indemnifie them from the *Europeans* that have Factories in *India*. Our Cargo consisted of such things as could not be vended at *Bassora*, as Indico, Cloth, Dates, Chests of Glass, Venetian Looking-Glasses, and a good quantity of Money to buy *Indian* Commodities. I hired a Cabin, and laid in Provision and Water, fearing in so hot a Voyage, the latter might grow scarce; and it was not without precaution, for so it happened. Setting Sail, and getting clear of the Islands, we steered South-west, and had Water, at 5, and 8 Fathom, 2 Men being continually heaving the Lead, least we should fall on Shallows, or Rocks that are under Water near the Shoar.

It will be endless to tell you the often shifting of the Wind, the Calms we had, and the Tackings we made; therefore, let me say with some difficulty we got to the Island of *Carek*, the first place the Ship designed to Traffick at. This Island reaches in length, from South-east to North-west, is very narrow about 3 or 4 leagues in circumference, and 50 Leagues from *Bossara*; it is partly Hills, and partly Plains, yielding Grapes, Barley, Wheat, Dates, and good store of fresh Water, which is a precious commodity in those Countries: There are Wells dug on the top of Rocks 10 or 12 Fathom deep, and have Steps to go down, and from the bottom of these Wells the Water passes, and runs under ground into the Plains. Near to the Wells there is a neat Mosque on the Hill, and on the Island is 150 indifferent Houses, and near it a Pearl Fishery. The King of *Persia* is Lord of it, and great numbers of Boats come to Fish for them in *May, June, July,* and *August*. Here we unladed part of our Goods, but sold little, by reason a Dutchman had been there before and forestalled us, giving out this Ship would not touch there, by which means over and above, he took in a great many Passengers, and Lading for *India*.   I   Being

Being thus disappointed, we soon weighed Anchor, and steered away South South-east with a very gentle Wind, but were soon becalmed for many Hours; then sprung up an Easterly Wind, and we stood away to the South, and soon had the Isle of *Rischer* on our Larboard, which is very near the main Land, and makes a little Port, called *Bender-Rischer*, which is guarded by a Fort. and standing away, we came up with the Island of *Coucher*, and left it on our Larboard; this Island is large, and indifferent Fruitful; and so Sailing on, passed Cape *Verdestan* at 3 or 4 Leagues distance; and as we Sailed, we had often a faint view of the main Land of *Persia*, especially where it lay high and Mountainous; but before we came to the Island of *Lar* we lost our Long-Boat, which was a great disappointment to us.

Lar is a little Desart Island, bearing nothing but a few Trees at the West North-west end of it; we passed by this, and the next that presented was *Andravia*, a little low Island near the main Land; and passing by we had *Kies*, another Island to the South-West; it is indifferently Inhabited, the Houses lying up and down in it; but Coasting *Paloro*, and leaving Mount *Sennas* on the Main Land to the Larboard, we made *Congo*, a little Town in the Kingdom of *Persia*, 27 Degrees, 15 Minutes North Latitude; it stands on the Sea-side, near the Foot of a black Rock that shelter the Town from the North Winds, and behind there is a white Rock, or Hill, and many such along the Coast. The Town lies from West North-west, to East South-east, and is defended by a little Castle, where 3 pieces of Cannon are mounted, and has a safe Road for Shipping to Ride in, though they are very much tossed in high Winds, about it are 5 Gardens replenished with Fruit-Trees, as Figs, Lemons, Quinces, Oranges, Pears, &c. Large Pomgranates, Mellons, and Palm-Trees; there are also the *Indian* Mangoes; they have *Schiras*-Wine, and Brandy, made of Dates; there are near it Hills, producing
Sulphur,

Europe, Asia, Africa, *and* America 115

Sulphur, which is dug and transported to the *Indies*. The Custom is easie, half of it belonging to the King of *Portugal* by Agreement, beside five Horses the King of *Persia* presents him every Year; and to this end there is a *Portuguese* Agent residing in the Town, who has the Colours of that Nation on the Tarras of his House.

Leaving this place after the sale of some Goods, and taking in others, we set Sail for *Sindy*, being the first Town of *India*, where the River *Indus* discharges it self into the Sea; but here we narrowly escaped falling into the hands of the *Zinganes*, a sort of *Indian* Pirates, who lie with their Boats behind the Rocks, to surprize Vessels as they come near them, and if they board a Ship, in the first fury, till they have mastered and secured the Prize, they put all to the Sword, and the rest they Lame, by cutting the Sinew above the Heel, and make them Slaves to keep their Cattle; they so use them to prevent their running away: Their Arms are only Swords, and Arrows, therefore our watchfulness, and the fire of our great Guns made them retire again among the Rocks, so soon as they prepared to attack us. But having little to do here, we set Sail for *Surat*, having now on Board us, by taking in many Passengers 116 Souls, and passing many small Islands, and some Promontories, came to *Queschimo*, a large low Island, so that Sailing by it, one may see the Mountains of the main Land over it; it lies from East to West 20 Leagues in length, but indifferent in breadth. There is a Fort where Ships Anchor at 6 Fathom Water, and this formerly belonged to the *Portuguese*. On the South East of it lies *Nabdgion*, or *Pilombo*, a little low Desart Island; and East of it *Tonbo*, affording little besides Antelopes and Coneys; but Ships have here the Advantage of many Wells to Water at, yet the entrance is dangerous, because of the Banks that lie under Water about it; the *Portuguese* were once Masters of most of these Islands, and exacted Tribute from Ships that Traded there, but their

I 2   Strength

Isle of *Angem* to the North-east, and on the South-east a Port of *Arabia Fælix*, called *Julfer*, to which many *Indian* Barks come to buy Dates and Pearl, the latter being fished all along the Coast from *Mascat* to *Babrem*, and bring *European* Money to purchase them. The next that stood with us were the Isles of *Salame*; these are four Rocks over-against Cape *Mosandon*, one of them bigger than the rest rising a little into a point, there is a dangerous Chanel passing between them, all Rock at the bottom, so that many adventuring to pass it have been cast away.

Having passed these, we met with great storms of Hail, accompanied with prodigious Thunders and Lightning, insomuch, that the Sea seemed to be all on Fire. This made us furl our Sails, and though the Air on Head of us was as dark as Night, there appeared a Rainbow on our Starboard.

Upon the breaking of this Storm prodigious Spouts began to rise out of the Sea to our Larboard, and at length, encreased almost on all sides of us, some being very near, which put us into a considerable fright, least falling on our Ship they should sink it, they being extraordinary large, insomuch, that all affirmed they had not seen the like in their Lives, so that all Hands were employed to secure the Ship as well as might be, from the threatning danger, for we as good as gave our selves to be lost; however, trusting in the Creator of all things, and taking to my self more Courage than ordinary, I took a view of these watery Prodigies: The first that appeared was about a Musket-shot from us, as we were steering North-east, and before it rose, the Water in that place boiled up prodigiously, more than a Foot above the surface of the Sea, foaming and looking whitish, and over it something representing a black Smoak (which the *Banians* foolishly
said

Europe, Asia, Africa *and* America. 117
said was the Devil sucking up Water to drown them.) This made a hurrying noise like a Torrent running in a Valley, mixed with a hissing like that of Serpents, or Geese. A little after appeared a dark puff of steem, this seemed to be a Pipe as big as ones Finger, the noise continuing, this tapered as it were up to the Clouds, and the light put it out of our sight, so that we knew that Spout was spent; but then there was another to the Southward of us, which began in the same manner as the former, soon after another to the Westward, and another to the side of the second, the most remote of the three; and all these appeared like so many bundles of Straw, a Foot and an half, or two Foot above the surface of the Water, smoaking to appearance exceedingly, making the same noise as the first. A little while after I perceived so many Pipes reaching down from the Clouds upon these Risings, and every one of them had a large end joyning to the Cloud, widening like the end of a Trumpet, and the lower end resembled the Teat, or Dug of a Beast, stretched perpendicularly down by the force of some weight. These Pipes appeared to be of a paleish White, which I conjecture was the Water in them, for no doubt they were formed before they drew it up, and being emptied disappeared; for though the Pipes descended small, fvelled with the Water they grew larger, to the thickness of a Man's Arm, or more.

These Spouts are dangerous things, for falling on a Ship they entangle the Sails, and lift her up, then leting her fall again sink her if she be small, but if the Ship be too heavy to be lifted, they split the Sails, and emptying a vast quantity of Water into her with a violent force, sink her, and thus I believe Ships have been lost, Sailing in those, and other Seas where Spouts are, and so going down in a Minute or two, have never been heard of. Some that were on Board brought a large black handled Knife, to cut the Spouts at a distance, which Superstitious Fancy is thus put in practice: One of the Ships company kneels down by the Main-Mast,

I 3 and

a. d holding in one Hand a Knife with a black handle he Reads the Gospel of St. *John*, and when he comes to these Words, *viz. The Word was made Flesh, and dwells in us*, he turns to the Spout and cuts the Air a thwart, and then they hold the Spout, though at a great distance, is cut, and lets down all its Water with a great noise. But the Master looking on this silly fruitless Fancy as a piece of Conjuration, would not let it be put in practice. In the *Mediterranean* they shoot Cross bar-shot at them, which hitting, is more probable of the two to cut; however, these spent themselves without doing us any harm, and at length through infinite Mercy, we weathered the Storm which raged furiously all the time and kept on our Course, having the main Land of *Arabia* on our Starboard, and on our Larboard that part of *Persia* called *Marjan*, which bore South east of us, and we made particularly one Hill of Land shaped like a Sugar Loaf, and here, in *November*, *December*, and *January*, the East Winds commonly Reign, and therefore, to go from *Persia* to *India* in a short time, the best Season is *March*, *April*, and the beginning of *May*, for then the *Mouson*, or Trading Wind blows. However, we held on with the help of the Current, which from the end of *July* to *January* sets towards *Ormus* from *India*, and from *January* till *July* from *Ormus* towards *India*.

In our Passage another Storm arising, we saw 3 new Spouts, but they were at too great a distance from us to apprehend much danger. In our way, off *Bembaceca*, we overtook 3 Ships bound to *Surat*, as we were, but proving slow Sailers, the Master would not stay for them, but resolved to make the best of his way, so contrary to the mind of the Mate, we left them to Sail at their leisure.

CHAP.

CHAP. XVIII.

The Arrival at Surat; *a discription of that Town; the manner of the People; Travels into the* Indian *Provinces, with Observations of what is Rare and Remarkable in the vast Dominion of the* Great Mogul.

AFter many dangers in Coasting *Persia*, and a great part of *Arabia*, we knew by the Snakes we saw at Sea, a kind of spungy Froth floating in great abundance on the Water, which pricks, and makes the Hands of those that touch it burn, that we were not far from the main Land of *India*; we kept Sailing by many small Islands, of which those Seas are plenty, till we made *Daman*, a Town belonging to the *Portugueses*, who have strengthened it with a considerable Fort: It lies in 20 Degrees North Latitude. From this Town to Cape *Comorin* is a range of very high Hills along the Coast, yet this Town has no other Harbour but a little Chanel which remains almost dry when the Tide is out. Here refreshing our selves, we took the advantage of an Easterly Gale, and weighing Anchor bore away Northward, having no more than five Fathom and an half Water in an Hours Sailing; but then coming into deeper Water we Sailed more boldly, and came up with the Bar of *Surat*, in 6 Fathom and an half Water: Here the Custom house-Officers came aboard us, and narrowly search'd and viewed every thing they had an opportunity to see; after that Boats came to fetch off the Passengers and their Goods, and we were had to the Custom-house, and again searched in a very odd manner. The entrance

Travels and Voyages in
entrance for Veſſels of Burthen is very difficult, and we were a-ground twice before the Tide could carry us in; we paſſed then by the Caſtle of *Surat* on our Right Hand, and dropped our Anchor before the Cuſtom-Houſe.

Thus being happily at Land, after a two Months troubleſome Voyage, I and others reſted and refreſhed our ſelves. The Bar, ſo called, by reaſon of Sands, and is 6 French Leagues or more from *Surat*, yet their Ships of great Burthrn muſt unload before they can come up the River.

Being impatient to ſee *Surat*, of which I had heard ſo much diſcourſe at home. I went in a Boat on the River with divers other Paſſengers, but by reaſon of the Stream being againſt us, we were a conſiderable time e'er we reached the Town; and the Cuſtom-houſe being open, upon the Signal given we came on Shoar, without which we might not do it: then paſſing a large Court, we entered into a Hall, where the Cuſtomer waited to have us ſearched.

The manner of their ſearching, as I ſaid, is odd, and very ſtrict, they making their ſearch from Head to Foot, feeling your Nakedneſs in every part, looking alſo into your Mouth, as if they would tell you your Age by your Teeth; and the Waiter demands of every Paſſenger, as his Fee, an Abaſſy, which is worth about 18 d. and the Bark has half a Roupe, which is about 14 d. a Head for every Paſſenger. If they find one ſmugling in the leaſt, he is fined ſeverely, if not Caved. All the Baggage is brought into the Cuſtom-houſe to be ſearched, and when that is done, every one is called in his turn, to pay, and take them away for Money; they take two and an half *per Cent.* for Merchants Goods, of Chriſtians four, and of the *Banians* five *per Cent.*

India is a very large Country, of which I ſhall ſay ſomething, before I enter upon particulars. It is bounded on the Weſt with the River *Indus*, on the Eaſt with *China*, on the North with *Tartary*, on the

Europe, Asia, Africa, *and* America.

the South with the Ocean, and is properly divided into two divisions, *viz. India intra Gangem*, and *India extra Gangem*; the first contains nine Kingdoms, *viz. Narsinga, Malavar, Ballasia, Cambaia, Mandao, Bengala, Aristan, Comora,* and *Dellia.* The second, seven, *viz. Macine, Aracan, Couchin-Chian, Baram, Siam, Pegue, Malavar.* The whole Country seems to take its denomination from the vast River *Indus,* which runs 1000 Miles e'er it falls into the Sea; and the Empire of the Great Mogul is the Principle, many of the others being petty Kings, some of them paying him Tribute, and his Territories are usually called the *Mogulistan.* The present Great Mogul is held to descend directly from the line of *Tamarlan* the *Tartar*, whose Successors setled in the *Indies,* and took to themselves the Name of *Moguls,* to distinguish them from those to whom that Prince left *Zagalay, Persia, Coraffau*, with other Countries to be Govern'd after him; and they concluding this Name would contribute to the Glory of the Family, because the People would be the more easily perswaded they are of the Race of the great *Ginguiscan,* the first Emperour of the Ancient *Moguls.* It has been successively maintained for many Generations, and is a mighty Empire established in *India.*

As for *Mogul,* is was anciently the Name of a mighty People Inhabiting a Country at the extreamity of East-*Tartary*, inclining towards the North, which others have called *Mongul* and *Mongal,* some *Mogulistan,* where *Ginguiscan* was Born, and that Emperour reduced it wholly under his Obedience, before he proceeded to the Conquest of the rest of *Asia*; and both himself and Subjects were called *Moguls.* The Great Mogul is said to carry 300000 Horse into the Field with him when he makes War, beside a considerable Army of Foot; yet the most knowing *Indians* say, though he pays so many, there is not above half of them in Arms at once. The great Men that Command, usually, for their own advantage, it being the most they have to live on,

double

double the Muster-Roll. He has in his Dominions, 20 Provinces or Governments, and those that have made them more, have mistaken, by making two of one.

The true bounds of his Empire to the West, are, *Macram*, or *Sinde*, and *Candabar*: On the East it reaches to the River *Ganges*; on the South it is limitted by the Gulf of *Bengala*, the great Sea, and *Decan*: on the North by a part of *Tartary*. It extends from East to West, above 400 Leagues, and from North to South 500; and this vast space, some Mountains and Desarts excepted, is very much replenished with Cities, Towns, Castles, Boroughs, and pleasant Villages; and the Country about them very fruitful in Corn, Rice, Fruits, &c.

In the Province of *Guzerat*, in this Empire, is the Town of *Surat*, of which I have spoke something already. It lies in 22 Degrees 7 Minutes North Latitude, watered by the River *Tapty*. The Walls were formerly of Earth, but they are framing now of Brick, 2 Fathom and an half thick, and of the same heighth, being cautioned so to do for its better defence, upon its being plundered by *Raja Savegi*, who made himself Master of great Riches, though he took not the Castle, nor was able to force the Factories of the *Europeans*, who had Fortified them with Cannon, and making a stout defence, saved their Goods from the spoil. This *Raja* had his Government in the Mountains, and did great mischiefs in *India*; though *Aurenzeb*, the Mogul, or Emperor, did all he could to prevent it.

In building the new Wall, a great many Houses are left out of the Town, especially those built of Cane. When the Mouson, or Monson, a Wind that serves for Trade of Shiping, blows, the Town is full of People, so that 'tis difficult to get any Lodging: and this is in *January*, *February*, *March*, part of *April*, and sometimes all that Month.

It is Inhabited by *Indians*, *Persians*, *Arabians*, *Armenians*, *Turks*, *European* Christians, and some few other Nations; though the proper Inhabitants are

divided

Europe, Asia, Africa, *and* America. 123
divided into 3 Orders; the first of these include the *Indian Moors*, and others of the *Mahometan* Religion; the second are *Gentils*, or Heathens, who adore Idols, the third are the *Parsis*, who are likewise called *Guares*, or *Artechpirest*, adorers of Fire, professing the Religion of the ancient *Persians*; and these retired into *India*, when *Caylif Oman* reduced *Persia* under the Power of the *Mahometans*. The *Banians* are here the richest Merchants, some of them being held to be worth 8 Millions of Crowns. The *Dutch* particularly, among other *Europeans*, have driven a great Trade here, as did the *English*, and these had Houses assigned them for their Factories, called Lodges, very neatly built.

The Castle is built on the side of the River *Tapty*, and is a Fort of moderate bigness, and of good strength; it stands at the South end of the Town, and defends the Entry against those that would attack it. It is square, and flanked at each corner with large Towers: The Ditches on 3 sides are filled with the Sea Water, and the 4th which is on the West, is washed by the River. In this Castle the Mogul's Revenues gathered in the Province are kept, and never sent to Court without Order.

On the West side there is a stately Gate to enter at, which is in the *Bazar* or *Meiden*, and this Castle has a particular Governor, and the Town has another. The Houses of the Rich are but meanly built, of Timber, Brick, Lime, and Tiles, and most of these being fetched a great way renders building very dear, by reason there is no Stone in this Province: They make their Laths of Bambous Cane, and they chuse, by reason of the excessive heat of the Sun, which drys and craks so fast, to build when it Rains, rather than in dry weather. As for the Houses of the ordinary sort, they are made of Cane, and covered with Palm branches. The Streets are large and even, but not Paved. They spare the Oxen here to Till the Land, and carry Burthens, feeding on Cow-Beef, especially for the most part; they have good Mutton, and abundance

of

of Poultry, and eat with their Meats the Oyl of *Cnicus Sylvestris*, or wild Saffron, the best in the *Indies*; also that of *Sesamum*, which is common, but not so good. They have white and red Grapes there, but they make an eager and unpleasant Wine, because the heat is so excessive they have not deliberation enough to ripen; nor is the strong Waters drunk there much better; it is made of *Jagre*, a a kind of course black Sugar dissolved in Water, with the bruised Bark of the Baboul-Tree, and so Distilled.

They make strong Water likewise of Tary, and draw a Brandy from Rice, Sugar and Dates, which, however, is but very sorry stuff, and kills many of the *Europeans*, who coming a long Voyage, too suddenly fasten on those Liquors and drink intemperately. They infuse these ingredients likewise in Water, and by setting them in the Sun make Vinegar.

At *Surat* are sold all sorts of Stuffs and Cotten Cloth that are made in the *Indies*, likewise a great many *European* Commodities, and those of *China*, as Purceline, Cabinets, and Coffers, adorned with Turquois, Agats, Cornelian, Ivory, and all sorts of Embellishments; here are Diamonds, Rubies, Pearls, and most sort of precious Stones that are found in the Eastern Country; also Amber, Musk, Myrrh, Frankincense, Manna, Sal Armoniac, Lac, Indico, Quick-silver; the Root Rænus for Dying Red, and all sorts of Spices and Fruits that are to be found in the *Indies*, and other Countries of *Levant*; and here Merchants buy up Drugs to transport into all parts of the World; so that this Town, though not large, may be said to be the Emporium of the *Indies*.

Having pretty well viewed this place, and taken such things as I was informed were necessary for such hot Countries as remained for me to Travel in, and considering *Amedabad* was the Chief City of *Guzerat*, I directed my Journey to take a view of it. This Province, a few Ages since was an entire Kingdom,

dom, Govern'd by *Mudafer*, a young Prince, who by the advice of his Guardian, called in *Mogul Echbar*, to make his party good againſt the great Men who were troubleſom to him; but the Mogul getting ſtrong footing, impriſoned him and his Guardian, where they died miſerably, and ſeized the Kingdom, annexing it as a Province to his Empire, and it is the pleaſanteſt of *Indoſtan*, though not the largeſt, for it is well watered with the Rivers *Nardabad* and *Tapty*, with ſome other Rivers of leſſer Note, ſo that the Fields look green all the Year, by reaſon of the Corn and Rice that cover them, and the various kinds of Trees that continually bear Bloſſoms and Fruit.

Setting out from *Surat*, with ſome others in company, I Travelled Northward, and 2 Hours after croſſed the *Tapty* in a Ferry, as I did the River *Kim*, near the Town of *Beriao*, and came to *Oucliſſer*, and paſſing the River *Nardabad*, arrived at *Baroche*, diſtant from *Surat*, and the Sea, about 10 French Leagues, or 20 *Indian* Coſſes, which is a meaſure amongſt them of about half a League. This Town lies about 22 Degrees North Latitude; it has a large ſquare Fortreſs ſtanding on a Hill, and the Town lies upon the ſide, near the Foot of it, looking towards the River *Nardabad*, encompaſſed with a Stone Wall 2 Fathom high, flanked with Towers between 30 and 35 paces diſtant one from another, and is the ſtrongeſt in the Province. The *Bazar*, or Market-place is a large Street at the Foot of the Hill, where are made the Cotton Stuffs, called Baftas. Here are Moſques and Temples of the Heathens, with Pagods or Idols in them, to whoſe ſenſeleſs Shrines they pay devout Adoration. Here are plenty of Agats, and alſo abundance of Peacocks.

Leaving this place, I continued my Journey Northward, and came to the little Town of *Sourban*, 7 Leagues from *Baroche*, and croſſing the Brook *Dader*, and ſeveral little Villages, I entered *Debea*, where a barbarous ſort of People Inhabit, who, a few Years ſince fed on Man's Fleſh, ſelling it publickly

lickly at their Shambles, so that Strangers always go armed here, for fear of being robbed and mischiefed by them, which made us make but a short stay; but passing the Lake, or River *May*, we came to *Pesnad*, about 7 Leagues from *Debea*, and saw in our way 2 great *Tanqueze*, and a number of Monkies, who came and crossed us in the Road, fearless of our shouts, but rather mockingly answered us again, crying *Pou*, *Pou*; the Tanquiez are standing Ponds, or reservatories for Rain Water, paved at the bottom, and kept very choicely. Leaving this place I Travelled with my Company to *Soufentra*, and so to *Mader*, which place is very Woody, and there the Monkies were in greater numbers than before, in the Fields, Roads, and on the Trees; and Travelling 5 Leagues from this place, I came to *Gilbag*, where I met a great many *Collies*, a People of the cast off *Gentiles*, who wander up and down, and have no fixed Habitation; their chief business being to pick the Cotton Wooll. In *Gilbag* there is a handsom Garden that belongs to the Mogul, and in it are kept a number of Peacocks; it is finely Watered, and well Planted with Fruit-Trees, and from hence it is two Leagues to *Amedabad*, to which I went the next Morning.

    This, as I said, is the chief City of the Province, and is about 86 Cosses, or half French Leagues from *Surat*, and the Sea. It is Govern'd by an *Omra*, or *Indian* Lord, under the Mogul: It lies 23 Degrees and some Minutes North Latitude, on a lovely Plain, and is watered by the River *Sabremetty*, which when the Rains fall, much overflows the Plains. There are large Gardens, enclosed with fine Brick Walls; these Gardens have reservatories for Water, and each of them a fine Pavillon at the entrance, and at the end of most of them there are convenient Lodgings. The Houses in the Suburbs are scattering, and many ancient Tombs are to be seen about the City, into which you enter by a straight large Street; the Walls are pretty strong, composed of Stone and Brick, flanked with great round Towers

ers and Battlements. It is about a League and an half in length, and has 12 Gates, which are strictly watched, for fear of a surprize from the *Raja*, of *Bandour*, whose Territories are near, but almost inaccessible Mountains, which gives him an opportunity to make inroads thereabouts, and safely to retire with much Booty, not regarding the Mogul. In this City are many curious Arches, and large Squares. There is a Kervanserai in the *Meidan*, furnished with curious Balcony-Lodgings, supported with Pillars; and the King has a Pallace in this City of curious Work, where the Musicians resort to Play on their Instruments Morning, Noon, Evening, and Midnight, for which they have a Sallary allowed them; in the Apartments there are several Ornaments of Folages covered Gold; there is the *Juma*, *Mesgid*, or *Fridays*, whither on that Day the People all Flock; it is very beautiful, and is the fairest of all others, though there are many more; on the outside of each Gate is a fine Steeple, with a Balcony, where the *Muesins*, or Bedles, with their thundering Voices call the People to the Mosque, for in this Country they have no Bells; and when they repair hither they appear very devout, for I saw above 400 *Faquirs* who held their Arms cross behind their Heads without stirring all the Prayer-time. I visited another Mosque which had been a Pagod Temple, before *Aureng-Zebe* caused a Cow to be killed in it, which caused the *Gentiles* to forsake it. It has abundance of Figures of naked Women in it, sitting after the Oriental fashion, as also, of Men, Beasts, and Monsterous Creatures; but they are somewhat disfigured by their Noses being cut off, which *Aureng-Zebe* caused to be done out of a pretended Zeal, which raised him to the Throne over the Heads of his Father and two elder Brothers.

In this City is the place where the famed Magician was Buried, whom many of the *Indians* hold for a great Saint, and visit his Tomb with great Devotion: It is a square pile of Building, having on each side several little Domes setting off a great one the middle. The entry into it is by 7 Ports that take up the whole Front; the Pavings is Marble, the Doors are of the same, inlaid with Chriſtal and Mother-Pearle: The Tomb is like a bed, covered with Cloth of Gold, and over it 7 Canopies of different coloured Silk, one higher than another: The Pavement is uſually ſtrowed with white Flowers, which the devout *Mahometans* bring when they come to ſay their Prayers at the Tomb.

Near to the Burying-place of the Ancient Kings of *Guzerat*, which is a very fine Building, and curious Arched Vaults under it, where the Aſhes of the Dead are in Urns, is the Sepulcher of a Cow, under a Dome, ſtanding on 6 Pillars, but either they knew not, or declined to tell me the reaſon why ſhe was buried there; but at another place I heard, one of their Kings was driven out by the People, who flying to the Mountains, was there ſupported by the Cow's Milk till he was recalled, whereupon, dying ſoon after, he left a Pention to keep this Cow ſo long as ſhe ſhould live, with Commands, that ſhe ſhould be Buried in this manner when ſhe Died; and the People on certain Days go to the Sepulchers of their Kings to bewail their loſs.

The next thing I viſited, was a famed Well, 8 Story deſcending, every Story ſupported with Arches and Pillars; it is 4 Fathom broad, and about 24 long; very lightſome, having in it curious Springs. They ſay it was built by a King's Nurſe, and coſt 20 Millions of Roupies, but I believe a great deal leſs finiſhed it.

Though ſome may think it ſtrange, and ſcruple crediting it, yet certain it is, here the Gentile *Indians* have an Hoſpial for ſick Beaſts, and another for Birds, which they feed and look after till they are well, and then they ſell them to their own Sect, but not *Mahometans*, whom they count Cruel, becauſe they miſuſe and kill Creatures, and often they buy them out of their Hands at dear rates, purely out of a charitable compaſſion to ſave the poor Creatures Life, for they hold it a Sin to kill any thing.

thing. Near this City are large Forrests, in which they take Panthers, and the Governor has those that teach them to be tame and tractable, and then he sends them to the King as presents to divert him in Hunting. I saw likewise a Beast there that had the Head of a Coney, the Ears, Eyes, and Teeth of a Hare, the Muzzle round and Flesh-coloured, the Tail of a Squirrel, in the fore Feet it had four Fingers, and a Claw in the place of the Fist; the hinder Feet had 5 Toes, each of which were long as well as the Claws; the soles of its Feet flat, and like an Apes, of a Flesh colour; its Hair on the sides, long, course, and of a dark red, but greyish on the Belly, like the Wool of a Hair; and from Head to Rump, about a Foot and an half long; few could tell what to make of it; they told me it was brought from *Moca*, yet, probably, it was no other than a Squirril. The Commodities mostly traded for here are, Velvets, Skins, Taffatas, Tapestries, with Gold, Silk, and Woollen Grounds, Cotton, Cloth, Indico dried and preserved, Ginger, Sugar, Cinamon, Tamarines, Mirabalans, Cumin, Lac, Saltpetre, Opium, Honey, and some Schites, or painted Cloth.

Cambay being in this Province, by the Sea, I resolved to visit it, but on my way found little worth mentioning. Let it suffice then that I arrived there. This Town lies at the bottom of a Gulf of the same Name, which is very dangerous for large Vessels to come in, by reason of the Flats, and banks of Sand, and for those of less force by reason the *Malabar* Pirates lie sheltering under the Rocks to surprize them. This Town is much larger than *Surat*, tho' not near so Populous, for the causes I mentioned. The Walls are Brick, about 4 Fathom high, with Towers at certain distances. The Streets are large, and have all Gates at the ends of them, which are kept close shut at Night. The Houses are very high, built of Bricks baked in the Sun, and the Shops are stored with Aromatick Perfumes, Spices, Silks, Stuffs, Ivory, Bracelets, Agat, Cups, Caphlets, and Rings: The Agats are got out of a Quarry, near a Village called *Nimodra*, about 4 Leagues from from *Cambaya*. Moſt part of the Inhabitants are *Banians* and *Raſpouts*.

The Caſtle where the Governor reſides is large, but not beautiful. In this Town there are ſo many Monkies, that ſometimes the Houſes are covered over with them, as it were a Dovecot, and theſe miſchievous Creatures never fail to hurt one or other in the Streets, if they can find any thing to throw at them. There are many Gardens about this Town, and a ſtately Marble Tomb is to be ſeen very ancient, and the Building about it ſuitable, adorned with Porphery Pillars, &c. There are the Ruins of other old Tombs to be ſeen near it, held to be thoſe of Ancient Kings. The Suburbs are near as big as the Town, and great ſtore of Indico is made there. As one Travels from this place there is great danger of Robbers who lie concealed, and by a ſlight throw a nooſe about a Man's Neck, pull him down, and ſtrangle him in a trice, and ſo rifle him, and therefore it is proper to go in a good company, though there is a cuſtom to carry a *Techeron* Man and Woman with them, who declare to the Robbers, that the Party is under their Protection, and if they injure them, the Man proteſts to cut his own Throat, and the Woman ſhows them a Raiſor, with which ſhe vows to cut off her Breaſt, and this they ſay, has often deter'd the Thieves from offering violence to Travellers, becauſe the Heathens who are moſtly the Robbers, look on it as a horrid and unpardonable Crime to be guilty of the Death of a *Techeron*, becauſe, ever after, the Party who is the cauſe of it is hated by his Caſt, and turned out of the Tribe, and continually upbraided with the Death of a *Gentil*, though I could not underſtand this takes now adays, for few of them will kill themſelves, though they proteſt it, but have a cunning fetch to excuſe it, alledging, after they have whiſpered with the Robbers, they have compounded, and ſo get Money out of Chriſtians, which no doubt they ſnack between them.

This

Europe, Asia, Africa, *and* America 131

This Province has several other considerable Towns, as *Goga*, on the other side the Gulf, between 20 and 30 Leagues from *Cambaye*, *Patan* lying more Southward, towards the great Sea, where many Silks and Stuffs are made: It is defended by a Fort, and has a Fine Mosque in it, which was formerly an Idol Temple.

Diu, belonging to the *Portuguese*, fortified with 3 Castles, at the Siege of which, an Army sent by the last Sultan but one of *Ægypt*, named *Campson Gaurus*, perished, and Sultan *Solyman* the great Emperor of the *Turks*, sending another Army under *Solyman* Bassa, which was joyned by a vast power of *Indians*; the valliant *Portuguese* Governor named *Siveira*, so well defended it, that after a long Battery, they were forced to raise the Siege, and leave their Tents, Artillery, and Ammunition, with 1000 wounded Men in their Camp, though the *Turks* in their Passage, had seized *Aden* by Treachery, and strangled the King of that place. At *Diu* is made the Stone *Cobra*, so famous for antedoting the biting or stinging of Serpents; it is composed of the Ashes of a burnt Root, mingled with a kind of an Earth they get under the Rocks, and making these into a Paste, they form the Stone of it; then they prick the Wound, and letting a little Blood out, they apply the Stone, leaving it till it falls off of it self; it has the same effect on Wounds made by Poyson'd Weapons, and after that put into Womans, or Cows Milk, it leaves the Poyson it has sucked in, and if it be not so used, it will burst.

There are two other Towns of Note in this Province, *viz*. *Nariad*, and *Mamadebad*, where they make store of Stuffs; the latter furnishing this, and adjacent Provinces, with Cotton Thread. The income of this Province to the Mogul's Treasury is accounted Twenty millions and five hundred thousand French Livres yearly.

Travelling on, I entred the Province of *Agra*, which I reckoned the largest in the Mogul's Territories;

K 2

ritories; *Agra*, which gives it the Name is the Capital Town in it. It is distant from *Surat* 210 Leagues, and is seated on the River *Gemna*, in 28 Degrees and an half, North Latitude. The River has its source in the Mountains to the North of *Dehly*, and increasing by the way, it is here considerable, and passing through large Countries, empties it self into the great River *Ganges*, at the Town of *Halbas*.

Mogul *Ecbar* made *Agra* a City, it being before but a Borough, and establishing the Seat of his Empire there, called it *Ecbar Abad*, or the Habitation of *Ecbar*, joyning several Villages by other Buildings to enlarge it: He fortified it very well with a Castle and Walls of great heighth and strength, and had his Pallace in the Castle, containing 3 Courts with Porches, adorned with Gilding and Painting; nay, some pieces plated with Massy Gold. There are many stately Sepulchers, Baths, Pillars, and other things of great Antiquity. And here *Aurengzebe* Imprisoned *Cha-Gehan*, his Father, when he mounted to the Throne, and in that confinement he died, who has a little Sepulcher erected to his Memory. There are in *Agra* a great many Christian Families; some reckon 5000, but the computation is not agreed on. The *Dutch* hold a Factory in this Town, and for the greater encouragement of Travellers, the *Fourfdar*, an Officer in the nature of a Sheriff, is obliged to make restitution to those that are Robbed, and this is punctually observed in all, or most of the Provinces.

Here are Elephants, Antelopes, Leopards, and other Beasts that they use in their Games for fighting. I saw here Green Pidgeons, and the *Indians* have a cunning way to catch them in the Water, for they go into the Rivers Naked, and keep their Bodies under Water, their Heads only remaining above, which is covered with a Cap of Feathers in the Form of a Water-Fowl, so without scaring them, draw them under Water by the Legs.

In the Mountains, about 5 days Journey from hence, they Hunt, and take store of *Merovers*, or
wild

wild Cows, of which Hunting they make great advantage. Their Pictures in *Agra* are pretty well done, but moſtly in bandy Poſtures, exceeding Active, being purpoſely drawn to ſtir up lacivious deſires, and therefore I ſhall paſs them over. The *Agrians* are the beſt Workmen I ever met withal in working Gold on Agat, Chriſtal, and other brittle things, which few of our Lapidaries, or Goldſmiths can do, or if they can, fall ſhort in equalling them.

Paſſing from *Agra*, I came to *Fetipour*, once the Seat of the Empire, but now not much conſiderable, except for its lovely Meidan and Moſque; the entry of *Ecbar*'s Pallace, and ſome ſtately Pillars ſcattered up and down; it was ſlighted, as they ſay, becauſe all the Springs about it were brackiſh, and unwholeſome. I was informed, in this Province there are upwards of 3400 Towns and Villages, of which, next to what I have named, theſe are the Chief, *viz*. *Bernzabad*, *Chitopour*, *Bargant*, *Mirda*, *Hindon*, *Ladono*, *Chalaour*, *Byana*, *Canova*, and *Scanderbade*, moſt of theſe produce Manufactures of Stuffs, Silks, Tapeſtry, &c. and the Revenues of this Province mount very near to that of *Guzerat*.

Next we entered the Province of *Dehly* by difficult ways, becauſe the Rains had made the Rivers ſwell in many places. It bounds on *Agra* to the North; and *Dehly*, the Principal Town of the Province is about 45 Lergues from *Agra*, and Mogul *Cab Gaban*, and *Aureng Zeb*, made it the Royal Seat of the Empire; the way is all along planted with curious Trees in a Line, and each half League is marked with a kind of a Turret, and there are conveniencies by the way for Travellers to ſhelter and reſt in: There is by the way likewiſe, an ancient Heathen Temple, viſited by the *Gentiles*, who provide neceſſaries for a great many Apes that are kept there, and they pay a kind of a blind Devotion to them, as the Creatures of the Pagods. *Dehly* ſeems to be compoſed of certain Villages, and there is the Ruins of a Town, which the *Indians* ſay, was the Regal Seat of King *Porus*, famed in Hiſtory for the Wars he he maintained against *Alexander* the Great. There is to be seen a Piramid or Obelisk of Stone, with an Inscription in very ancient Characters; which they say, *Alexander* erected in Memory of his Victory over *Porus*, but the Character not being Greek renders it doubtful.

This City lies in an open Champion Country, washed by the River *Gemna*; it has a Fortress half a League in circumference, with a strong Wall, and a round Tower, every 10 Battlements being secured by a Ditch wharfed with Stone, and a Garden round it. In this Fortress the Mogul holds his Pallace; and keeps the Ensigns of his Royalty; and from hence he beholds the fighting of Elephants, and other pastimes at Land, as also on the River; and towards the Town is a large place where the *Rajas* in the Mogul's Pay Encamp, as his Guard. The Market is kept in a fine Square, where abundance of Juglers, and Fellows pretending to Conjuration, shew Tricks. All the Mogul's Attendance in the Pallace shew him a profound Reverence, standing demure before him, with their Hands a-cross upon their Breasts, none daring speak unless Commanded, and at Noon every Day he gives Audience to such as have recourse to him for Justice, administring it Impartially, without respect of Persons.

There is a stately Hall, wherein he gives Audience to his Ministers about affairs of State, and those of his Houshold; and in this Pallace is a Throne of Massie Gold, set with Flowers of Diamonds, Emerald, Rubies, and other precious Stones, and a Peacock made out in all its Colours, with Gold, Silver, and precious Stones, insomuch, that it resembles the Life, and is of vast value: They say these were begun by *Tamarlan*, and finished by two succeeding Moguls: Some hold these to be worth 20 Millions of Gold.

There is a stately Mosque, with its Dome of white Marble, and the Karvanserai of *Begum Saheb*, Daughter to *Cah Gahen*, and Sister to *Aureng Zeb*. There are two extraordinary fair Streets in the City,

Europe, Asia, Africa, *and* America. 135
ty, very wide and streight, of a considerable length, having Arches all along on both sides serving for Shops, and on the back-side many convenient Warehouses, also Tarrassed Walks over the Arches, where they take the Air, and have a fine Prospect; and these Streets end in a very fine Square and Castle: There is nothing else considerable, for the ordinary Houses are built mostly of Earth and Canes, the other Streets are narrow and incommodious, by reason of the vast Crouds of People that flock to Court, but when the Court is absent, there is Room enough without jostling; for the great Men, when there with the Mogul, have large Trains, and his Officers are very numerous; he has also a Guard to his Person of 35000 Horse, and about 12000 Foot, and most of the Soldiers have their Wives and Children to attend them; so that by what appears, the Residentary Inhabitants do not appear to be two thirds of the number by a considerable deal, if we reckon the Merchants and Artificers that follow the Court where-ever it removes, into the account of the former.

They have Elks and Rhinoceroses here that are as large as Oxen; they have many Bufflers, and they breed up Dogs brought from *Bengala*, who are held to have been originally brought from *England*, for their pastime in hunting Lyons, and other furious Wild Beasts. They have Elephants both small and great; those are the biggest and strongest that are brought from *Ceilan*, and some of these will carry 40 Men of 80 pound weight each; they are very ductil, he that guides them can direct them to do what he pleases with his Voice, and a small Wand: the Elephant's Trunk serves him instead of a Hand to feed himself, and take up Water, *&c.* they show many Tricks as their Guide directs them, and will do no hurt unless provoked, or in their Lust, and then the Guide who rides on their Necks is in great danger, for they run furiously, and turn all topsiturvy till they are stopped by Fireworks, which they throw before them. They decoy the
K 4 he

he wild Elephants in the Woods and Mountains with a tame Female Elephant, entangling him in toiles whilst he is in Copulation, and then keep him without Meat till he is almost Famished, and so overmastering him, they lead him away, by coaksing of him and feeding him with Balls made of Paste, for they soon fall in Love with those that seem to be kind to them; sometimes they catch them in Pits, covered over with rotten Hurdles and Earth; they are not seven Years with Calf, as some ignorantly hold; but when the Females are young and lusty, they bring forth at the end of 12 or 14 Months. Some say they worship the Moon, because they have been found kneeling, and throwing up Herbs and Flowers at its Change; and usually about that time they wash themselves in Rivers, if they have an opportunity.

 The *Indians*, as well as the *Moors*, often kill them in the Mountains for their Teeth, they having two exceeding large ones: Some are found Dead with their Trunks off a good way, and this misfortune happens to them when they go to Water at *Ganges*, or *Indus*, which Rivers are pestered with huge Crocodiles, who bite off the ends of their Trunks, when they dip them in the Water, and so the poor Beast is starved for want of wherewithal to feed it self. Some hold these Creatures live an hundred Years.

 At *Dehly* they have very curious Pictures representing the History of their King's Wars, and such like Figures, and their Colours exceeding ours, render them very Lovely and Ornamental. The richer sort here have abundance of Jewels, especially the Rajas, who preserve them as an Inheritance from Generation to Generation. They have a kind of Tin here brought from *China*, that in Luster nearly resembles Silver. To the North-east of the Province of *Dehly* is that of *Azmer*; the Country of *Sinde* bounds it on the West, *Agra* to the East, *Multan* and *Pengeab* to the North, and *Guzerat* to the South: It was formerly divided into 3 Provinces,

viz.

viz. *Bando*, *Geffelmere*, and *Sorat*, but now bears the Name of the Capital City; it lies between 25 and 26 Degrees North Latitude, at the Foot of a very high and almoſt inacceſſible Mountain, at the top of which is a ſtrong Caſtle, and it is above a League in turnings and windings to come to it.

The Town of *Azmer* is walled with Stone, and has a good Ditch about it; without it there appears the Ruins of many ſtately Buildings that ſhew great Antiquity; in the Town is to be ſeen *Cogea-Mondy*, a *Mahometan* Saint; it is a curious Building, having three Courts paved with Marble, the firſt is extreamly large, and hath on the ſide ſeveral Sepulchers of pretended Saints, with a reſervatory of Water, and a neat Well about it; the ſecond is not ſo large, but much more beautiful, and many Lamps burning in it; the third is more beautiful than the reſt, and therein is *Cogea*'s Tomb in a Chapel; the Doors of it are adorned with various Colours made into Flowers, and other curious Devices with Mother-Pearl: There are other Courts and Lodgings for the Imans or Prieſts who read the Alcoran, and many go a Pilgrimage from far Countries to this Tomb. The common Building of the Town, as all over *India*, is but indifferent, yet there are many particular pleaſant places in it.

There is a great Feaſt held every New Years day, and a Fair kept by the Ladies of the *Seraglio*, and others of the beſt Quality, who expoſe their Jewels, Cloth of Gold, and other rich Things to Sale, and indeed themſelves, for the wittieſt and handſomeſt uſually get Husbands, if they be not Married before. They have a ſumptuous Feaſt at the Mogul's Charge; and he is preſented by them, the great Men, and their Ladies, with a vaſt deal of Treaſure, and in the ſeveral Provinces whilſt this Feaſt holds, he has ſeldom leſs than 14 or 15 Millions given him. There are curious Shows of Elephants, Fireworks, and other pleaſant things to divert them; and when he is preſent with his Begums or Princeſſes, he lays aſide the ſtiffneſs of Majeſty, and is very familiar

with

with his Nobles, returning them Presents, but of no great Value in some parts of this Province, and very ordinary in others. The *Indian* Girls are Married at 8 or 9 years old, and have usually Children at 10: Those of the more rustick sort go naked, except a Rag to hide their Privities.

They have a Beast here no bigger than a Hare, which has on its Belly a swelling, or Bladder, that fills with corrupt Blood, which being taken off becomes pure Musk, but the Beast lives not long after it. They use Oxen for most sort of Labours, as to ride on, carry Burthens, draw in Coaches, Carts, Chariots; the white ones are esteemed the best, and bear an extraordinary price.

They make store of Salt-Petre in this Province, which is done in this manner. They dig a fat black Earth, and put it into Pits, mingling it there with Water, and beating it with great Wooden Beaters, so let it stand till the Water has imbibed the saltness, then they draw it off in Pots, Refine and Boyl it till it Rocks, and being dried in the Sun, they sell it to the *Europeans*, who carry it home as Ballast, and vend it at good Rates. This Province is held to pay the Mogul between 30 and 33 Millions a Year, by way of Tax and Customs.

Departing from hence mostly through a Country indifferent Fertil, and watered with some small Branches of Rivers, I entered the Province of *Sinde*, or *Sindy*, which by some is called *Tatta*, bounded with *Azmar* to the East, and the Mountains that border partly belonging to one Province; on the North with *Multan*; on the South with a Desart and the *Indian* Sea; and on the West by *Macram* and *Segestan*: It reaches from South to North in length, on both sides the River *Indus*, and the Orientals call that vast River *Sinde*, or *Sindy*. On the Banks of it was fought a Famous Battle, between *Ginguiscan* first Emperor of the *Tartars* and the Antient Moguls, and Sultan *Gelaleddin*, which alotted the Empire to the former, in his gaining a Victory wherein 200000 Men were Slain, so that he utterly vanquished quifhed the *Caezmian* Princes, who had for a long time been Mafters of *Perfia*, all *Zagatay*, and the greateft part of the Country of *Turqueſtan*. This River runs 1000 Miles, and receives many other Rivers into it; its Banks are thick of Towns, but there is no great ſtore of Fiſh in it, by reaſon of the Allegator, or Crocodiles that deſtroy them.

The chief Town in this Province is *Talta*, though there are ſeveral others of Note and Trade, as *Died*, or *Diub-ſind*, it lies between 24 and 25 Degrees North Latitude. At *Talta*, particularly, there is a great Trade, where the *Indian* Merchants come from all parts to buy up the Goods made there, the Inhabitants being very ingenious in all kind of Arts. The great River mentioned, makes many Iſlands towards this place which are very Fruitful, but little Inhabited, yet renders the Town very commodious, were it not for the great heat that reigns there in the Summer Seaſon.

At *Lourebender*, 3 days Journey from this Town upon the Sea, there is a fine Road for Shipping, being reckoned by many the moſt commodious in the *Indies*, which cauſes a great Trade, where the Palanquins of *Talta* are vended, being the neateſt in *Indoſtan*. The beſt and neateſt Chariots and Coaches made in *India* are found here, though the *Indians* Travel in Palanquins, which are a kind of Couches with 4 Feet, having on each ſide Balliſters, 4 or 5 Inches high, and at the Head and Feet a back-ſtay like a Childe's Cradle: This Machin hangs by a long Pole, called Pambou, by the means of 2 Frames nailed to the Feet of the Couch, theſe Frames have great Rings, through which Ropes paſs, and alſo the Pole or Pambous, and ſo the Planquin is carried on Mens Shoulders, who ply for that end for a ſmall matter. Theſe Machins are very richly adorned, every one doing it after his own humour, as he is able; ſome with Tiſue, others with Cloth of Gold, or rich Embroidery; for as the *Indians* are generally Neat, ſo they are moſtly Proud, taking a delight to ſhow their finery to Strangers.

The other Provinces of the Mogul's Empire are, *Multan, Candahar, Caboul* or *Cabouliftan, Cachmir* or *Kichmir, Lahors, Ayoud* or *Haoud, Varad* or *Varal, Becar, Halabas, Ouleffer* or *Bengala, Malva, Candich, Balagate, Doltabud, Telenga,* and *Baglana*; but thefe, and fome others in *India,* not under the Jurifdiction of the Great Mogul, for want of an opportunity, and an indifpofition I had, by reafon of the intemperatenefs of the Air, upon often changing Climates, not giving me leave to take a ftrict furvey of them, I hope the Reader will pardon fome Omiffions, and be pleafed to guefs at them by what I have faid of many in particular, fince as to Trade, People, Building, Manners, Cuftoms, &c. they little vary, only I fhall fay fomething of the Famous River *Ganges,* and then conclude my Travels in this Torrid Country, with General, but very Material Obfervations.

The *Ganges,* as well as *Indus,* is a vaft River, full of pleafant Iflands, covered with lovely *Indian* Trees, which delight the Paffengers for 5 or 6 days Sailing. The Heathens, or Gentils, *Indians,* efteem the Water: They have Temples, and Pagods near it, and here have a freedom of Worfhip; the chief Pagods are that of *Jayanat,* which is at one Mouth of the *Ganges,* and that of the Town of *Bonarous* upon the River; thefe are fuperftitioufly decked with Gold and Jewels; Millions of People repair thither, and Feftivals are kept for many days together, when they carry their Idols in Triumph.

The Great Mogul drinks commonly of the Water of the *Ganges,* though many affirm, that if it be not boiled it caufes a Flux. This River having received a vaft number of Brooks and Rivers from the North-eaft and Weft, difcharges it felf by feveral Mouths into the vaft Gulf of *Bengala,* at the heighth of about 23 Degrees, and this Gulf begins in 8 Degrees North Latitude, and is reckoned 800 Leagues over: On the fides of it, to the Eaft, is many Towns, belonging to divers petty Princes, who are Sovereigns, with whofe Subjects, as well as the Moguls,

Europe, Asia, Africa, *and* America. 141
Moguls, the *Europeans* Trade for rich Commodities. On the banks of the *Ganges* are Herds of Deer, grazing, but the Crocodiles destroy many of them by pulling them into the River when they come to Drink, and then devour them: I saw a Negro Boy pulled under by one of them as he was Swiming, but saw him no more. The Ships that Moar in the River where these most haunt, keep Guard by Night to prevent their clambering on the Decks, and surprizing the Men a sleep.

CHAP. XIX.

Of the Marriages, Apparrels, Superstitious Customs, the keeping the Mogul's *Birth-Day, and other Things observed by the* Indians, *as the Funerals of their Dead,* &c.

HAving described many Things worthy of Note in *India*, I now proceed to others which I purposely omitted, that for Brevity sake I might have the conveniency of collecting and placing them together.

The Marriages of the *Mahometan Indians*, especially those of Note, are celebrated with Pompous shows, and much Magnificency: they are Married by a Moula, or *Mahometan* Priest, and then the Bride in rich Ornaments, is carried to the Bridegroom's Apartments on an Elephant. The Females Marry very young as at 8, 9, and 10 years of Age, and some sooner, but those that Marry early leave of Child bearing at 30, and are very much wrinkled. The Wedding Ceremonies of the *Gentil Indians* is this; the Bramen, or Priest, after having said

some

some Prayers over the Couple, puts a Cloth between them, and orders the Man with his naked Foot to touch the naked Foot of the Woman, and so the Ceremony is compleated. The Women are very Fruitful in this Country, and easily Delivered.

As for Apparel, they wear Cotton, Stuffs, or Silks, as loose of they can; the Man has Linnen wraped round his Head, like a little close Turban, and the Woman a kind of a Carchief, though their Habits, according to the Casts, are various, yet of as many Colours as they can have them.

They often do Pennance by Abstinence, and some are put in a hole for that purpose, where, they say, they remain 6 or 7 Days without Eating or Drinking; but this is mostly in the Temples of their Pagods, of which they have numbers, many with vast Labour being cut out of natural Rock; some like Men, and others very Monstrous: And in some Provinces great Hills and Rocks, with prodigious cost and pains are cut into such Forms or Shapes, which shews their Superstition.

At *Bengala*, and other places, they Sacrifice to the Sea, throwing in Coco Nuts, which little Boys swim for, and make much sport and pastime in strugling for them, and this they call the opening of the Sea, because, for some Months, Trade is stopped, by reason the Mounson, or Trading-Wind, serves not, and this they do with a great deal of Devotion and Solemnity.

The Casts, or Tribes of the *Gentil Indians*, are reconed to be 84, and though they profess to be all of the same Religion, yet they differ mightily in their Ceremonies. Every one of the Tribes follow a particular Trade, and their off-spring must not quit it under the Penalty of being counted Infamous, and turned out of his Cast. They are generally very Charitable, especially to Strangers in their Sickness or Distress, and will streighten themselves very much to relieve them. The Bramens, who are their Doctors, make the first and head Tribe.

The

Europe, Asia, Africa, *and* America. 143

The Mogul's Birth-Day is kept with great Feasting and Rejoycing, and then he is publickly weighed in Golden Scales, and precious Stones tied up in bags are the Weights: The Weight of him is Regiſtred, and if that Year he weighs more than the former there is great Rejoycing; and for Trifles he gives amongſt his Nobles and Favourites, he receives a vaſt Treaſure in Preſents; if he weighs leſs, they conclude him to be Languiſhing, which abates much of their Merriment, and that Day particularly, the *Indian* Women adorn their Ears and Noſes with Rings and Jewels, if they are forced to borrow them, though at other times the better ſort wear them; thoſe they wear in their Ears are flat, either of Gold, Silver, or Copper.

Among the *Indians* they have a Liquor called Tary, which is the Juyce of a Palm, or Coco Tree, or rather the Sap, which they love ſo much, that in many places the Women make it in their bargain before they are Married, that they ſhall be allowed to Drink it, and to go abroad ſometimes to ſee their Neighbours: It is gotten by wounding the Trees, and taſts ſomething like Whitewine. The Coco Nuts are about the bigneſs of an ordinary Mellon, and are very much eſteemed for the Liquor they produce. The *Dutch* at *Batavia* have a Market kept under theſe kind of Trees, and the pleaſantneſs of the Shade brings them in a great income for Standings; beſide the advantage of the Fruit. As for the Swords, Daggers, and other Arms of the *Indians*, except Bows and Arrows, they are heavy and clouterly made, after the ancient Faſhion of the *Engliſh*. There are in *India* many Hermophradites, partaking the Genitals of both Sexes; theſe, though they go in Womens Aparrel, wear a Turban on their Heads to diſtinguiſh them, under a great Penalty.

As for the belief of the *Indian Gentiles*, it is, that every Man may be ſaved in his Religion or Sect, provided he exactly follow the way that God has directed him, affirming, when they bow to Idols,
they

they worship them not, but have God in their Mind; they say those that take ill courses will be Damned, and doubt not, but their Religion is the first of all Religions, and that it was established in the days of *Adam*, and preserved by *Noah*, believing that there is a Heaven and a Hell, for Rewards and Punishments, but none shall enter before the Universal Judgment: That they show Honour and Respect to a Cow, because she affords them more subsistance than other Creatures. The *Pythagorian* Doctrine or Opinion of Transmigration of Souls, is held by many of the Casts, which makes them refrain killing Beasts or Birds, least the Souls of some of their Tribe, departed, should be in them, and they often rescue them by purchase from the *Mahometans*, who are about to kill them.

They call their God *Ram*, and say he was produced out of the Light, and in that consideration, they render him Divine Honours in their Pagods, and elsewhere. In saluting their Friends they repeat his Name twice; their Adoration consists in joyning their Hands, as if they Prayed, and letting them fall very low, then gently raising them to their Mouth, and last of all, over their Heads. They say *Chitta* was *Ram*'s Wife, and when they see the Picture of the Virgin *Mary*, they affirm it is *Chitta*'s Representation, saluting and bowing very low to it, bringing Offerings of Fruit, Oyl, and Wax-Candles, for none of their Sacrifices are Bloody, but consist of bringing to their Pagods, things of Ornament, and such as may be Eaten, and taking the Bramen's Directions, they anoint the Body of the Image with Oyl, and say their Prayers before the Idol they intend to Invocate; they present their Oblation, and return out of the Temple, and when the Bramen has taken what he thinks fit, the rest is distributed to those of any Religion that will come for it. Besides the Bramens, the *Gymnosophists* of *Porphyrus* are the Priests, and Doctors of the Heathen *Indians*. But the *Mahometans* have a Mufti, and here I omit their Opinions, as being spoken of elsewhere. They

Europe, Asia, Africa *and* America. 145

They have many strange Ceremonies in the Funerals of their Dead; they first wash them in Water near the Temple of some Pagod, and then in some places siting uncovered in a Chair, is carried with beat of Drum to a Funeral Pile, attended by the Wife, and the Relations, in the richest Attire, and after the usual Absolution, it is laid on the Pile, and the Wife who had followed in Triumph, has a kind of a Throne seated there, in which she places her self, adorned with Gold, Jewels, and Silver of her own, and lent her by her Friends, seeming willing to die, singing and rejoycing, that passing with him through the Flames, she shall have the Honour and Happiness to accompany him in the other World; and when the Bramen sets Fire to the Pile, the Relations throw in Spices, Oyls, and Odours, till both the Bodies are consumed. This, by the wife, is looked on as a piece of Priestcraft, to get the Riches that are found in the Ashes, as Gold, Silver, and such Jewels as resist the Fire, for the Ashes being accounted Sacred, none but the Bramen has the medling with them; and the Woman is counted Infamous among her Cast that refuses to undergo this Cruelty.

Some are buried with their Husbands, up to the Neck, then strangled and quite covered; and some of the Maids, for the love they bear their Mistrifs, will in like manner accompany her in Death; but this is rarely used now, for the Mogul, and other *Mahometan* Princes of *India*, have strictly forbid it, as Inhuman, and Barbarous, which secures many Women from the Infamy they would otherwise undergo in their Cast; yet though the Governors pretend all that in them lies to restrain it, some are still burnt, for by earnest Sollicitations, and large Presents, if the Wife Petition for it, which some of them do, leave is obtained; but it is thought they are incited to it by the crafty perswasions of the knavish Bramen, who promises them inestimable Joys and Pleasures in another Life.

L   Having

Having somewhat satisfied my Curiosity, and, as I think, given a satisfactory account of the places I visited, the Customs of the People, &c. the Fame of *China* invited me to take a very tedious Journey to visit that Kingdom, and hearing that a Caravan of Merchants every Year passed from *Lahors* thither, I found a convenient opportunity by Land and Water, to arrive at that City a little before the Caravan was about to depart, which consisted of about 500 Men, and 7000 Camels, Horses, &c.

CHAP. XVII.

Travels through divers Countries into China, *and a satisfactory Account of all that is remarkable in that Kingdom.*

IN our Passage to *China*, for brevity sake, I shall not be particular in every thing I saw, as not being remarkable in such wild and desart Countries. Let it suffice then, that setting out we passed over vast Plains, Rivers, Mountains, and Rockey ways, in danger of wild Beasts and Robbers, there being but few, and those inconsiderable Towns, till we came to *Athec*, where recruiting with Provisions, and refreshing our selves, we Travelled on in much the like ways to *Paſſaur*, and so by several small Towns till we came to a City called *Capherſtam*; the Country it stands in is very Fertil, producing good Wine, and one thing I observed, that they go to their Temples in Mourning Weeds; and 25 days Journey from this, we came to *Gtrideli*, in 20 days more to *Cabul*, and so to *Ciracar*, and *Paroua*, the last Town in the Mogul's Territories, after which we were often forced to pay Tribute to petty Princes

that

Europe, Asia, Africa, *and* America 147

that govern'd the Cities and dependancies in our way. Then to *Aingharan* we journied over exceeding high Mountains, and leaving that place, came to *Calcia*, then to *Gialalabath*; here recruiting, we passed to *Talkan*, and *Cheman* in the Kingdom of *Samarhan*, and by a troublesom way from thence, came to *Badasciam*, and *Chiarchiumar*, where we rested for some time, and then kept on our Journey to *Serpanel*, and so entered the Country of *Sarcil*, full of Villages, and in 6 days passed over *Ciecialith*, a vast Mountain covered with Snow, in which Passage some of the company perished with Cold, and in a tedious Travel attained *Tanghetar*, in the Kingdom of *Cascar*, and passing *Jaconich*, came to *Hiarchan* the Royal City, where, for a good Sum, the Master of the Caravan obtained the King's Passport to further our Journey more quietly: Then we kept our Journey through *Jocil*, *Hancialix*, *Aleghet*, *Hagabateth*, *Egriar*, *Marcetelec*, *Thalec*, *Horma*, *Thoantac*, *Mingrieda*, *Capetalcol*, *Zelan*, *Sarc*, *Guebedal*, *Cambasci*, *Monserfec*, *Ciacolo*, and *Ascu*; we passed these by a very tedious way, over Stones, Sands, and the Desarts of *Carcatha*, and so to *Oitocarach*, *Gazo*, *Casciani*, *Dellai*, *Scregabedal*, *Ungan*, and *Cucia*, then to *Pucian*, and *Turphan*, a Fortified City; thence to *Aramuth*, and so to *Camul*, the last City of the Kingdom of *Ciales*, and from *Camul* to the North Wall of *China*, through which we had admission at a place called *Ciaicum*, after a 6 Months Journey, and so passed to the City of *Socive*, and thus being entered *China*, I shall proceed to speak of it, as far as I could learn, during my stay there.

As for the vast Kingdom of *China*, it has gone under many Denominations, as the Princes has been pleased to new Name and call it, as they severally ascended to the Throne: Uuder the Reign of the first King it was called *Tae mim que*, that is, *The Kingdom of great Brightness*, and by several other Names. But when the *Tartar*, whose Race are now in the power, Conquer'd it, they called it *Tai Ciroque*, *A Kingdom of great Purity*; and since it was called

Chin, to which the *Portuguése*s, the first *Europeans* Trading there, adding an A, it has since amongst us been called *China*, and so it is generally accepted.

It is seated in the extremities of *Asia* towards the East, and lies under 20 Degrees from North to South from the Fortress of *Cai Pim*, placed on the Frontiers of the Province of *Pekim*, in the Latitude of 41, to the Meridional point of the Island of *Hai nan*, in 8 Degrees of the Elevation, and to the South of the Province of *Quamtum*, so that according to the *Chinese* account, it is from North to South 5750 Li or Furlongs, which make 575 French Leagues, at 25 to a Degree; and from *Po* point, a Sea-Port Town in the Province of *Che-Kiam*, to the extreamity of the Province of *Suchven*, in a streight Line from East to West it is 426 French Leagues, though Geographers taking it another way, make it much longer, *viz.* from the last place to the North-west of the Province of *Leaotum*, called *Caiyven* to the last City of the Province of *Yunnan*, called *Cin-tien-Kiu-min-Fat*, and so the length is accounted 750 French Leagues, and the breadth taken from *Tam Chan*, the most easterly place of the Country of *Leaotum*, joyning to the Kingdom of *Corea*, to *Tum-tim* to the Westward of the Province of *Xensi*, it is 500 French Leagues.

This vast Kingdom, or Empire, contains 15 Provinces, larger than some considerable Kingdoms, mostly Rich and Fertile, which are ranked according to their Antiquity and Precedency, in this Order, by the *Chinese*s.

Pekim, Nankim, now called *Kiam-nan, Xensi, Xantum, Ho-nan, Xansi, Chekiam, Kianosi, Huquam, Su Chuens, Fokien, Quamtum, Quamsi, Yunnan, Quei Cheum*, and *Xantum*; many of these have Towns commodiously on the Sea, and others on great Rivers and Lakes, the whole Country being plentifully watered, by which means it is exceeding Fertil, and saves them abundance of Land Carriage.

The

Europe, Asia, Africa *and* America. 149

The *Chinese* brag much of the Original of their Kingdom, and some of their Books place it many thousand Years before the Creation of the World; but most agree, it has preserved its form of Government during the Reign of 22 Families, and from them have descended 236 Kings, during the space 4034 Years, for so long they allow it to have been a Kingdom; yet there is amongst them another more probable account, *viz.* This account reduces the beginning of it to about 400 Years after the General Deluge, and if any pretend to dispute it by Writing, or word of Mouth, it is enough to endanger their Lives, for they look upon it as a disparagement to their Kingdom, as being the proudest, and most conceited People of all Nations, thinking themselves the best in the World, and that all others are insignificant to them, making in their Maps *China* very spacious, and other Countries like little Rocks in the Sea, and they hold a firm opinion, that *Europe* is no more than 2 small Islands; they also hold, all their Neighbours for *Barbarians*, and paint them in Monstrous and Ridiculous Forms; and to make them seem Cowards, though they have often experienced them to the contrary, they report and paint them as little Pigmies, who tie themselves in bundles when they go abroad, least the Eagles and Kites should carry them away; and when any one argues learnedly to them, they start, as in a surprize, demanding whether they have their Books in their Country, and when the Strangers Answer no, they reply, why then how came you by that Learning? They hold their Religion the purest and ancientest of all the Religions in the World; However, it is to be believed, that their Chronicle is the ancientest that is to be found, and is so well connected, the Reign of one King hanging so well to the other, that it cannot reasonably be suspected to have been Written upon trust, by Conjecture, or Imagination.

They divide the Heavens into 28 Constellations, and *China* into so many parts, allowing each part

L 3   one,

one, and leave none for any other Nation; and in brief they give their own moſt lofty and magnificent Titles, but to Foreign Countries, moſt barbarous ſcornful, and degrading Names, to exalt their Kingdom by the diſparaging others, which Pride I am apt to believe proceeds from their Ignorance, though ſome of the Nobles are more moderate and diſcreet. but then it is ſuch as have Travelled abroad, though but a few of them are permitted, and even theſe dare not ſpeak much in the praiſe of other Countries leaſt they ſhould be looked on as undervaluers of their own, and conſequently as Enemies. Some of their Kings have had the vanity to ſtile themſelves Child of the Sun, and Emperor of the World. They are, however a very induſtrious People as appears by their vaſt and ſtately Edifices, Manufactures and other curious Matters, for there are no idle People in the Kingdom, the Lame, Blind, and Deaf employ themſelves in one buſineſs or other, as they are capacitated, and get a living by it, inſomuch that they have a Proverb, which ſays, *There is nothing in China caſt away;* and let it be never ſo vile, it may turn to Profit one way or other in the City of *Pekim* which is the chief of the Kingdom. Many thouſands of Families live only by making and ſelling Card-Matches, and Wicks for Candles, and as many by what they pick up about the Streets. They have in every City a Bell, and a Drum-Tower, on which Watchmen ſtrike, to give the Hours, and the quarters in the Night-time, and both the Drum and Bell are exceeding large, being heard many Miles, anſwering one another in a Muſical Harmony. They burn an Incenſe made of Sweet Woods and Perfumes in their Chambers, and before their Pagods, making Candles of the ſame and other mixtures. which in burning caſt a fragrant ſmell, and ſome they make ſo large to place in their Temples before their Idols, that they will continue burning 20 or 30 Days and Nights, and burning to certain windings and marks, they, by that, diſtinguiſh Hours and Days, in burning ſuch and ſuch exact

act proportions; and those that burn them in their Chambers, when they would rise at a certain Hour, tie a little Brass weight by a String to a mark that specifies the Hour, and the string burning, the weight falls into a brass Bason set under it, and strikes like a Larum-Watch.

They have many other curious devices, as Chariots that will run swiftly without Horses, only a Man that sits in it turning a Winch, which by certain Springs turns the Wheels round with great Rapidity. But passing over things of this Nature for the present, I will proceed to describe, in some measure, the City of *Pekim*, the Metropolis of *China*, where the King has his chief Court.

This famous City is seated in a Plain, forming a vast Square, each of its sides being 12 *Chinese* Furlongs in length; it has 9 Gates, 3 upon the South side, and 2 upon each of the other sides: it is now Inhabited by the *Tartars*, and their Troops are divided into the 8 quarters, or, as they call them, Banners. But considering, under the preceeding Kings, the numerous Inhabitants had not a sufficient place to contain them, though the Nine Suburbs answering to the Gates were as big as Cities. There was a new City built like the old one, square in Form, having its North side joyning to the side of the old one; this has 7 Gates, and every one a Suburb answering to it, so that taking that in, with the Suburbs, it is of a vast circumference, yet many who have writ of it, have made it much larger than it is; the one and the other are divided into 5 Jurisdictions, or Tribunals, of which I shall speak hereafter. The principal Streets run to the 4 direct Points, or Winds; they are long, streight, and broad, so well proportioned, as if they had been marked out with a Line. The little Streets run all from East to West, being very fair, and divide the spaces between the great Streets into equal and proportionable Islands, having each a particular Name, and there is a Catalogue to be sold of them, with Notes and Directions, that Strangers, and those whose business it is to go on Errands

Errands, may the easier find them, for they are very numerous.

The fairest of these Streets is called *Cham gan Kiai*, or the Street of Perpetual Repose; it is about 30 Fathom broad, and of a vast length: The Houses are low built, which, they say, is done in respect to the King's Pallace, that it should appear more magnificent, though besides the King's, there are Pallaces belonging to the Nobility very stately, yet they are built backward, so that nothing but a great Gate appears to the Street. The old and new City are crouded with swarms of People, as the Shops are with store of rich Commodities, so that one would suppose there was a continual Fair held in it.

The King's Pallace is seated in the midst of the City, and Fronts towards the South, as almost all others do in this Country; it is encompassed with a double enclosure of Walls, in form of a long square; the outward enclosure is extraordinary high and thick, plaistered on both sides with a curious red Plaister, and covered with a small Roof of varnished Brick of a Gold Colour; the length of it from South to North is 8 *Chinese* Furlongs; it has a Gate in the middle of each side, composed of 3 Portals, the middlemost never being opened but when the King passes, and these have a Guard upon them, but not very considerable; there are also many Elephants kept in a spacious place for service, and to divert the King, where are Stables compleatly furnished for them, and no Persons that have any considerable deformity are suffered to enter the Pallace; the inner Wall that immediately incloses the Pallace is very thick, and high built, embellished with well contrived Battlements, and extends from North to South 6 Furlongs, and a Furlong and an half in breadth, and the Pallace is about four Miles three quarters in circumference; it has 4 Gates with large vaulted Arches, those to the South and North being like to them of the first Inclosure, and upon the Angles of the Walls are 8 Towers of an extraordinary bigness,

Europe, Asia, Africa, *and* America.   153

bigness, and good Architecture, Varnished with beautiful red, and adorned with Flowers of Gold, covered with Tiles of a Gold Varnish, and there are Guards kept in them all, except *Madarin*'s of the Tribunals within the Palace; and the Officers of the King's Houshold are forbidden to come within this Wall, unless they shew a little Table of Wood, plated with Ivory, wherein their Names, and the places they serve in are set down, with the Seal of the Mandarin to whom they belong. It has a curious Mote round it full of Fish, and every Gate a Draw-Bridge, unless the South, which lies over an Arch. In the vast space between the two Walls are many stately Palaces that might suit the entertainment of great Kings, they being richly adorned with pollished Stone, and curious Gilding.

On the East side close by the Wall runs a River, over which are several Bridges of Marble, with Draw-Bridges in the middle of them: On the West where the space is large, there is a lake full of Fish, 5 Furlongs and a quarter in length, made in the Form of a Bass-Viol; where it is narrowest there is a very beautiful Bridge which answers the Gates of the Wall, at the end of which stand Triumphant Arches of 3 Arches a piece, very Majestick, and of excellent Workmanship. The Lake is environed with little Pallaces, or Houses of Pleasure, partly on the Water, and partly on the Land; and on the Lake are many beautiful Barges for the King's use; the remainder of the East and West spaces not taken up by the Lake, are beautified with Palaces, and the Officers Houses, all very Stately and Magnificent, as also of those of Artificers that belong to the King's Pallace.

The inward Pallace is low built, according to the fashion of the *Chineses*, containing many Pallaces, or Courts, one within the other, so that it seems a little City of Pallaces, guarded by a great number of Turrets, or Towers; and particularly in the King's Apartment is to be seen nothing but gilded Cielings, Pillars inlaid with Ivory and costly Stone;
his

his Throne is exceeding Rich and Magnificent, valued at many Millions, by reason of rich Stones and Gold that adorn it: There are also some Temples erected within this enclosure, and so many other things, that it would require a Volume to describe them particularly.

Besides the Temples in the Pallace, the King has 7 others, in which he Sacrifices once a Year, *viz*. 5 in the New, and 2 in the Old City, very large, and exceedingly beautified with Gold, and costly Paintings. In the first of these called *Tien-Tam*, or the Temple of Heaven, he Sacrifices to Heaven at the time the Sun comes to the Winter Solstice, Offering Hogs, Oxen, Goats, and Sheep, which is done with great Solemnity and Humility, the King laying aside his Golden Robe, yellow Vesture, and precious Jewels, and putting on a plain Habit of Black, or Sky-coloured Damask. The second Temple is called *Ti-Tam*, or the Temple of the Earth, and here the King before he is Crowned, Sacrifices to the God of the Earth, and then putting himself into the Habit of a Ploughman, he Ploughs a little piece of Ground with a varnished Plough, drawn by 2 Oxen with gilded Horns, and in the mean time the Queen and her Ladies dress him a homely Dinner, which they Eat together. To the North of these stands another Temple, called *Pe Tien-Tam*, or the North Temple of Heaven, he Sacrifices at the time of the Summer Solstice, and at Vernal Equinox he Sacrifices in a Temple to the East, called *Ge-Tam*, or the Temple of the Sun, and at the Autumnal Equinox, at the Western Temple, called *Yue Tam*, or the Temple of the Moon; and to prepare for the Sacrifices, there is a Fast held in *Pekim* for 3 days, during which time, no Flesh nor Fish is to be eaten, under great Penalties; and this they say they do in a thankfulness for the Benefits they receive from the Earth, by the Seasons of the Year, and the influence of Heaven.

In the sixth Temple called *Ti vam miao*, or the Temple of the past Kings, is a rich Throne, and the

Europe, Asia, Africa, *and* America. 155
the Statues of all the Kings of *China*, from the first King, named *To hi to Xum Chi*, Father to the present Prince. here the King performs an Annual Ceremony to his Predecessors. The seventh Temple is called *Chim-Hoam Miao*, or the Temple of the Spirit that guards the Walls; but here the King never Sacrifices, but appoints Mandarins, and other Nobles, to do it at his Charge, so that the Ceremony is performed with much Royalty; and in every City there is such a Temple Dedicated to the same end.

Having proceeded thus far, I shall entertain you with an account of his Pomp, and Magnificent Attendance, when he goes out of his Palace; and this he rarely does but upon two occasions, *viz*. either to Hunt, and take the Air, or to Sacrifice, unless necessity forces him to the Wars; upon these occasions he takes a Guard, and all the Nobles that are near have notice, and attend him in their best Equipage; they most consist of between 12 and 13000, adorned with Embroideries of Gold, Silver, and precious Stones, their Horses traped with the same, and all their Servants that attend, at a distance, in very rich Attire.

First, there appear 24 Men with large Drums, in two Files, then the like number of Trumpets in the same manner, next as many with long Staves, varnished with red, and adorned with gilt Folinges; then 200 Halberdiers, the Heads of their Halberds being like a Crescent; these were followed by 100 Men carrying Maces of gilt Wood, with Staves as long as a Launce; then 2 Royal Poles, called *Caffi*, varnished with Red, and gilded with Flowers at both ends; after these 400 large Lanthorns richly adorned, with many curious pieces of Workmanship; these were followed by 400 Flambeauxs curiously Carved, and made of an odoriferous Wood that burns long, and casts a curious shining light; then 200 Launces fringed and adorned with the Spoiles of Wild Beasts; these are followed by 24 Banners, on which, in Gold, and Rich Imbroidery are represented the Signs of the Zodiack, which

the

the *Chinefes* divide into 24, contrary to us; after thefe come 56 Banners, with 56 Conftellations painted on them, under which they comprehend the whole number of Stars; then 2 large Flabels, fupported with Poles, and gilded with Suns, Birds, Beafts, and other Things; thefe are fucceeded by 24 Umbrellos richly adorned; then 8 forts of rich Utenfils for the Kings ordinary ufe, as a Table-Cloth, a Bafon and Eure of Gold, &c. after thefe 10 led Horfes all white, Traped with Imbroidery of Gold and precious Stones, followed by 100 Lanciers, and on both fides them the Pages of the King that particular belong to his Chamber, and in the middle, between them, the King himfelf, with an Air very Majeftick and Stern, mounted on a ftately Steed, covered with a rich Umbrello, coftly, beyond the belief of fuch as have not feen it, fhading both the King and his Horfe; he is followed by petty Kings, the Princes of the Blood, and a great number of the Principal Nobility in their richeft Attire, and ranked according to their Degrees; then 500 young Gentlemen belonging to the King, followed by 1000 Footmen clad in red Robes, Embroidered with Stars and Flowers of Gold and Silver; then fucceeds an open Chair, or Litter, carried by 36 Men, attended by another clofe Litter as big as a handfom Room, carried by 120 Men; then 2 vaft Chariots, each drawn by 2 Elephants; after thefe another large Chariot drawn by 8 Horfes, and another which is lefs, by 4; thefe have very rich Caparifons lined with Silk, and the Governors in coftly Liveries, each of them attended by an Officer and 50 Soldiers; next to thefe follow 2000 Mandarins of the Learned Tribunal; and to clofe all, 2000 Military Mandarins, with the King's Train: The People every where receive him with profound Veneration and Refpect, many Kneeling, and others lifting up their Hands, with Prayers for his Profperity.

Befides the numerous Veffels in Seaports, on Lakes, and Rivers, many of which have places in them

Europe, Asia, Africa, *and* America.   157

them like Rooms and Chambers, wherein the People belonging to them live and breed. The number of those that are appointed to carry Provisions to the Court are near 1000; those that are to attend the Mandarins are very numerous, and the rest, without great difficulty are not to be numbered, for all the Lakes, Rivers, and Ports are so full of Vessels, that they seem so many floating Towns, or Cities, and no less than 4 Millions of People are imployed in their Navigation. Their Rivers are many, and exceeding large, so that on the River *Kiam*, which is called the Son of the Sea, one may Sail for 3 Months. The Vessels that are only to bring the King's Habits, Silks, Stuffs, &c are 365, for every day he has a Change of rich Garments. What shall I say? The People adore him as a God, and think all the valuable things on Earth too little for him, and therefore it would be endless to describe all the Magnificence that attends his State, and every thing he is served withal. Let it suffice then, that no Prince on Earth that ever I saw, or heard of, equals him in Grandeur, for his Subjects look on him as the Son of Heaven, and that it is not only their Duty, but a main incumbent of Religion to Honour him in all they can. They bring their Timber, mostly by the Rivers, not in Vessels, but in Floats, some of 3 Leagues length, fastened together with Rushes and Osiers, and on the Floats are little Wooden Houses for those that guide them to lodge in by turns, and dress their Provisions: And indeed they bring plenty of all things by their Rivers and Lakes, which stores their Cities and Towns very plentifully, which are very numerous; for according to their own Printed Account, of those walled in are 4402, which are divided into two Orders, Civil and Military; the first of these comprehend 2045, of which 175 are Cities of the first Rank, which the *Chineses* call *Tin*; 274 of the second Rank, which they call *Cheu*; 288 which they call *Hien*; 205 Royal Hosteries, or places of Entertainment of the first, and 103 of the second

Rank:

Rank; and these are Govern'd by Mandarins, who, in their Governments are a kind of Viceroys.

The Nobility of this Kingdom, as generally taken, is no more than an illustrious Grandeur that has continued for several Ages, but these are subject to many casualties, for when the Reigning Family expires, they are generally put to Death, because they are very powerful in the Country, and give a jealous suspition, so that new upstarts are put in their Room, which renders those more safe who acquire this Honour, by the Gown or Military Employments, because that Honour is recalled at pleasure, and the Grand-Child seldom enjoys that, or their Estate. There is but one of the Ancient Families now remaining that I could here of, *viz.* that of the Famous *Confucius*, who was Born under the third Imperial Family, called *Cheu*, 551 Years before the Birth of Christ; and this Family has great Priviledges above others, as to be exempted from Taxes and Tribute in the Provinces they Inhabit. They give a Title of Honour of a lower Degree to their learned Men: and Philosophers are in great Veneration amongst them, and to some of them they have given the Epethite of Saint, and give the same Veneration to their Memory as to their Pagods, though they take it as an affront to be taxed with it, for they call them Kings without Command, by which imploy they were worthy of Crowns for their Learning, Virtue, and Wisdom, but desteny prevented them. *Confucius*, a Learned Man among the *Chineses*, who, though long since Dead, is admired and adored amongst them: He modeled their Law, or Rule, to be observed, into nine Maxims, which he called *Chum yum*, or the Golden Mediocrity, wherein he lays down, that a good Prince ought to have 9 Qualities, or Virtues. 1. To Govern himself well that he may show a good Example to those he Rules over. 2. To Honour and Cherish Learning, and learned Men, and to encourage Virtue, frequently to consult and converse with the Learned, on the Affairs of the Kingdom.

3. To

Europe, Asia, Africa, *and* America. 159

3. To Love and highly respect his Kindred, the Princes of the Blood, and to grant them the Favours and Rewards they merit. 4. To be Courteous and Respectful to the Nobility in general, and give them their due deserts. To incorporate himself in a Friendly and Amicable manner with all his Subjects, to equalize his Heart with theirs, and to regard and esteem them as his own proper substance and Person. 6. To Love his People with a true Affection, unmixed with Dissimulation; to rejoyce at their Prosperity, and be afflicted at their Misfortunes. 7. To invite to his Court, and encourage Artists, for the quick dispatch of publick and private business. 8. To Treat carefully, and with all civility, Embassadors sent from Foreign Princes, that they may see in Words and Deeds, the effects of a Princely and Generous Mind. 9. To Cherish and Embrace all, that he may engage them to him, to be the Bulwarks and Fortresses of his Kingdom. And these Rules well practised may serve other Kings, to render them great and happy.

The King has a Privy, or Supream Council of the Learned Mandarins in his Pallace, who are called his Council of State, which is the most Honourable Dignity in the Kingdom; these consult and transact all the weighty Affairs, and these have several Magnificent Halls in the Pallace, wherein they meet, to consult according to their Degrees; and when he advances any one to this Dignity, he adds to his Name, the Name of one of these Halls. Besides these, there are 11 other Tribunals of Mandarins, 6 for Ecclesiastical and Civil, and 5 for Military Affairs: The first of these are called *Lo-pu,* and the last *U-fu,* and these are of ancient Institution, the *Chineses* dating it 2000 Years before the Birth of Christ; and to these Tribunals People repair for the determining their Affairs, and for Redress; besides, they dispose of Offices and Trusts, and confirm Honour and Dignities. Their Power is great, for they have a jurisdiction almost over all that belongs to the Court, and it is absolute over all

the

the Provinces, so that they are much feared, and dreaded, because they can place and displace at pleasure, and examine into all Frauds and Abuses to the Crown, and into Ecclesiastical matters. They are fearful of doing any injustice, by reason there is a Mandarin, in the nature of a Controller, or Overseer to every Tribunal, who examins publickly or privately all that is done, and if he finds any injustice or disorder, he is bound to make the King acquainted with it; he is called *Coli*, so that seldom any Corruptness or Partiality is found amongst them, and if it be, the Offender is severely punished. There are some other dependent Tribunals in *Pekim*, and to every one of the Provinces there belongs a Supream Tribunal, which has the oversight of inferiour Courts, so that business is managed and dispatched with little difficulty.

They have made prodigeous Works in this Country to secure the Rivers within their bounds, yet notwithstanding, sometimes encreased by the violent Rains, they break out to the destruction of vast numbers of People, Cattle, and Houses, as it happened in the Year 1668, after violent Rains, which almost destroyed the new City of *Pekim*, and they had much ado to secure the Flood from overturning the Walls of the old City, and in this Deluge which was accompanied by an Earthquake, for it had a long time before been a very dry Season, near a Million of People perished; and though many got upon Trees, Hills, and Out-Houses, they were there starved for the most part, for want of Boats to fetch them off, and the rapid Flood tumbling Rocks along with it, broke down two Arches of the Famous Bridge, which is about a Furlong over: This Bridge is the most beautiful in *China*, but not the largest; the River overflowing is called *Hoen Ho*, or the Muddy River, because the rapidness of its Stream, carries with it a great quantity of Earth, tore from the Banks and Windings, which renders it muddy all the Year, but it is little Navigable, by reason of the many Cataracts, or Falls in it; yet

for

for bringing vaſt Stores to *Pekim* from the Southern Provinces, a Canal is opened 3500 *Chineſe* Furlongs, through ſeveral Provinces, accommodated with 72 Sluces, every one having large Folding-Gates, and theſe are only open in the day time, ſome of them being very difficult to paſs with Barks of great Burthen, becauſe the Falls are great; but they are drawn up againſt the Stream by the ſtrength of 4 or 500 Men, and let down in the like manner, with many Ropes faſtned to them, to prevent ſetting on the Piles, or plunging, and they are guided by long Poles, with Iron Heads at the end. The Chanel begins at *Tum Cheu*, about 2 Leagues and an half from *Pekim*, where there is a River, with the Currant of which, Veſſels drive till near the Sea, and then it falls into another, through which Veſſels Sail, till they come to the Chanel; and Sailing about 25 Leagues, a Temple preſents it ſelf, called *Fuen Hui Miao*; or, *The Temple of the Spirit that divides the Water*; hither they Row againſt the Stream, but when they come at the Temple they Row with the Stream, for on the Eaſt-ſide, about half a days Journey is a large Lake between high Mountains; this Water ſwells a great River that bent its courſe towards the Sea on the Eaſt, but they ſtopped up the out-let, and with prodigious labour cutting through the Mountain, opened a Canal by which they brought the Water to the Temple, in that part they hollowed 2 other Canals, one towards the South, and another towards the North, with ſo true a proportion and regular Line, that the Waters coming to the middle before the Temple, take leave of each other, one running to the North, and the other to the South in one and the ſame Canal, which is very admirable, and diſcharges it ſelf into a large rapid River, called the *Yellow River*, the Water being ſo coloured by the yellow Earth on the Banks, and Gold coloured Sand and Slime at the bottom; upon this River they Sail 2 Days, and then entering another Paſs to another Canal running towards the City of *Hoaingan*, and running by and through ma-

M   ny

ny Cities, comes to *Yamcheu*. The vaſt Wall of *China* that excludes the *Tartars*, is no leſs to be looked on as a work of Wonder; it runs from Eaſt to Weſt, and in length 405 *Portugueſe* Leagues, making 33 Degrees 10 Minutes, reaching from the City of *Cai yean*, Seated in the extreamity of the Country, called *Leao Tum*, to that of *Cɒnſo*, or *Can cheu*, Seated on the borders of the Province of *Xenſi* in a ſtreight Line, for ſhould the turnings and windings in the Mountains be reckon'd it would make much more; it is guarded by 1327 Towers and Fortreſſes; the Wall is 2 Fathom thick, and 4 in heighth, built moſtly of Stone, though in ſome places Brick appears, where it is ſuppoſed to be mended or altered, ſo that were it vigilently guarded, and no Treachery, which too often happens by the Captains of the Watches, being bribed with part of the Plunder, the *Tartars* would be too feeble to ſurmount it, for upon this Wall and Frontier only, there are 90254 Men kept in Arms and Pay, and thoſe that keep the Watch-Towers give the Signal of the Enemies approach by a Flag in the day time, and in the Night by Fire.

Theſe are but part of the King's Forces, for the Auxiliaries that lie ready to march to their aſſiſtance, are in a manner innumerable, for the Horſe only amount to 989167, and the Foot are many more, their Pay yearly amounting to 5034714 Livres, though they in ſome ſort maintain themſelves by their Induſtry, and no doubt as great, if not a greater number guard on the other Borders, ſo that there are ſeveral Millions in Pay, for in the Kingdom there are 2357 Fortified Places, beſide a great many, that are Garriſoned upon almoſt inacceſſible Mountains and Rocks, that being ſtrong by nature, have no Walls.

In the 15 Provinces there are 332 Famous Bridges, 2096 Mountains famous for their being cut into the ſhapes of Monſterous Idols, for their Fountains, Minerals, or Fruits, their Waters, ſuch as are Lakes full of Fiſh, hot Fountains wonderfully

Europe, Asia, Africa, *and* America 163
ly Medicinal, large Navigable Rivers and Streams, are 1472.

There are 1099 pieces of Antiquity to be seen, as Statues, Paintings, and curious Vessels; 1159 Towers and Triumphal Arches erected at Sundry times, to the Memories of those that were renowned in War, Learning, or Virtuous Actions; 272 Publick Libraries, stored with variety of Books, many of them covered with Gold and Silver Plate, adorned with precious Stones.

There are yet remaining entire 709 Temples, which the *Chinese* have Erected at several times to the Memory of their Ancestors, of curious Architecture, large and beautiful, and the Names of those to whose Memory they were Erected affixed on Pillars, and in these the several Families of the deceased Assemble at a prefixed Day, and prostrate themselves on the Ground, in token of Love and Veneration; then they burn Incense, and afterwards make a splendid Feast at several Tables, richly set forth.

They account 480 Temples of Idols exceeding Rich and Magnificent, beside many of lesser Note, attending on these are 300000 *Bouzes*, a kind of a Religious Order amongst them, some Married, and others not permitted, besides a great number that Travel up and down, called *Licentiates*, having their Licenses to Authorize them from the Tribunal of the Ceremonies.

Their Mausoleums, or Tombs, are very stately, to the number of 680, besides many of lesser Note; but they Bury their Dead after they have kept them as long as they please without the Cities, according to the manner of the Eastern Countries; their Coffins are very Rich, so that one of them sometimes costs 1000 Crowns. The Catacombs of the Grandees are stately Arched Vaults in Mountains, or Plains, over which, when the Body is in, they raise a little Mount, planting Fragrant Trees in good order on it: Before this they Erect a large Altar of white pollished Marble, or Alleblaster, fixing Candlesticks,

dlesticks, one upon it, and one on each side. They Place Statues, or Figures, in Rows, representing a History of the deceased's Actions, and are very curious Artists in resembling Passions of Grief, Joy, Fear, &c. to the Life. The *Chinese* reckon 3036 Men Famous for their Virtues and Valour; Two hundred and eight Virgins, and Widows, Renowned for Piety, Chastety, &c. whose Memories are Celebrated in their Stories, and Poesies; they are also honoured with Titles, Temples, Inscriptions, and Triumphal Arches.

There are in this Kingdom 32 Princes, or petty King's Pallaces, resembling that of the King's, but much less. The Cities are Govern'd by Mandarins, as I before hinted; and when any one gets the King's Letter to the Tribunal to be admitted, the Names of the Cities are Written on thin Boards which are cast into a Vessel, and on their Knees they draw, and he whose Name comes up is allotted the Government of that City; yet there is jugling in this, for the Tables are so, where Money is given, that they seldom fail of a rich City, though it is but for a set time, *viz.* 3 Years, least they should corrupt Justice, or gain on the Affection of the People to raise Rebellion; however, they are Reverenc'd like petty Kings, and abundance of Royal Hosteries are built in Cities, and on the Roads, to entertain them in their Travels, at the King's Charge, where every thing is in a Magnificent readiness, when they know there is a Mandarin on the Road: There is also places for the Entertainment of the Curriers, and to furnish them with fresh Horses.

The Mountains yield Gold and Silver, and therefore the Country is stored with Treasure, though Gold indeed is more a Merchandize than a Coin amongst them; the presents therefore that they make are excessive, as 10, 20, or 30000 Crowns at a time. The King eats in Gold Plate, and all his Nobles, and those that are invited, at a vast number of Tables in Silver and Porcelain, so that the Furniture

Europe, Asia, Africa *and* America. 165

niture at a great Feast amounts to 5 or 6 Millions, for there are Cups set with Diamonds, and other Stones of vast value; some are entire Stones, very Rich, and the Noble imitate the Court, as far as their Ability will allow them, they being very Rich, for they usually get in their 3 Years Government, as Viceroys of Provinces, or Mandarins of Cities, a Million of Crowns; and those that are of the Council of State, called *Calaos*; or, the upper Tribunals, much more by Bribery; for though they protest against it, and there are severe Laws in this Case, no Office passes the Seal without a considerable sum of Money underhand.

There is in this Kingdom vast quantities of Copper, Tin, Iron, and other useful Metals, of which they make great Guns, Idols, Statues, Dishes, Cups, and other Things: their Workmanship is very fine: of Copper and Tin they make vast quantities of Money, with little holes in the middle to string the pieces, and so they pass as ready told, in 500, or 1000 on a String; and 1000 of their Deniers is given for a *Chinese* Tuel, or Crown. Their Exchange is made in Bank, or places appointed for that end; on one side this Money is the Name of the Reigning Prince, and on the other that of the Tribunal that caused it to be Coined. Their Gold and Silver is not properly to be called a Coin, as being only cast into Ingots like Boats of different weights and value; some of those of Gold are vallued at 20 Crowns, and those of Silver at half a Crown, and some more.

When they bury their Dead they burn a great many gilded Ingots, which they call Loans of Gold and Silver, vainly fancying the Ashes turns to Copper in the other World, and serves their Friends to purchase Houses, Horses, and Provision, likewise to bribe the evil Spirits that they should not injure them, and that so the good Spirits may be Fee'd, to hasten their Transmigration, suffering their Souls to enter into Men, and not into Beasts.

There is abundance of curious white Silk, and Wax in *China*, and by reason of the vast Silk Manufactures made all over the Kingdom, the Ancients stiled it the Silken Kingdom, so that many Vessels and Caravans are loaded with it for other Countries. Most of the Men, nay, the very Lackeys, and the Women all of them wear Silk, and the richer sort have it Embroidered with Gold, Silver, Pearl, and other Ornaments.

The fine Wax peculiar to *China*, is not made by Bees; but a little Fly as big as a Flea lays an Egg that breeds a Worm, which piercing the Wax Trees to the Pith, it issues out and hangs upon the Branches like drops of Dew, and by the Sun and Wind, is hardened and whitened, in such quantities, that it serves the Court, the Nobility, and Temples, to make fine transparent Tapers.

Furs are in this Kingdom in vast quantities, and almost every one wears a finer or coarser sort of them, as they are able, for the Linning of their Garments, Seats, Chairs, Couches, &c.

To mention the several sorts of Fruits and Provisions, would be almost endless, they have allmost all we meet with in *Europe*, and a large addition of what we have not in variety of Fruit, especially of delicious taft. During 3 Months of Winter, they have vast store of Game, and on the Rivers they pitch Nets 200 Yards long, and set dead Wild-fowl on their feet, as if they were alive, for stakes to decoy the living; as Ducks, Phesants, Wild Geese, &c. of which, and other Fowl, so many are taken, that they are sold for little or nothing. They have 3 sorts of Bears which they Hunt, one called the Man-bear, the other the Dog-bear, and a third the Pig-bear, because their Snouts and Faces a little resemble these. Their Paws boiled and well ordered, are a great dainty among the *Chinese*, and the *Tartars* much admire their Fat, which they eat: These are scarce, but for Deer, wild Boars, Ellands, Hares, Conies, and the like, they are in vast plenty in most of the Provinces.

After

Europe, Asia, Africa, and America. 167

After all this, the Weather is piercing cold in the Winter Season, and very hot in the Summer; so that in the former, they keep Fires in Stoves, and in the latter, retire the better sort into cool Vaults and Cellers. Their Firing is a kind of a Stone-coal dug in the Mountains, and sometimes in the Plains, except in Woody Countries, and they are at great charge in Carriage: It gives as violent a heat as Charcoal, and the heat is very lasting. They sleep on Mats, or Carpets, and in the Day-time sit together in clusters on them, the better to preserve the Heat, for the Colds are sometimes very Excessive; the richer sort have Beds, and the Stoves are under the floors of their Rooms, which sometimes by reason of the excessive Heat take Fire, burning the House, and surprizing in the suddain Flames, all that are sleeping in it.

The *Chineses* that they may be Magnified by Strangers, take a pride to be very civil to them, and give them the upperhand at their Feasts, seating themselves according to their Degrees; yet the Eldest give place to those who come from the remotest parts.

When any Ambassador arrives from the *Dry*, his Embassy is allowed till his departure: he is furnished with all manner of Provisions, Horses, Letters, Barks, and lodged in the Royal Palace, where every two days the King sends him a sumptuous Entertainment of all sorts of Varieties. They take great care, and a kind of pride in their Apparel, the poor among them going very Neat and Decent. The learned Men affect a grave Gesture, and count it a sin to appear in any thing contrary to the Rules of decent Behaviour and Urbanity.

The Women affect Modesty, Chastity and Honesty, keeping themselves covered, so that when they present any thing to their nearest Relations, they lay it down, their Hands being covered with their Sleaves, and retire with Silence: They rarely stir abroad, and are exceeding Submissive and Obedient towards their Husbands, there being nothing, they

they command them, though never so difficult, but they willingly Enterprize.

Upon their Festival Days, they have a great number of Illuminations, and Fire-works, representing divers Creatures and Figures in the Air; so that on a Hill at a distance, one would think all the Cities were on Fire. The Lanthorns in the Pallace, and Royal Halls, are vastly Big, *viz.* 20 Cubits, and sometimes more in Diameter, holding 100 Lamps, or Tapers, so that they cast a glorious Light, and Figers turning in them by the force of the Smoak, represent in swift motions many curious Actions, as Fights, Dances, Hunting, Hawking and the like.

CHAP. XIX.

Travels through Tartary to Muscovy, *and what is observable on the way in those vast desert Countries; the Nature of the People; their manner of living, with a particular Discription of* Astrakan, *and the Sturgeon fighting in the River* Volga.

HAving visited *China,* and learned what I thought convenient, for it is not good to be too Inquisitive, for fear of being taken as a Spy. I began to be weary of the Fatigue, and of so long an absence from my Native Country, wherefore I resolved to take the first opportunity to return home, and it was not long e're Fortune befriended me to pass by Land; (for the way by the *Caspian* Sea is very dangerous, for that little Sea, or rather great Lake, is full of Flats and Shallows, very tempesteous in most Seasons, and has a great number of Rocks

in

in it, with dangerous Eddies, or Whirl-pools, by reason about 100 large Rivers discharge themselves violently into it;) for there was a Caravan going from *Pekim* to *Bokara*, and in it I entered my self with all Necessaries for my Journey, and in 15 days the Weather being very fair, and our Stages large, we reached *Soezi*, the last Town of *China*, without the great Wall; and here I stored my self with abundance of good Ruburb that grows in their Gardens, which stood me in much stead when I came into the cold Countries; and from hence we journeyed mostly *North-west*, and the principal Towns in our way, was *Baretola*, *Kechemire*, *Kiboal*, *Samark*, and some others, which by reason of my Indisposition on the Road, I shall not undertake to describe. Let it suffice then, that the *Tartars* inhabit mostly this vast Track of Land; in some places very Mountainous, in others, vast Deserts and Forrest, the ground Sandy and Stony for the most part, and all along I could see Snow. On the tops of the high Mountains, though in the beginning of Summer, the People are Rude and Simple, most of them living by feeding Cattle, which they drive from one place to another, carrying their Wives, Children, and all they have along with them; pitching Tents in their Encampments, especially where they find pleasant Springs, and stay there till the Grass is Eat up, and then they remove: The *Tartars* are a very numerous People, and spread a vast track of Land in *Asia* and *Europe*, and Principally they are thus divided, *viz*. The *Precopenses*, *Asialica*, *Antiqua* and *Cathur* from their Principal Provinces, which may be termed, though there are other numerous little Divisions too many here to mention; and though they are a cruel kind of People, our Caravan met with no on-set by the way, though we see numerous Hoards of them on either hand. As we see their Houses are mean and inconsiderable, and their Diet mostly raw Flesh in many places, and above all, they are great lovers of the Fat of Bears, yet they give not their Minds so much to Robberies as the *Arabs*, or other untractable Nations, because few of them know the use of it, or at least have no great esteem for Money; some are *Idolars*, and some *Mahometans*.

This Track abounds in Furs, and there are some Mines of Gold and Silver found in many parts, but they little regard Diging it; and so barbarous are they, that many of them dress their Children at great Feasts, to entertain their Guess, as the choicest of Dainties; nor do they refrain from Feastings on their Dead: There are a great many strong Stags and Harts I saw in my Passage, which they use to Ride, carry Burthens, and draw their Waggons, or Sledges. Mulbury-Trees grow in some places along the Roads, especially bordering on *China*, which are laden in their proper Seasons with Silk-worms that produce much Silk, but they little regard it, it being mostly gathered by the *Banians*, who live scattered among them, who send it to *Persia* and other Countries, and have rich Merchandize in return; for here the coldness of the Country obliges them mostly to habit themselves in Furs, and thick course Cloathings. They trade much in White and Black Fox Sables, Hart and Fawn Skins; they have vast Forrests of Black Wood, wherein many huge Bears lurk to surprize Travellers, which made us keep close together when we passed such places, and have our Eyes about us, as well as our Fire-arms in readiness; and so keeping the Road, though not without many turnings, and ruged ways, when we had passed *Samark*, and it brought us to *Bockar*, where I staid some time to refresh me, for I had been ill of a Flux by the way, which still held me so, that I took no great pleasure to make any curious remarks here, and had I done it, as I was informed, there is nothing worthy of Note in the Town, the Houses being plain and low Built, the Streets crooked, and no Antiquities memorable. Here the *Moscovites* and *Yousbecs Tartar* are driving a considerable Trade together in Furs, and other Commodities.

Having

Europe, Asia, Africa, *and* America. 171

Having here pretty well recovered, by the assistance of a *German* Physician, I found in this place, I thought, a convenient opportunity to pass to *Astrakan*, which in a few days, I had, passing part of the way in Sledges, drawn by Harts, that run with them very swiftly; and another part, by taking Horse, there being a kind of a little Caravan, made up by the meeting of divers Travellers. The *Muscovites* use Sledges, that in the Winter they slide swiftly over the Snow and Frozen Rivers, having Beds in them, and covered over with Tilts like Waggons, so that they are a warm Convenience; notwithstanding in Winter, Travellers have been Frozen to Death in them.

Astrakan is Seated on the Great and Famous River *Volga*, which at 70 Mouths, or Channels, discharges its Water into the *Caspian* Sea, and so forcibly, that it keeps its stream unmixed with the Salt-water for many Leagues. In this River, the *Muscovites* have a great Fishery for Sturgeon, which they catch in abundance very large, so that the Eggs sometimes found in one of them, may weigh 100 Weight: As for the Flesh, they pickle up and send it into divers parts of *Europe*, some they press to make Oyl, and the Eggs they salt to make Ragous to serve them instead of Butter, which in *Lent* is denied them, and this is the Cavere so much used in many Countries. In the Summer, there are so many *Muskela's*, or *Sting Gnats*, about this River, that Passengers are miserably Stung and Blistered by them, though they wrap themselves up, and defend them all they can.

We were forced to stay before this City, till we obtained leave of the Governor for admittance; which after a little attendance, was granted: It is Seated in 48 Degrees *North* Latitude, in an Island of the *Volga*, 13 Leagues from the Mouth of the River, and appartains to the Great *Czar* of *Muscovy*. It is encompassed with a double Wall, without any other Fortification, except some few Towers, half Musket Shot one from another. The Great Guns planted

planted there are fine pieces, and about 80 in number, it ſtands low on gravelly Ground, ſo that the heat is exceſſive in Summer, and the People are conſtrained to Bath themſelves in cool Water in Troffs placed in Vaults; yet the Soil produces good Fruit of ſundry kinds, they have ſtore of excellent Mellions, eſpecially the Karpous, or Water Mellions, their Rhinds Green, but of a Roſey Red within, of a pleaſant taſt, cooling and delicate to quench Thirſt. There are divers ſorts of Grapes, of which they make a kind of pleaſant Wine, but it ſoon Sowers: All this while, no private Perſon dares touch a Grape till the Governour has made choice of them, and other Fruits, for the *Czar's* Table. There are divers Nations inhabiting here, drawn by the Conveniency of Trade, and the ſweetneſs of the Air. The *Armenians* entirely poſſeſs one Suburb, and the *Nogais Tartars* an other, which reſemble a City, being Fortified with Wooden Ramports, and the Deputy Governour Commands there; within the Encloſure ſtands a pretty convenient Moſque, but the Houſes for the moſt part are made of Bullruſhes, of which there are about 2000. They keep a Market in the Morning in their Quarter, and the *Maſcovites* keep theirs in the Evening, in the middle of their City; yet this City is often inſulted by the *Calmuc Tartars*, which conſtrains the Inhabitants for their better Repoſe, to ſend them Preſents, which the *Tartars* call a Tribute of Bread, Fiſh, Fleſh, and other Proviſions, and they drive a Trade with them for Furs and Horſes, of which they bring great plenty; beſides the *Muſcovites* are many times obliged to them, for their aſſiſting them with Men in the time of their Wars.

CHAP

CHAP. XX.

Travels in Muscovy, *and Observations of what is worthy of Note; as to the Towns, Rivers, Mountains, Commodities, Heats and Colds, Laws, Religion, Manners and Customs of the People, &c. and from thence through* Poland *and* Germany *into* Holland.

Having a desire to see *Muscovy*, and particularly *Moscow*, the chief City, I made it my business to find an opportunity to leave *Astrakan*, and pass thither.

As for this vast Conntry, it is bounded on the *West* with *Lithuania* and *Livonia*; on the *East*, with *Tartary*; on the *North*, with the Frozen Ocean: on the *South*, with the *Caspian* Sea, the *Ottoman* Empire, and *Paulus Mæotis*. It is branched with many large Navigable Rivers, as the *Tanais, Borhistenes, Volga*, &c. It is divided into 9 Provinces, *viz. Novog, Radia, Valadomira, Plescovia, Rhesen, Servia, Parmia, Condoria, Petrosa* and *Muscovy*, though from this last, the whole Track takes its Denomination.

Towards the *Southern* parts, it is pretty plentiful of many things of Value, yielding Corn, Cattle, Furs, Flax, Hemp, Wax, Honey, &c. but the *Northern* parts lye very cold, the Earth being so long covered with Snow, that the Ground is chilled, and produces not its Fruits kindly; yet Furs are gotten off of White, Black and Red Foxes, Grey and Red Squrrils, Minever Ermins, Wolverin, or wild Dogs. The Woods which are generally Fur

and

and Birch, abound in Ravenous Creatures, particularly, Wolves and Bears, which in the extremity of Weather, pinched by Cold and Hunger, comes in great Clusters to the Villages near the Forrest, and puts the Inhabitants to flight many times, killing and devouring them and their Cattle, so that at such times, by way of prevention, they are forced to be on their Guard. But as to these, and other matters of the like nature, I shall take them in course, as my Travels lay in this Country, which is of vast extent from *North* to *South*, if you measure from *Cola* to *Astrakan*, which bendeth somewhat *Eastward*, which is reckoned the length of it is accounted 4260 verst or russ Miles, though one of them makes not above 3 quarters of our Miles though *Northward*. Beyond *Cola*, there is a large Country unto the River *Tromschua*, that runeth 1000 verst Miles, but the ridged Winter Frost renders it not much inhabited, and little fruitful in Summer. As for the Breadth, if one goes from that part of the Czar's Teritories, that lies farthest *West*, on the *Narve* side, to the utmost parts of *Siberia* Eastward, where are divers Garisons, it is 4200 verst Miles: But to come near as a Traveller, considering how to get the safest and easiest way to *Moscow*, it being in *June*, when the Rivers were open, I was perswaded to Embark on the *Volga*, which I did with a Merchant of that City, who shewed me a great deal of kindness, the Vessel being his own; for from *Astrakan* to *Moscow*, it is accounted 18000 verst Miles. We sailed till we came to the Mouth of the River *Cama*, which dischargeth its Waters into the River *Volga*, and so made our way by Water and Land to *Cazan*, which the *Muscovites*, a few Ages since took from the *Tartars*, and is the Metropolis of a Kingdom. It is a City of considerable Tade, it was formerly walled with Timber and Earth, but upon annexing the whole Kingdom to the Crown of *Muscovy*, the great Czar *Vasiliwich* walled it with Free-stone. The Building is not Stately, yet very Commodious, for the Inhabitants, who are a mixed People, as they are

on

on all the Borders; we lodged and refreshed our selves here, and passed in a 11 days through a fine Country, well Watered, and very Fruitful, to a considerable fair Town, which we reached in 10 days, called *Nisnovogrod*, where *Occa* falls into the *Volga*. This is the head of a Shire, or County of that Name, and from hence by *Rezan*, and so passing a tedious Journey through many difficult ways, we came to the River *Moscow*, on whose Banks the City of *Moscow* stands. I should have told you I left my Merchant Trading up the River *Camaon*, on whose Banks are several and pretty Towns, but he took care to provide me a Guide, who accompanied me to *Moscow*, the nearest way over the Land, and to help me to Imbark where the Rivers offered to lessen our Journey, for I did not think fit to fall directly down the *Volga* into the *Caspian* Sea, which would little have furthered me.

Being arrived at the head City of *Moscow*, I entered on the River side, and finding some *English* there, I was not long destitute of a Habitation, and being Evening when I entered, I thought fit to rest that Night, and the next day went to take a view of the City, which is very large. The Form of it is in a manner round, with three strong Walls, circling the one within the other, the Streets lying pretty commodiously within all the Heart or Center inclosed by the inmost Wall, is called the *Czar's* Castle, or Pallace, very large in Circle; the Houses of ordinary Persons are but indifferently built with Timber, Loam and Mortar, covered with Boards or Bark of Trees; but the Houses of the Nobles are pretty Stately. The Churches are many, and they are Adorned on the tops with Globes of Copper, and guilded Spires. That of *Blaneshina* or *Blessedness*, is of curious Architecture, after the Fashion of the *Greek* Churches, whose Tenents in Religion, the *Muscovites* devoutly hold; the Church of St. *Michael* is nothing inferiour to it, but above all, the Cathedral called, *Our Ladies Church*, is large and stately; in it the Czars are Crowned by the Patriarch. The

Market

Market is kept in the Castle, or within the inward Wall, unless the River be Frozen over, and then it is partly kept thereon, and sometimes alltogether; so that upon the Ice bareing all sorts of Carriages, there appears to be a kind of a Fair, because the People bring vast quantities of Goods from remote places on their Heads. The Castle is on a rising Hill, well Watered and Fortified, and the Princes's Palace very conveniently contrived, but his Attendance upon publick Occasions, as at the Audience of Ambassadors, and the like, is more Magnificent, they being in great Numbers mostly Arrayed in Cloath of Gold and Silver, rich Furs, Velvets, Pearls and pretious Stones; Battle Axes of Gold are carried before the Czar, and his Robes exceeding rich of Goldsmiths Work, poudered with pretious Stones and Imbroderies of Pearl'; their Feasts are served up in Dishes of Gold, the meanest Vessel being Silver, and both kinds very numerous. The Diet is choice, and well dressed, according to the *Russian* Fashion; their Drink is Wine, Meath, and sometimes strong *Aquavitæ*, which among them is called *Russ* Wine.

In this City are still to be seen some Ruins of the Walls the several Fires have made, for I was told it contained 41500 Houses before the *Crim Tartars* reduced it to Ashes, *Anno* 1571. and in it destroyed 80000 People, and besides the Houses, 1500 convent Churches and Chapples. The *Poles* burnt it *Anno* 1611. and *Anno* 1676. an Accidential Fire happened Burning 20 days, but now Guards are appointed, to take care of Fire, and have Sallaries allowed them. There is one thing Admirable, which is a Bell raised in a large Tower; this Bell is 24 foot in height, and I was told, though it has been chipped off some Tuns of Mettle to make it ring better, that it weighs 176 Tun, and the Clapper 4 Tun, which is pulled by a Rope to sound it on particular occasions, for it cannot be raised by reason of its vast weight.

Provisions are very plentiful here, as Fish, Fowl, Venison, Hares, and other Dainties; for the Woods, Rivers, and Lakes, which are very many and large, abound with these, and divers other useful Creatures, and in some parts of *Moscovy*, they draw their Sledges with Rain-deer, who do the Office of Horses, and run more swiftly: In my passing *Tartary*, I observed the like; they also used there great Dogs for the same purpose, and on the Borders, I met several riding on Elks.

I saw in this City many Bath-stones, and other Stones, which in the Winter are used in all places, which prevents their being pinched by the ridged Frosts, which are extream from *October* till *March*, accompanied with vast Snows, so that in that Season, there is little stiring abroad: for the Air is so piercing, that many have been stifled with it going out of their Houses, especially too early; and they report in that Season, it is frequent to find People frozen to Death in the Streets, and many are brought in Dead in Sledges frozen, though they have Beds there to lye on, and Tilt Coverings of Furskins over them; and for this time all the Rivers and Lakes are locked up, the Ice usually a Yard thick or more, yet they have store of Grain, as Wheat, Rye, Oats, Maize, &c. Plums, Pears, Cherries, black and red, Hurtle Berries, Apples, Rasps, Strawberries, and other delicate Fruits; for so the Almighty Wisdom has ordained it, that when the time of Thaw comes, which is usually the end of *March*, the Snow being cleared off the Ground, after that becoming dry in 14 days, Flowers, and all other products of the Earth sprout out and flourish incredibly; the Woods show a pleasing Green, and the Birds every where warble Mellodiously, especially Nightingals, who Sing more distinct and clear than any where else. The Storks busy themselves in Building in ruined Edifices, Hawks of all kinds in the Rocks and Sea-shoar-cliffs, Eagles in the rockey Mountains more *Northernly*; the Hare in Winter is White, sheds her Coat, and becomes the colour of ours.

The

The Lakes and Rivers are stocked with Swans, and variety of other Water Fowl, so that the face of things seem admirably changed, and the Country is so pleasant, that those who should see it in Winter how Dismal, and in a manner Desolate it appears, (and knows no more) would conclude it impossible, or take it for quite an other Climate. Therefore I took my opportunity of Travelling here, whilst it was seasonable, for the dreadful Stories I heard of Winter, made me sometimes allmost fancy I had an Ague in my Bones at the Relation of them; but the *Muscovites* are hardy, answerable in a good degree to the Climate, and are more patient of Cold and Hunger than others, by which means they have the advantage of their Enemies, in tiring them out by Winter Camps, and other Fateigues: For a *Russ* Soldier told me, he had often made his Bed in the Snow without any Tent, only hanging up his Mantle against that part, from whence the Weather drove, and turning his back to the Wind, his Drink being the cold Stream, with a little Oat-meal dusted into it; and the Forage for his Horse, consisted in that Season, of Twigs and Bark of Trees, and yet performed well the service undertaken; others to harden and inure themselves to the Cold the better, go abroad Hunting the Beasts that bare the Furs, have come sweating out of their Bath Stoves in the ridged Season, and leaped Naked into a River, where the Ice has been broken; and it is a remedy among them against the Numbness of their Limbs, occasioned by cutting Winds, to rowl themselves in Snow; yet for all this, there are many tender among them, that cannot endure these hardships.

The Women are much confined at Home, and very Obliging and Obedient to their Husbands, yet so much Heat as they endure, being closed up in Winter, tending their Fires, makes them but of a bad Complexion, yet they mend their Faces by their Husbands allowance, with a Red and White Paint, but easily discernable; yet being the Fashion, is not minded, and especially, among the Vulgar: If a Man sometimes beats not his Wife, she will be Sullen, and fancy he loves her not, and they have a Custom, when they first pretend Courtship, among other Presents, to send a Whip to show the Woman what she has to trust to, if she prove Disobedient, and this they take more kindly than the rest; but I find these matters, though proper to be known, yet some digression from Travels, have drawn me to launch too far this way, therefore now I come something more home to the purpose.

The next chief City of *Moscovy* is *Novogrod*, pleasantly Seated, and a place of considerable Trade; the Building mostly of Wood, as generally the Building is in all this Country, the Streets in many places not paved, but planked with Furr, jointed and laid in so, that it shoots the Water off commodiously; it is the head of a Province or Shire, where the Court of Justice do determine matters, is held by a Duke and Dyack, the Latter acting in the nature of a Secretary; and these Courts are held in all chief Cities, but an Appeal lays from them to the Office of the four Chetfrids at *Moscow*, who are chief Judges of the four Quarters, or Divisions of the whole Country of *Muscovy*, each holding an Office for his District or Quarter, and all the Shires or Provinces apply themselves to the Office of that Lord of the Chetfrid they are under, then the matter is laid before the *Czar*'s Council, and what they Determine, is sent back to be put in Execution.

Vologda is an other principal City, seated on a River of that Name, where is a great Trade for Furs, Hides, Tallow, Corn and other Merchandize, bringing in a considerable Revenue in Customs and other Taxes to the Prince, who has a part in this an other places, for almost every thing that is sold, so that his Incoms are very great, accounted no less than 13 Millions of Rubbles a Year, and a Rubble is reckoned according to Exchange, a Mark English.

Voldomir is an other City of considerable Trade, and gives name to a Province; it is built very regular, and pretty well Fortified, and is watered by a confiderable Stream, at leaftways very near it: But befides *Mofcow*, the Towns or Cities of chief ftrength, are *Vobsko* and *Smolensko*, *Cazan* and *Aftrakan* lying on the Borders, and defending the Country againft the Inroads or Incurfions of the *Tartars*. *Jaruflave*, an other fair City for its commodious Scituation on a high Bank of the *Volga*, is in great Efteem: The Country about it is exceeding Fruitful in Corn-pafture, Fruit-trees, and has a great Fifhery on the River. In this City, they fay, dwelt the *Rufs* Prince *Vlademia*, Sir-named, *Jaruflave*, who at the Mediation of *Sneno*, the Dane, married the Daughter of our King *Harold*.

Periflave is a confiderable City, commodioufly built on the Banks of a great Lake, yielding in it abundance of Fifh, and enriching it by Trade from fuch Towns as border on that Lake, or the Rivers that fall into it.

Roftove may be numbered among the reft; for here is a great Trade for Furs, and other Commodities, bought up to difperfe into other parts of *Europe*, and Merchants come hither as far as *Perfia*, fome fay from *China*, beyond the great Wall built to exclude the roving *Tartars*, of which I have already fpoke of. There are a great number of other Towns, the Country being moftly to the *Southern* parts full of them, but not fo confiderable as thefe I have named; for the Houfes are of Wood, moft without any Lime or Stone, built very clofe and warm, with Fur-trees plained and piled over one another, faftned together with Notches or Dents at every Corner; and between the Timber for warmnefs they ftuff in Mofs, and the Houfes have Stairs leading out of the Yard into the Chamber, and this manner of Building feems more agreeable to the Country than any other, as being far warmer than Stone or Brick in the extremity of Winter, and in Summer, the Mofs being pulled out of the Chinks, lets in the cool breathing Air to refrefh them; and of this Timber, they have fuch plenty, that for a

fmall

Europe, Asia, Africa *and* America. 181
small matter a House may be Built with many Appendages, or Conveniences for Shops, Merchants, Ware-houses, or private Families, for 20 or 30 Rubbles, or little more; and when the Houses fall to decay, they store them considerably with Fireing and other Necessaries, as *Perma, Weelinda, Totam, Kentisma, Solovetsky, Ocona, Bombasey,* and *None-nosks,* are famous for their Salt-pits, where great quantities are made, and out of which the *Czar* has a considerable Revenue, as 3 *Russ* on every hundred Weight.

The Rivers that water this Country, besides what I have named, are *Wichida,* a long and large River which rises out of the Country of *Permia,* and falleth into the *Volga. Duna,* that empties it self into the *Baltick* Sea, by the Town of *Riga. Onega,* that falleth into the Bay of *Solovetsko,* ninety Verst from St. *Nicholas.* This River below the Town of *Cargo Polia,* meeteth with *Volock,* that falls into the *Finland* Sea, by the Town of *Yama,* so that from the Port of St. *Nicholas,* into the *Finland* Sea, one may go by Water to *Suchana.* This River floweth into *Duyna,* and so into the *North* Sea; there are abundance of Fish in it, and in the open Season it is in a manner covered with Water-fowl. *Duyna* is many hundred Miles long, which falleth *Northward* into the Bay of St. *Nicholas,* a Bay so Named by one *Chancelour,* an *English* Man, who first found a *North-East* passage to *Russia,* in 1553. and called the Bay St. *Nichola's* Bay, from an Abby Dedicated to that Saint standing near it; and upon notice of his arrival, was sent for with great Joy by the Czar to *Moscow,* whether he went on Sledges 1500 Miles, and was received in great Joy, and highly Feasted with great State and Magnificence, the Court appearing in all its Splendor overjoyed now in hopes of an open Trade by Sea, for before they were obliged to carry their Merchandize through the *Hastill* Territories of *Poland, Sweeden,* and other Countries, to ship them for these parts; and hereupon Ambassadors were sent to *England,* and a free Trade
granted

granted with large Priviledges, whereupon a Company now called the *Muscovy* Company, settled Factories at *Arch Angel*, and other Towns adjacent, having Lands allowed them, and an Agent, or Consul permitted to reside at *Moscow*, though since the *Dutc*, and other Nations, have found the way and interloped upon them: This Bay lies in 64 Degrees *North* Latitude, yet the Country about it is very pleasant in the open Season, and in the River stands an Island called *Rose* Island, where are Roses Damask, Red, Violets, and abundance of pleasant Flowers and Fruits. There is a Monastery near it of 700 Monks, who live after the Greek manner, and have large In-coms, for they receive rent for the Lands lying many Miles round them. However, there is in this Country many desarts and waste places, especially to the *Northward;* with rockey Shores and craggy Mountains; but on the latter, they breed Goats, and a kind of wild Horse, Volverins or wild Dogs, but the latter mostly in the Woods near the Rocks, they find a Fish called *Morso*, a Sea Monster, who by the help of his Teeth, clambers up to get his prey of Eggs that the Wildfowl lay in the Pits, and hollow places his Teeth are about two foot long and better for use than Ivory, of which they make Knives and Sword hafts, &c. They fancy that in pursuing these on the Ice, and the Flakes breaking away, some of their People were driven by the Currants and Winds on the coast of *America*, and stocked in a great length of time that large fourth part of the World, because there is some resemblance between them, but I fancy this opinion Groundless. They Hunt likewise the Seals on the Ice, and kill them by striking them on their Noses with Clubs, and make good Merchandize of their Skins, and the Oyl they get from them.

As for the Nobility of *Muscovy*, they are four-fold; The First are called *Udeelney Kna Zey*, and these are of chief Authority, as being the Ancient Nobility, that is, exempt or priviledged Dukes.

The

The second are the *Bojazens*, such as the Czar honoureth, besides their Nobility with the Title of Counsellors.

The third are the *Vayavodey*, or such as have been Generals of Armies, or done some great Exploits for their Country.

The Fourth and lowest degree are such as have the Title of *Knazey*, or Dukes, but descend from younger Brothers of the chief Houses; all of these have priviledges suitable to their Degrees, and make a considerable Figure.

The Parliament is held at *Moscow*, composed of the Clergy and Nobility, summoned by the Czar, who sits in his Throne in that Assembly, and others according to their Degree. Then the Dyack, or Secretary, reads what is purposed by the Prince to be propounded to them; the Patriarch, with his Bishops, and other Clergy, are hereupon required to give their Opinions first in order, who generally consent to what is propounded, and the Nobles agree with them, as thinking such Holy Men cannot Err; then is it drawn up and sent to be proclaimed as standing Law in the principle Cities and head Towns of the Empire. The *Moscovites*, as to their Religion are Christians of the Greek Church, very superstitious in their Worship; for they often in their Devotion beat their Fore-heads against the floors of their Churches, till they are Swelled, and sometimes Bloody; they pay a Veneration to Saints, and particularly, to St. *Nicholas*, whom they stile their Patron, they Reverence the Virgin *Mary*, St. *Peter*, and others. They have the Cross and Holy Water in high esteem among them, and their Bishops go in Procession to hollow the Rivers once a Year, at which time the People strive for the Water; many leap into it, and dip their Infants, though the weather be extream cold: This Water so Hollowed, is likewise given to the Sick, with a fancy it will restore them, or by cleansing, make them fit for another World. They keep four *Lents*, and then they abstain from strongs Liquors, and all gross sort of of Food, as Flesh, &c. they observe certain Vigils, watching in their Churches by Night, repeating Arisons, and bowing their Fore-heads to the floor a certain number of times.

Their Marriages are celebrated as ours, but with some odd different Ceremonies, *viz.* The Bride stoops down and knocks her Head against the Bridegrooms Shew, in token of her Submission and Obedience, and the Friends of the Bride bow to him; then they break Bread and Eat it among them, intimating that by this Marriage, the Friends on either side are united as the crumbs of Bread were in the Loaf, and that they are to account themselves as one Man, and one Family, &c.

The Funerals of their Dead are very solemnly performed; they Wash and Apparel the Body very neatly, then are their Mourners appointed for some days to Howl over it, and often to demand what was the occasion it died, seeing it wanted nothing of Wordly Goods, as Meat, Drink, Riches, &c. naming the sorts and kinds, and then set up a hideous Lamentation, much like the wild *Irish*: If it be in the open Weather, it is put into a Grave in a few days, but in the hard Weather, when the Ground cannot be dug, they pile the Bodies up in a House, they call God's House, and when the Season is practicable, every one fetches away his Dead, and buries it.

The *Muscovites* are generally very Corpulent, and of a large size, strong, and of late grown Dexterous in the feats of Arms, particularly Fire-arms; they have abundance of great Ordinance, some carrying Bullets two foot Diameter. They are curteous to Strangers, unless they get in Drink, and then they are very Rude and Mischievious; and this they often do, for the Men and Women are excessive Drinkers, so that many have been Murthered by them in their drunken Revels; before Dinner they usually drink a Cup of *Aquavitæ*, which they say, gets them a good Appetite, and after Dinner carouse stoutly of Meath, and other strong Liquors, and then to sleep on Benches. The

The better sort wear exceeding Rich Garments, as Scarlet or Velvet lined with Furs down to their Ancles, loose like the *Greeks*, and under them Vests or Wastcoats of Cloath of Gold or Silk Imbroidered; the Scull of the 12 Caps Imbroidered with Gold, Silver or precious Stones, according as they are able, and over it a Cap or Bordering of Sables, Ermin, Minever, or the like: the Women, unless Head attire, are cloathed almost like the Men, with open Sleeves down to their Fingers; they wear Girdles Imbroidered, or Plated with Gold and Silver, but with the poor Mousack, or Country Peasant, tho' he keeps the Fashion it is as hard as with us; his Garments are course Cloath, or Sheepskin, with the Wool on, but every one has a differently suiting to Winter and Summer, for in the Latter Season it is very hot, more then commonly in *England*, yet it lasts but *June*, *July*, and *August*. They much delight in Musick, tho' it be but Indifferent, for I heard nothing like that of other nations whilst I remained amongst them; as for Learning the lower degrees affect it not, addicting themselves to Husbandry, and Handicrafts; very obedient they are to their Prince, never disputing his Commands, or Injunctions, what ever they be, paying their Taxes and Customs, tho' somewhat heavy, very chearfully. If in a Law controversie the Judge cannot decide it, he demands if they will kiss the Cross on their Affirmation, or denial; if the Defendant does it, he is acquitted of his Debt, or Injury done; if both require it, then they draw Lots, and he that has the better Lot, is only allowed it, and concluded to be in the right. But in Criminal matters they use Tortures, and those very severe ones, to extort confessions, but if the party hold out against them he is acquitted. They have one sort of Execution very odd, which is, by putting Criminals under the Ice to be smothered in the Waters, but cannot be done at all times, wherefore they have many more, as Hanging, and the like. These

These are the Principal matters I observed, or was Informed of in this Country, worthy to be placed in a History of this Nature: and now fearing to be Winter locked after my having been in so many warm Regions, I bethought me of Removing nearer home, because the cold Season was approaching, wherein I was very sensible, it would be very Incommodious for a Stranger to travel in these parts, and therefore I took an opportunity of a Caravan going for *Poland*, part of which Country I passed, but had little or no time to take a survey of it, only thus much I shall say in General. The *Borbistenes* bounds it from the *Muscovite* Empire on the East, on the West it has the *Vistual*, on the North the *Baltick* Sea and *Sinus Trinitus*, on the South *Hungary*; and is divided into 10 Provinces, viz. *Luconia, Lithunia, Vollina, Samogita, Pedelia, Russia, Nigra, Podlasia, Musovia* and *Poland*; and the Latter giving the Country its generally accepted Name. These Provinces are Branched with several Navigable Rivers, as *Vistua, Raben, Bog, Mimel*; its Metropolis is *Cracow,* or *Craconia,* where usually the King has his Residence. It is an Elective Kingdom, and at present the Regal Lot by free choice of the Nobility and Gentry, is fallen on the Vallian and Renowned Duke of *Saxony,* who is crowned King of *Poland,* and has received the Homage of the greater part of the *Poles. Cracow* is Scituate on the Banks of the River *Vistua,* Navigable 400 Miles, being as it were Encompassed with distant mountains, and fortified with strong Walls; the Buildings are very fair. This Country produces Tar, Rosin, Pitch, Wax, Honey, Barly, Oats, Amber, Tallow Hides, Minerals, and other Commodities; and therein by Trading are found the Commodities of divers other Nations: we stayed not here, but passing some other Province Entred *Germany,* by the Way of *Hungary, Austria,* &c.

This Famed Empire is bounded on the North with *Denmark,* and the *Danish* Seas; on the East witn *Prussia, Poland* and *Hungary*; on the South with

Europe, Asia, Africa, *and* America. 187
with the *Alps*; on the West with *Flanders, Holland*, &c. The Cities and Towns of this Empire may be properly divided into 3 parts, as first, the *Hans* Towns, that enjoy large Previledges and Immunities, about 70 in Number. 2. Those called Imperial Cities, by reason of their great Privileges above the rest, in Coining Money, bargaining, acknowledgement of Subjection, unless to the Emperour, whom they acknowledge their Protector, and pay him Annual Tribute so. And 3*dly*. those under the Electoral Princes, which are commonly called Principalities; the chief Rivers are the *Danube*, and *Rhine*; the first runs about 1500 Miles, and receives 58 Navigable Rivers to swell its Stream, and at last falls into the Black Sea : the second passes thro' *Germany* and *Belgia* 800 Miles, and falls into the *German* Ocean.

This large Country produces Silver Mines, Copper. Lead, Tin, Iron, Corn, Wine, Allum, Quick Silver, Linnen, Woollen, Linnen-Stuffs, Silks, store of Cattle, and many other Commodities? and from hence by Land and Water I reached the Low Countries, and briefly, I so directed my way, that I cam to *Amsterdam*, the chief trading City in the Province of *Holland*. It is seated on the River *Tay*, which on the North side of it, flows like a large Sea; when on the South the River *Amster* running through 3 Lakes, entereth its Streets, and falleth into the River *Tay*; and by the Addition of a new City to the old, it is become very Commodious, and Strongly fortified; and in it are to be found the Commodities of almost all Nations, tho' the Country produces nothing very considerable of its own, but these things come by Navigation, for most of the Inhabitants are Merchants, who's Goods are brought by Vessels to their Doors, and Warehouses; and the People are generally Frugal, Industruous and Rich.

CHAP.

CHAP. XXI.

A Voyage from Amsterdam *in* Holland, *to* Cales *in the* Spanish *Dominion, and* Thence *to* America; *giving an Account of what happened on the Sea, and in some Islands; touched at,* &c.

BEing at *Amsterdam* I began seriously to consider of my Travels, and whilst I Ruminated on many things, a strange fancy came into my Head, that I had not compleated my first undertaking, in visiting the several Parts of the World, because I had not been in *America*; though the fatigues and dangers I had run thro' might have been a sufficient Motive to have put a stop to my further Progress in strange Countries, and give me satisfaction enough to have returned home; but the report of the Golden Mountains, and other things, egged me on, made me seek for an opportunity to pass to *Cales*, where I doubted not but by one means or other, to get a Passage into the *Spanish Indies*, for that was it I Aimed at; for the other I understood are little considerable, as to Travellers, and have nothing Extraordinary to be found in them, and besides are mostly very well known to my Countrymen: therefore in describing *New-England, Virginia, Barbadoes, Jamaica*, &c. I should have furnished their Curiosity with nothing that is rare, and new to them. I had not waited a Week before an opportunity offered, and I Embarked with such necessaries, as I had procured. Entering the Bay of *Biscay*, we were taken with a violent Storm, and sprung our Mizen; it held us for 24 Hours, so that every moment we thought we should become a prey to *Neptune*'s Watery fry, and this Storm was more terrible, and threatned more danger than any I had seen before, which made me repent my attempting so rashly, as thinking God was angry with me for my presumption, and then concluded if I could get safe ashoar I would rest quiet, with what I had seen and felt; the Storm at last blew over, and then a fresh gale, Providence so ordered it, that we reached the desired Port.

Being now on Land again at *Cales*, or *Cadiz*, in the Dominion of the King of *Spain*, such is man's frailty, I found my desire of Travelling not so much quenched, as in the Tempest I fancied it. A secret Inclination promised, and urged me on, that seeing I had made so many weary steps in 3 parts of the World, I should now venture upon the proposed fourth, held to be Larger and Richer than any of the other three, and as fortune would throw it in my way, to make me more resolved on it, a *Spanish* Merchant whom I had been Intimately Acquainted withal in *London*, I renewed my Acquaintance with him, and he Entertained me very civilly, but when I opened my Mind, and unbosomed my Intentions, he told me it would be a very difficult undertaking, because the Officers of the Port had very strict Orders not to permit Strangers to Embarque for the *Spanish Indies*, least they might be sent thither as Spies to discover the Havens, and Strength of the Forts, and other things that might be prejudicial to the Government. I told him I had no such Intention, that curiosity was only to inform my self, as a Travellor, of what was rare to be observed in a World, which the alwise God had so Admirally framed and ordered, and when I gave him a general account in what Parts I had been, and showed him my Papers of Memorandums, and curious Remarks, he was satisfied, promised to do his Endeavour for the furtherance and security of my passage, and to furnish me with Money sutable to the Country, upon Bills I gave him to receive by Exchange in *London*; and then he let me know he was a Part-owner in one of the

Ships,

Ships, that was to accompany the Galeons, called the St. *Johns D' Ulua*; and to be brief, when the Fleet was ready to Sail, he gave the Master private orders to conceal me in his Cabin, and use me as a puculiar friend of his. I had pretty well learned the *Spanish* in *England*, which with little more attention I doubted, not to Improve so well in my Voyage as to be taken for a *Spaniard* among the Native *Spaniards* of *America*, who, I was Informed, but corruptly spoke the Language of old *Spain*. In a little time a warning Piece was fired for the Fleet to weigh Anchor, and tho' our Ship was narrowly searched, I so well wraped my self up in a Ticking, and lay instead of a Bolster at the Bedshead, that I was not discovered, tho' they turned up the Quilt, and other covering to see if any had absconded under them, that were not Licensed to depart.

Anchors weighed, and the Wind being fair, we set Sail with a prosperous Gale till we came to *Golfo d' Yeguas*, a very turbulent Sea, where the Ships and Galeons rowled and tottered extreamly, the Waves dashing violently, by reason of an Eddy occasion by a current that set into it, and the Galleon who went only a Convoy, having convey'd us thus, left us as concluding we were out of danger; especially of the *Barbary* Corsaries, and then by the Masters advice I showed my self on the Decks, as not fearing to be carried back again, or hindered in my further passage; and having the Wind constantly favourable, we steered our course without meeting with any thing Remarkable, till we made the Land of *America*, about 6 Weeks after we set out from *Cales*. Here I saw many Dorados, or Golden Fish, sporting in the Water, so called, because their Skins are of the Colour of Gold, and the Sailers with Hooks and Lines catched a great many of them: they Eat something like a Herring, but more short and Sweet. The first Land we stood in with, was *Desseada*, or as the *Spaniards* have named it, *The desired Land*, as being first
found

Europe, Asia, Africa, *and* America. 191
found by *Collumbus*, when he discoverd the Western *Indies*, but passing by it we stood with another Island, called *Margalanted*; Passing by that and *Dominica*, we arrived at *Guadalupe*, where we before designed to Refresh ourselves, and casting Anchor in a safe Road before the Island, as many as would, had leave to go on ashoar. The *Indians* who Inhabit it, no sooner saw our Ships, which they had long waited for, and Expected by their Recoining the Course of the Moon, which is the account of the Months they keep, but they came running to the Shoar with Provisions to wellcome and refresh us: which were Sugar Canes, Plantons, Tortois, and some Fowl, and for it they received Knives, Beads, and such like Trifles; and many Rowed to the Ships in the Canoes, Boats clouterly made like Troughs out of the main body of a Tree. These People were naked Except a cloath to hide their Priveties, and many of them like the Antient *Britains* had scarified on their Faces, and other Parts, the Figures of Flowers, Suns, Moons, Stars, Birds, Beasts, and the like; and rings in their Nose, which they looked on as their chief Ornament. They are Idolaters, worshipping the Host of Heaven. The Commanders gave some of them Wine, that came aboard, which they Eagerly coveted, but a little soon made them Drunk, and kick up their heels on the Decks, as being only used to drink Water, and a Liquor that Distills out of the Plantain Tree. Yet for all this kindness, we could not but suspect they Murthered two of our men, who went into the Woods to gather wild Fruit, for tho' we searched and stayed for them, they returned not, nor could be found, which made the rest more cautious to venture too far.

Leaving this Island we Sailed within sight of the Land of *Puerto Rico*, and then of *St. Domingo*, a very large Island, and here the Ships separated to the several Ports they were bound, as *Havana*, *Honduras*, *Jucatan*, and others; yet we kept together 4 Sail, being bound for the *Mexicaian* Province

vince, and came into the Sound, where we found the Sun, it being in *August*, exceeding hot, and afflicted us the more because we were becalmed, and one of the Sailers in the Evening leaping into the Sea to cool himself by Swiming, was unfortunately seized on by a Monsterous Fish, which they called a Tiburon, a kind of Crocadil, that pulled him under Water, and devoured him; who's surprizing Tragedy became a warning to the rest, yet hoping to be revenged, we let down two large Hooks, fastned back to back, with a strong Rope, and Baited with a stone of flesh, and took one of these Fish, but not the Murderer, as we found by his Gorge, when we opened him; he was as much as Sixteen men could Hawl on the Deck, tho' they let down a noose Rope under him to hold him fast hampered; he proved to be 12 yards long, and being killed the *Spaniards* cut him up, and salted part of his flesh, which had something of the Tast of Beef in it, being very firm and hard; and soon after a fresh gale Springing up, and we had sailed a few Leagues, the man at the Topmast-head cryed out, Land, which did not a little rejoyce us, for the hot weather on those broad Seas had rendred us faint and sickly, but it being near Sunset, and the Coast dangerous to enter on in the night time, we lay off till the next morning, and then stood into a part rockey on either side, and presently discovered it to be *Vera Crux*, otherwise called St. *John d' Ulliua*, and came so near in 6 Fathom Water, that by a Cable we fastned our Ship, that entered foremost by Cable Ropes, to the Rings that were placed for that purpose in the Wall of the Fort, which we saluted with our Guns. In this place *Hernando Cortz*, the famous *Spanish* Captain, first entered, when he made his Conquests in *Mexico*, sinking his Ships that his Souldiers might be the more resolute in the undertaking, as having all hopes of returning cut off, and with a Handful of men did such Exploits, that
made

Europe, Asia, Africa *and* America. 193
made the World Amazed, and this being the
Port to which our Ships were bound we went
Ashoar.

CHAP. XXII.

Travels from St. John D' Ulha *to the great City of* Mexico, *describing the Towns in the Way, Countries lying about them; with many other things and Relations, Antient and Modern; from the first Conquest made by the* Spaniards, *to this present time.*

THE proper name of this Sea-port Towns is St. *John d' Ulha*, the other *Vera Crux*, being given to it from the old Haven or Harbour of *Vera Crux*, lying 6 Leagues from it; for that proving dangerous for Ships to ride at Anchor in, by reason of the violent North Winds, it was forsaken, and the *Spaniards* removed hither, as being more safe by the means of a Rock which skreens off that Wind: and here were the first Majestrates, Judges, Aldermen and Officers of Justice named. Great was the Concourse of the People when we landed, and the Religious, who have Monasteries here, received us in procession, because they understood there were some Missionaries on board, sent out of *Spain* to assist in converting the *Indians*, and upon the Account of some of them, who took particular notice of me, during the Voyage. I had a very good Lodging appointed me, and great Feasting was made with store of Fowl and Fish, of which the Country
O try,

try is very plentiful, and as a laſt Courſe Sweet-meats and Chocolett were brought in; *Te Deum* was ſung in the Cathedral Church, and ſome Shows preſented, but my mind being bent an other way, I little minded theſe things.

I reſted the day of Landing with my Companions, and the next took a ſurvey of the Town, and places about it; I compaſſed it in 3 quarters of an honr, and found the Scituation to be on Sandy ground, except on the South Weſt, where it is Mooriſh, and full of noiſome Bogs at a little diſtance, which in hot weather cauſes it to be ſomewhat unhealthy: the People in it are generally Rich, and the Inhabitants may, as near as I could compute, be between 3 or 4000. The Houſes, Churches and Cloiſters are moſtly built with Timber, the Streets are few, yet have intercourſe by narrow Lanes, or other paſſages; ſo that it has been often much Indamaged by Fire: The Trade is conſiderable there from *Mexico*, as being the convenienteſt part alſo from *Cuba* St. *Domingo*, *Jucatan*, *Portoello*, and by the way of the latter from *Peru*, *Cartagena*, and all the Iſlands lying on the North Sea. There is a Caſtle on the Entrance, founded on a Rock, and another Rock that makes the Entrance of ſhipping unacquainted with the Harbour very difficult, each are the chiefeſt Strength of the Town, and under theſe the Ships lie ſafe at Anchor, ſheltred againſt the fury of the North Wind, which is many times there very violent, ſo that the Houſes in the Town Rock and Totter exceedingly, that the Strangers conclude they are falling on their Heads.

The next day I found a great many Mules brought by the Owners to be Lett, to ſuch as had a mind to leave the place and Travel further. I embraced this opportunity, and ſent on Board to bring my Baggage on Shoar, which I Laded on one of them, and retained another to ride on; and ſo taking leave of thoſe whoſe Buſineſs or Curioſity detain'd them longer, I ſet forward to viſit *Mexico*, a famed City,

City, and the chiefest in these parts, but at a considerable distance from St. *John de Vellun*. The Road from hence for three or four Leagues I found very Sandy, but open and convenient for Travelling, and without meeting with any thing remarkable, I came to *Oldvera Crux*, Inhabited by *Spaniards* and *Indians*; the *Indians* met us a considerable way from the Town, and offered us all the kind respect imaginable; sounding their rustick Musicks, and Dancing before us, Tuning their Voices, which was more Melodious than their Musick; and indeed entring the place, we were very civily receiv'd as Strangers, the people crowding to ask what News from *Spain*, and of the Affairs of *Europe*, we satisfy'd their Curiosity as well as the time would permit, and then they brought us Flowers and Sweet-meats, and we presented them with divers *European* trifles, of which they seem'd very fond, rather for the sake of whence they came than for their value.

They Conducted us to the Market-place, which is in the middle of the Town, and made Arbours of green Boughs under two large spreading Elmes, for us to repose in and refresh our selves, and thither brought us plenty of Sweet-meats, Diet-bread, and Chocolet, having before placed Tables and Benches for the purpose, and the *Indians* particularly Assembled about us in great numbers, welcoming us into the Country. This place is but of indifferent Building, and not of any considerable Trade, for want of a good Harbour; the Buildings are of Wood; and here I observe the Friars have a great Command over the people, for what they order them they immediately do, rendring to them profound Honours and Respects Having refreshed our selves here, we gave the people Thanks for their Civility, and so took leave, reaching a little before Night a small *Indian* Town, where we Lodged, and found very good Entertainment of Turkeys, Hens, Capons, and Fruits.

The next Town of Note we came to was *Xalappadela Vera Crux*, Confifting of about 2000 Inhabitants, *Spaniards* and *Indians*. This Town is a Bifhop's See, ftanding in a Fruitful Soil, yielding ftore of *Indian* Wheat, called *Maize*, and fome *Spanifh* Wheat; it is encompaffed with *Indian* Villages, Farms of Sugar, Cochinil, and Paftures, that breed a great many Mules, and other Cattel in the Town; there is a large Church and Chappel, both belonging to a Cloyfter of *Francifcan*-Friars, who live very loofely confidering the Vows they make when they enter into that Order, living Riotoufly, and forgetting Chaftity, many of them living more like Gentlemen of great Eftates, than Men under the ridged feverity of the Religious Order they profefs.

The next place we Arrived at was *La Rinconda*, which is only a kind of a Carevan-fair, or Inn, yet here we found ftore of Provifion, and particularly, pleafant Spring-water, which much refrefhed us, confidering the Heat we endured, for it being the beginning of *September*, the Weather was exceeding fultry in this Valley; the Countrey about it fhowed very Green and Pleafant, Confifting of a great number of Farms, producing Corn pafture, and Fruits; but Lodging here in the Night time, we were terribly peftered with the Gnats that ftung us intolerably, fo that when we rife we fcarce knew each other, though at Sun-Rifing they go away in fwarms, and come not again till after Sun-Set; we paffed fome Villages that Day, and by Night reached a Town called *Segura*, Inhabited by *Spaniards* and *Indians*, to the number of 1000. *Hernando Cartez* Built this Town as a Frontier, on the firft progrefs of his Conquefts in *Mexico*, againft the *Cullicacans* and *Tepeacus*, who were Confederates with the *Mexicans*, and much annoy'd the *Spaniards* in the beginning of their Enterprize, taking 12 of them, Sacrificing them to their Idol, and then made a merry Feaft of their Flefh, for which *Cortez* affifted by the *Claxcullan*

Indians

Europe, Asia, Africa *and* America. 197

nidians took *Tepeacus* by force, and brought them with all their Territories under subjection to *Spain*, Condemning them to perpetual Slavery, in Revenge for the Murther of his *Spaniards*, and overcame likewise the *Cullucacans*, destroying their Idols, and forcing the chiefest of them to attend him as his Servants or Slaves; here we found store of Plantains, Sappotes, and Chicosapotes, which are Fruits of a pleasant taste, very juicy and sweet, also fair Clusters of Grapes, so that here, and in many other parts of the Countrey, if Vineyards were allowed to be Planted, they would produce as good Wine, if not better, than that of *Spain*, but the *Spainish* Kings have prohibited it, least it should hinder the Trade between the two Countries; for indeed except Wine, *Spain* affords them little but what they have among them, or might reasonably be contented without.

Out of the Road to *Mexico*, a little *Westward*, stands the famous Town of the *Tlaxcallans*, who making an Alliance with *Cortez*, were faithful Friends to him in his Wars, after they had tryed his strength, helping him to atchieve those Victories, which for a long time scarce could be credited in *Europe*; for they perceiving their numerous Forces, could not prevail against his handful of *Spaniards*, concluded them to be Gods, and consequently innumerable, because neither of their two Arrows they carried on their Standard took Effect, though shot in, wounding many of them, they having a Prophecy, that when they missed, the Victory would always go against them. Upon which, after many bloody Battles wherein they lost 40 or 50000 of their Men, they submitted, and became ever after constant friends to the *Spaniards*, and utter Enemies to *Monte Zuma*, then Emperor of *Mexico*, and his Successor; and by their assistance, *Cortez* took that great City, and many other places, for which this Town had greater Priviledges allowed it, than any other in *Judea*: This Province of *Tlaxcallan* had then 28 Towns and Villages depending on it, containing 150000.

150000 Families, which are now moſtly inhabited by *Spaniards*; the *Indians* in this part being kept under, and very poor, having little other wealth than the Corn, called *Centli*, though in the Town of *Tlaxcallan*, there are Artifficers of both Nations, and the *Indians* out-do the *Spaniards* in making curious Earthen-ware, working in Gold, Silver, Feathers and other Manufactures. A little before one comes to this Town, there is the Ruins of their Ancient Wall that ſtood as a Boundary, and Strangers were forbidden to paſs it on pain of being Sacrificed in their Temples to the Idols, of which they had great Numbers, and for no other fault, *Cortez*'s Men underwent this Fate. *Tlaxcallan* is pleaſantly ſeated, there is ſtill a great Market kept in it, where ſometimes 5 or 10000 People aſſembled. It has ſeveral Churches and Chaples in it, and Cloiſters of *Tarians*, who grow rich out of the labour of the poor *Indians*, ſome being imployed to fetch them Wood, Water, and to Fiſh for them, being paid at the publick charge of the reſt. The two Streets of *Ocotelulco* and *Fizatian* are very fair, and the beſt inhabited of any other; the Town is not fortified, as indeed few in the *Spaniſh Indies* are, except the Sea-ports that are apt to be inſulted by the Buckaniers; the building is low, and very indifferent, it is a Seat of the chief Officers of Juſtice ſent from *Spain* every three Years, who is called the *Alcalde Major*, whoſe power extends to all the Towns within 20 Leagues circumference. The *Indians* likewiſe have among themſelves *Alcaides Regidores*, and *Alguaziles* ſuperiour and inferiour Officers of Juſtice, appointed yearly by the *Alçalde Major*, who keep them in awe, fleecing them at their pleaſure, and exacting their ſervice without any ſatisfaction.

Keeping on one way, we came to a City called by the *Spaniards*, *la Puebla de les Angeles*, or the City of *Angels*: I viſited this City during my ſtay, and found it very Rich, being peſtered with Cloiſters and Monaſteries, which is a ſign of Wealth, for in poor Towns they rarely ſettle. It is ſeated in a low and

Europe, Asia, Africa, *and* America. 199
and pleasant Valley, about 3 Leagues from a very steep Mountain, always covered with Snow, though the Heat in the Valley is very great; it was first Built and Inhabited in the Year 1530. being 20 Leagues from *Mexico*; it is a Bishop's Sea, and his Revenue is yearly about 20000 Duccats, the Inhabitants are accounted between 10 and 12000. They carry on a fine Cloth Manufacture there, which is sent over all the *Indies*, being as good as that of *Segovia* in *Spain*; there is a Glass-House and a Mint, wherein is Coined most of the Silver that comes from *Sacatecat*, to be sent to *Spain*; it has curious Gardens about it, replenished with Fruits, Flowers, and Fountains, and the Fields that Enclose them are very pleasant, abounding with Wheat and Sugar Farms. .

Continuing our Journey after a considerable refreshment, we passed through many pleasant Villages, leaving considerable Towns on either hand to *Guaco Cingo*, Inhabited by *Spaniards* and *Indies*, to the number of 6 or 700. There is in it a Cloyster of *Franciscan* Friars. This place is like *Tlaxcallian*, has many Privileges granted by the King of *Spain*, because it Confederated with *Cortez*, against *Montezuma*. The Friars here Entertained us with Singing and Dancing, boasting that they had brought up several of the Town to do it, some of which they produced, and made them Dance to their Gittars with Castinets, and this we found to be the last Town of note, till we came to *Mexico*, which lies about 20 Miles from the way, up and down, over rising Hills and descending Valleys, with a mighty high Mountain before us, that overlooks *Mexico*, and the vast Lake it is Seated on. This Mountainous Alp has perpetual Snow upon it, and in passing the Spurs we found a great alteration in the Air, for here it was very Cold, to what we had felt before. In this Mountainous way the *Mexicans* endeavoured to stop *Cortez*, by laying mighty Ceders a-cross, but not staying to defend the Barocades,

rocades, with some pain he remov'd them, and Marched his Army of *Spaniards* and *Indians* to the Plains of *Quichatipec*, in the Jurisdiction of *Tezculo*, where he gave 100000 of *Montezumas*'s Forces Battel, and Battering their Ranks first with his Field-Pieces, and then breaking in with his Horse, utterly defeated them; whereupon, divers Towns upon the Lake, and on the Borders of the Mountain, submitted to him; the Terror of him growing so great, that those who submitted not fled out of their City, which made him put out a Proclamation for their return, promising that no Injury should be done unto them.

CHAP. XXIII.

My Arrival at Mexico; a Description of that famed City, what it has been, and what at present it is; the manner of Building; nature of its Inhabitants; Riches, and plenty of the Mountains, Lakes, and places about it, &c.

After a tedious Journey, being Arrived at the great City of *Mexico*, the Head of the Northern *Spanish Indies*, I shall have occasion to speak more particularly of it, than of other places I passed through, as to what it now is, and in general as to what it has been, in its most flourishing splendor.

This City is large in Compass, and stands on two Lakes, which some have concluded to be but one, because of their nearness and Communication

Europe, Asia, Africa, and America.

cation of their Waters, but they appear different in three things particularly; *viz.* one ebbs and flows by the force of the North-Wind, and the other does not; the Water of the one is Sweet, the other is Salt and Brackish; one has great store of Fish, and the other is destitute of any, though they have both their source or Springs that feed them from the great Mountain that overlooks the City. The Houses in this City are Built more stately, especially those of the Nobility and Gentry, than in other places; the Vice-Roy of the *Mexacanian* Province has his Palace here, and so has the Arch-Bishop. The Churches are many, Founded mostly on the Heathen Temples, which were in the flourishing state of the City, very numerous, and had Pyramides in the Midst of a vast height, on which the Idols stood, to whom they offered Humane Blood in Sacrifice, and sprinkled the Walls and Pillars of the Idol-Altar with it; there are in the City several Spacious Streets, and great Markets, affording all sorts of Provisions and other Necessaries. The Lakes by reason of the abundance of Boats and Canoes that Trade on them, furnish the City with store of plenty, especially with multitudes of Fowl and Fish taken there, the former being allured by a certain Oily tough Scum on the Water, which they eat as Food; besides there are many Trading Towns on the Banks where the Boats take in Loading, and constantly supply the City. The Monasteries and Nunneries are a graceful Ornament to the rest, their being almost of all the Orders. The Churches have Curious Spires, with Guilded Crosses on their Tops, and the whole Fabrick's Built with Stone of rare Architecture. Water comes almost into all parts of the City, by small Conduits, for though the Streets were formerly watered by Channels from the Lake, they are now mostly stopped up, and firm Ground made where Houses are Built; for after the Conquest, *Cortez* divided the Ground where the Houses had been Consumed

by

by Fire, or void spaces, were some to the *Indians*, and some to the *Spaniards*, and free Leave was given by Proclamation, for every one to come in and Build, so that it was soon Rebuilt; but since the *Spaniards* have in a manner dispossessed the *Indians* of their part; for though many Live in the City, yet are they obliged to hire the Houses at dear Rates, that were formerly by Grant from the Court of *Spain*, their lawful Patrimonies, or Inheritance. The *Spaniards* Built their Houses in their own Fashion, and the *Indians* theirs according to the custom of the Countrey. *Cortez* Built his where King *Montezumas*'s stately Palace stood, which in the Siege had been consumed with Fire, and a vast number of Wild Beasts of all sorts that he kept there in Wooden Cages Burnt in it, lamentably roaring and howling as the Fire approached them; and this House is the most stately in the City, being the Seat of the Vice-Roy of all the Province, and is called the Palace of the *Marquess d' Valla*, for that Title the King of *Spain* conferred on *Cortez*, after he had obtained his amazing Victories, over such a mighty Nation, considering his Forces were but a handful of *Spaniards*; but that which seemed in all humane probability to give him success were the Bullets, and Chain-Shot, proceeding from his Thundring Artillery, for the *Indians* unacquainted with such Engines, took their roaring and breathing flame to be the Voice of the Angry Gods that fought against them, and when the Shot made Lanes among them, they took them for their Thunderbolts, or destroying Angels, sent as Messengers of their vengeance, to cut them off, not thinking any thing in nature could be of so violent a force, as to beat down Ranks of Men before them with such swiftness that the Eye could scarce trace the Deaths they gave. This, and the *Spaniards* Armour proof against their Arrows, made their Courage stoop and languish though otherways a Valiant people, as appears by their disputing it in

the

the City from Street to Street, and fortifying themselves with intrenchments as they Retreated, tho' by the Sword, Pestilence, and Famine, 10000 or more, lay Dead within the Walls. In this War *Montezuma* was Slain by his own Subjects, against their Wills, for being taken Prisoner, when multitudes of *Indians* assaulted the Palace, where *Cortez* and his *Spaniards* were, he was constrained to go to a Ballcony, or Battlement, to desire his Subjects to desist, and come to a Parley, when one of the inraged multitude not knowing him in the hurry, struck him with a sharp Flint on the Temples, which wounded him so much that he fell down, and soon after Died; yet at that time *Cortez* was forced to retire out of the City, to strengthen himself in *Flaxcallan*, and at his second time took it, by the help of the Vergantines, or Vessels he Besieged it with, on the side of the Lake, which stopping up all passage for Relief, Famine, and its attendant Pestilence, proved their worst Enemy, yet submitted they not, but disputed it, as I have said, till *Quahutimo C*———their New King, seeing things brought to the last extreamity, endeavouring to fly by way of the Lake, was surprized by the *Spanish* Vessels, and made Prisoner, at that time by *Cortez*'s perswasion (who would not give him his Wish to kill him, tho' he desired it,) Commanded his Men to lay down their Arms, and then about 60000 came out of their strength and submitted, have Lived a long time on the Flesh of the Slain; yet Famine notwithstanding had so pinched them, that they looked like the shadows of Men, Lean, Meager, and very Gastly.

Over again the Palace, they Built Arched Docks, to lay up the *Vergantines*, in perpetual memory of the notable Service they had done; but they are mostly wasted by Time; and other Vessels Trading on the Lake are in the wet Season laid up there. However this Great City is sometimes unhealthful, for as much as there arises at certain times

times a noyſom Vapour from the Lake, and at thoſe times the Winds blow little to purge the Air, becauſe of the Incloſure of Mountains. The *Spaniards* a long time ſtood on their Guard, after the taking of *Mexico*, the Citizens keeping 2000 Horſe and Arms, for Horſe-Men, always to be in a readineſs when the Trumpet ſhould ſound; but by what they have conſumed of the *Indians* in their Mines, and in working on the Lake, in making great Intrenchments, other Works, and particularly, by their Cruelty, they have ſo far exhauſted them, that thoſe Forces are laid aſide, and they live ſecure without fear of ſurprize; for the City lies open in moſt parts, and in all defenceleſs, except the ſtrength of the Inhabitants being deſtitute of Bullwarks and other conſiderable Fortifications, tho' an exceeding Rich City, and the Lading of 20 or more Ships are brought yearly to it, by the way of the North Sea, containing the beſt and Richeſt Commodities of *Spain*, and other parts of *Chriſtendom*, bought up by the *Spaniards* to this purpoſe, and from the South-Sea it Trafficks with *Perue*; it Trades alſo with ſeveral Eaſtern Nations, by way of the *Pilipinas*.

Money is daily Coined in the Mint to a great value, the Silver being brought on Mules from the Mines of St. *Lewis de Saccatecas*, about 80 Leagues more Northward, and beyond them the *Spaniards* by Conqueſt, and the voluntary ſubmiſſion of the Natives, have gained the poſſeſſion of very large Countries. There is in this City a Univerſity, which was formerly only a School. The Officers here are as in the great Cities of *Spain*, and it is Computed to have in the City and Suburbs 50000 Houſes, and to the latter, called *Guadalupe*, the *Indians* are moſtly confined. The *Spaniards* Styling themſelves abſolute Conquerors and Diſpoſers of their Perſons and Fortunes, being very proud and inſulting over them, a Conqueror among them being termed a Title of Honour, ſo that the moſt Beggarly among the *Spauiards*

Europe, Asia, Africa, and America. 205
iards will proudly boast to be descended from one of the first Conquerors, and Style himself a Don, though he has not one Foot of Land in Possession. There are many fair Gardens and Orchards about this City, with pleasant Summer-Fountains, and other things suitable for recreation in them.

The Buildings are with Stone and Brick, but not high, to prevent their being shaken, and overthrown by Earthquakes, that often happen in this Country. In the narrowest Streets 3 Coaches may go abrest, and in the broadest 6 ; They keep a vast number of Coaches here, some account them 15000. those of the Nobility and Gentry very stately, overlayed with Gold or Silver, and the Corners embolished with Precious Stone, Ivory, or Mother-pearl, the Lining and Seats are Cloth of Gold, Silver, or *East-India* Silks. The Shops are every where stored with Rich Merchandize, and by this you may guess at their Riches and dexterity in Workmanship. A Vice-Roy of *Mexico*, *Anno* 1625. sent the then King of *Spain* the representation of a Poppinsay, a Bird bigger than a Phesant of *Meltal*, and Precious Stones, so artificially placed, as to represent us several Colours, and all parts very lively, and it was estimated at half a Million of Duccats. In the Church belonging to the Cloyster of *Dominican*, is a Silver Lamp, curiously wrought, with 300 Branches, beside 100 little Lamps for Oyl set in it, each of different Workmanship, valued at 400000 Duccats, and with such like curious Works are the Streets made Rich and Beautiful from the Shops of Goldsmiths. The *Spanish* Women are here very Beautiful, and take a far greater liberty than allowed in *Spain*, in Gaming, Drinking, and making Visits ; nay, they will from their Windows, or Ballconies, invite Strangers as they pass the Streets, to play at Primera, and other Games, and such as accept the offer are plentifully Feasted with Wine, Sweet-meats,
and

and other Dainties, though this sometimes prove fatal, for the *Spaniards* though so far removed, have not altogether forgot the imbred Jealousie of their *Spanish* Ancestors, who brought it out of *Spain* with them: Many of the *Spaniards* Marry with the *Indian* Women, and beget a race called *Mollotos*, of a Tawney Complection; nor spare they to take away the *Indian*'s Wives, if they like them better than their own; they boast themselves to the poor credulous Natives to be the Valiantest and most Accomplish'd Men in the World, and that all Nations Tremble at the Name of a *Spaniard*, and by this, and other Artifices, they keep them in great awe and subjection, assuring them, that no Nation under Heaven is able to deliver them out of their Hands, or in Battel to stand before them.

As for the *Spaniards* Attire, the Fashion alters not here, but it is with the better sort excessive Rich, and the meanest will go as Fine as possible, though other Necessities crave the sparing of it. The best Silks, Damask, Cloath of Gold and Silver, Embroideries of Pearl and Precious Stones, are commonly worn amongst them; nay, among Trades-people, a Blackamoor, or Tawney Young Maid, will make a hard shift to be in the Fashion, with a Neck-Lace or Chain of Gold, Bracelets of Pearl, and Ear-bobs of large Pearl or Precious Stone; and though their Garments are very Rich, yet they overlay them with Gold, Silver-Lace, or Embroidery of Gold and Silver, and these sort of Wenches are allowed or wincked at to be Curtizans or Common Women, to satisfie the *Spaniards* Venery, to which they are insatiably given, and they have allways change of Apparel, especially for Summer and Winter, though the Winter here consists only in terrible Rains, and the overflowing of Lakes and Rivers, with innundations, occasioning many times the Destruction of Houses, People, and Cattel, and continues some Months. They are here very Superstitious

stitious, both *Spaniards* and *Indians*, for at the invitation of the Priests they make excessive Offerings to the Shrines of Saints, as Crowns of Gold, Bracelets, Precious Stones, Vessels of Silver and Gold, so that the Monasteries and Churches may well be said to enjoy the Profits and Pleasures of a Golden World; for their Revenues, or yearly Incomes, are more than in any part of *Europe*; nor do these Ecclesiasticks tie themselves to the strictness of the Rules of their Orders, but pass away the time in divers Recreations. They have pleasant Gardens, Fountains, Baths, Musick, and plenty of Provision to Excess, so that this exuberiance or super-abounding of this Country, has corrupted the Manners of the begging Friars, and rendred them as stately as petty Princes, particularly, their Superiors, who scarcely give place to any. Their Lodgings are stately, and the Roofs of their Cloysters and Churches adorned with Mosaick Work and Guildings of Gold; some Altars are of Massive Gold, others of Silver, Pillars of Brazil, and Marble of little esteem among them; and this Glorious shew of Pomp and Grandure draws the poor *Indians* to Admire and Adore them, though before their Heathen Temples were very Magnificent, but not comparable to these. They have Tabernacles of Gold and Silver, Christial, and other precious things to enshrine and carry the Host about in Procession; so that I may well say, the Riches of the greatest King or Potentate I have yet spoken of, may in some degree of Magnificence fall short of what I saw here, if I take the Clergy among the Laity.

In the Market-Place of this City, which is very Spacious, there are Arched Piazza's, and Shops furnished with Costly Wares, and before their Shops are all manner of curious Fruits Sold, that the Country affords; the Arches of the Vice-Roy's Palace, with the Walks of the House, and the Garden, belonging to it, takes up almost one side of the Market; at the end of it is the principal

pal Prison, strongly Built of Stone, and next it the Beautiful Street called *La Pateria*, or *the Goldsmiths-street*; where are to be seen the value of many Millions in Plate and Jewels. The Street of St. *Augustin* is very fair, where they Trade mostly in Silks. *Tabuca* is the longest and broadest, where mostly are Shops vending Iron-ware, Brass, and Steel, made into things fit for use and Service, and this is of very stately Building. In the Street *Del Aquilla*, the Houses of the Gentry are mostly seated. It is called so from an Eagle of Stone placed there, upon the Conquest of the City. There is a kind of a Park, or void place, shaded with Trees, where the Gallants and Ladies with their Trains and Equipages air themselves in the Evening, and here much mischief is done by quarrels, upon the account of Jealousie in Courtship, and hundreds of Swords at a time have been drawn, to Revenge or rescue a Revenger, and carry him off to Sanctuary, where being once Lodged, he is out of the power of the Law; yet after all, the Lake at present much undermines the City, for that the Springs permit but of few Cellars; in laying in Dead Bodies the Coffins are half covered with Water, and many of the stately Buildings sink, so that they are forced often to repair their Foundations, by laying new ones on the old, that seem as it were to be swallowed up in a quick-sand.

This City has but 3 ways to come into it by Causey, the one is from the West, and that is a Mile and half long; another from the North, containing 3 Miles; on the East there is no entrance by Land, but on the South the Causey is 5 Miles in length, and by this last way *Cortez* entred when he made his Conquest of it.

About this City, as well as in other places, are divers kinds of delicate Fruits, as the Nuchili of divers Colours, a Fruit which eaten, stains like Black-Cherries, and colours the Urine as red as Blood, so that Strangers unacquainted with its quality,

quality, really fancy they void Blood; this put the *Spaniards* into great frights at their firſt coming, and their Phyſicians being ignorant of the Operation applied Remedies to ſtanch Blood, till the *Indians* gave them to underſtand better; the skin of them are thick, and full of ſmall prickles, which touching the Lips ſtick in them, and make them for a time ſtick together, ſo that the Voice will faulter, but this skin is eaſily pealed off, and then the Fruit appears of a Scarlet Red. There are alſo Apples, Pears, Quinces, Pomegranets, Musk-mellions, Cheſs-Nuts, Wall-Nuts, Figs, Lemons, Oranges, Citron, and abundance of other Fruits, known in *Europe*. But one Tree more Admirable than the reſt, not known amongſt us, the Metel, which they Plant and dreſs as they do their Vines. It hath near 40 kinds of Leaves growing on it, which ſerve for divers uſes; for, when very tender, they make Conſerves of them, when more grown, Paper, Flax, Mantles, Shoes, Mats, Girdles, and Cordage; on other Leaves grow Prickles ſo ſtrong, that placing them in Frames of Wood they make ſaws of them; from the Root there cometh a Juice like unto Syrrup, which by heat is made into Sugar; they make of it alſo Vinegar, and a ſort of Wine, that ſtupifies the *Indians* to Drunkenneſs. The Rhin'd roaſted heals Sores and Ulcers, applying Poltiſces to them; and from the uppermoſt Branches diſtills a Gum, which diſſolved in Wine, Antidotes Poyſon: And to conclude with this City, there is nothing in or about it wanting, to make it happy; but the Temper of the people, who are reſtleſs, in a Countrey flowing with all Delights Nature or Art can afford them in any degree.

P   CHAP.

CHAP. XXIV.

Travels into divers other parts of the **Mexican** *Province, describing the particulars that are Curious, and worthy of Note ; As also in the* **Peruanian** *Province, as well Islands, as Continent; and all that is Rare and Remarkably found in* **America.**

HAving thus Travelled to *Mexico*, and described it as particularly as Prospect and Enquiry could inform me ; I now undertake briefly to do the like of the Country of *Americas*, as far as it is yet known to the *Europeans*, or *Indians*, I conversed with those parts.

The chief Division therefore of this great part of the World is two fold, *viz*. the *Mexicanian*, and *Peruanian* Provinces. *Mexico* gives name to the greater half of *America*, and is called *Nova Hispania*, or *New Spain*, from whence the Kings of *Spain* Style themselves *Hisaniour Reges*. The *Mexican* Track containeth chiefly the Northern Parts, comprehending many large Provinces, or Countries, already known, and many not yet well discovered, as the parts that lie between it to the Northern or Frozen-Sea, *viz*. *Mexico*, *Quivira*, *Nicaragna*, *Jucatan*, *Flerida virgina*, *Norumbega*, *Nova*, *Francia*, *Corteralis*, *Estoliland*, and some others, so that the Compass of this part already known is at least 23000 Miles.

The *Peruanan* part contains all the Southern Track, tied to the *Mexican* by the *Isthmus*, or
streight

Europe, Asia, Africa, *and* America 211

streight of *Darien*, being between 12 and 17 Miles over in some parts, from the Northern to the Southern Sea. This part contains the Provinces, or Kingdoms, of *Castella*, *Aurea*, *Gunia*, *Peru*, *Brasil*, *Chille*, in compass about 17000 Miles.

Mexico, as I observed, abounds with Gold sanded Rivers, producing many devouring Crocadils, tho' not so big as those in the *Nile* in *Ægypt*, which the poorer sort of the *Indians* take and feed on their Flesh, as a great dainty. There are several Mountains casting fourth Flames of Fire in it, as *Pepochampeche*, *Popocatapec*, and others, nay, all the *Southern* parts, as far as *Leon* in *Nicaragua* produces many of them, but the latter I have named, is one of the chief; it stands 8 Leagues from *Chollola*, it is a steep rockey Mountain. Ten *Spaniards* attended with *Indians* to carry their Water and Victuals, undertook to take a Survey of it, and approached so near the top, that they heard a terrible noise, occasioned by the Erruption of Fire; then the ground shaked so terribly, that they durst not approach no nearer, however, they perceived the Vulcan or Cavety whence the Fire Issued half a League in compass out, which Air and Fire proceeded, rebounding with a terrible Noise, Shrill and Whistling, so that the whole Hill trembled, and the top near this Mouth was covered with Ashes, about knee-deep, and as they were viewing it, such a shower of Fire fell, that had they not stept under the craggy over-hanging of a Rock, they had there been roasted to Death; but in an hour or two, it clearing up, they hasted down much affrighted, but without any harm: This Mountain before the coming of *Hernando Cartez*, had for ten Years dissisted sending forth Flames, and when it began again according to a prediction among them, the *Indians* looked for some great misery to befall them by change of Government. The Ashes blown in the Air, are many times scattered 10 Leagues from the foot of the Mountain.

Travels and Voyages in

This chief Province, called *Mexico*, is further divided into six Parts, viz. *Themiſtian, Nova-gallicia, Mechoacan* and *Gauſtachan*; the firſt is the nobleſt and greateſt, containing ſix Cities, of which the principal is the rich City of *Mexico*, the Seats of an Archbiſhop and *Spaniſh* Viceroy; the next is *la Richla de los Angeles*; the third *Vellazuca*; the fourth *Antiquera*; the fifth *Mexcioca*; the ſixth *Ottopan*, beſides theſe there are a great number of Villages, or large unwalled Towns on the Roads and Borders of Rivers and Lakes, inhabited by *Indians, Spaniards,* and *Meſtizoes,* a mixed Generation of *Indians* and *Spaniards.*

Near *Mexico*, is *Tacuba*, a pleaſant Town incloſed with Gardens; in the way to *Chapultepec,* is *Taluco,* a Town much traded to, and in the Woods breed Hogs, producing Bacon as good as our Weſtphalia. Travelling *Weſtward*, the Town of *la Piedad* preſents it ſelf at the end of a Cauſey, whether the People much reſort from *Mexico,* to pay Adoration to the Image of the Virgin *Mary,* inriched with Crowns, Chains of Gold, and precious Stones, valued at a Million of Duccats. There is a pleaſant Town bending to the *North*, called, *la Soledad,* or the *Solitary Wildernefs,* where the Bare-footed *Carmelite* Friars have their Reſidence; but if this be a Wildernels, few places can be accounted pleaſant, for it affords Fruits, Flowers, Shades. Fountains, and every thing that can delight Mankind. And heither reſort the Nobles and Gentry to take their Pleaſure, who bring great Preſents to the Friars, ſo that they live Fat and Plentiful on the outward appearance of Sanctity; for in their Oratory, and Cells made in Rocks, they hang Whips of Wyer, Girdles with ſharp pricking Needles to wear next their Skin, ſhirts of Hair, and other mortifying Materials; but one of them ingeniouſly told me, they were placed there more for ſhew, than uſe, to move Peoples Charity towards them, and brought them a vaſt income of Money, and all ſorts of Proviſions; and indeed though they have out of a deſign given this place

Europe, Asia, Africa *and* America. 213

place the name of a Wilderness, it seemed to me an Earthly Paradise. At *Tadubaya*, not much distance from this place, is a very rich Cloister of *Franciscans*, with curious Gardens and Orchards belonging to it; they have a stately Church there, and the *Indians* have been taught by the Priests to be Choiristers, and sing very fine.

I have spoken somewhat already of the Province of *Guaftachan*, which I passed in my Travels from St. *John de Ulhua*, to *Mexico*. It is a very plentiful Country, abounding in Sugar, farms Pasture, Corn, Cochinil, reaching as far as the Valley of *Guaxaca*, a very rich place, but having spoke of the most material Towns in my Passage, I shall pass to the third Province, called *Mechoacan*, which is about 80 Leagues in circumference. This Province is very rich, abounding in Mulberry-trees, which feed a great number of Silk-worms; also in Wax, Honey, Black Amber, divers coloured Feathers, of which they make curious Works, and the River abound with store of Fish. The chief City of this Province is *Valodolid*, a Bishop's See; the Towns of Note are *Sinfonte*, which before the Conquest, was the Residence of the *Indian* King of the Province *Pafcuar* and *Coliman*, inhabited by *Spaniards* and *Indians*. There are also two good Havens, called St. *Anthony* and St. *James*, or *Santiago*; the King of it, called *Caconzin*, was a great Friend to *Cortez*, and much assisted him in his Wars against the *Mexicons*, willingly yielding himself a Vassal to the King of *Spain*, though it was ill requited; for *don Nunio de Guzman*, first Ruler and President of the Chancery of *Mexico*, after the Conquest picked a Quarrel, and made War on this Province, took the King Prisoner, who was quiet and peaceable, not stiring against him; and when he had stript him out of 10000 Marks in Plate, Gold, and other Riches, he inhumanly burnt him at a Stake, with divers of his Nobles and Gentry, who seemed to rejoyce that they were accounted worthy to suffer with their King, and in Death bear him Company into the other World.

Nova

Nova Galia, or the fourth Province of *Mexico*, is well watered with two large Rivers, *viz*. *Piaſtle* and *Sanſebaſtian*; it contains many great Towns of *Spaniards* and *Indians*; the chief is *Xaliſco*; the next *Guadalajara*; the third *Coaza*; the fourth *Corupoſtalla*; the fifth *St. Eſpirit*; the ſixth *Capala*, now called *Nova Mexico*, a Frontier on the *Northern Indians*, from whence the *Spaniards* frequently make Inroads and War upon them, and much incroach that way, to the great Waſt and Deſtruction of thoſe poor People, who would live in quiet, and do good Offices to the *Spaniards*, if they might be permitted; but their thirſt after the Mines of Gold and Silver, they ſuppoſe to be in that Country, and not yet diſcovered, is the main incitement that makes them puſh their Swords ſo violently that way, though they often meet with their Match; for theſe naked People are very Warlike, and in their flights after a Diſcharge of their Vollies of Poiſon Arrows, chamber up and run upon the Rocks like Wild Goats; their dwellings are for the moſt part in the Woods, where they make Swamps, and fortified places of Timber and other Materials, rudely piled and faſtned one to another, and that which incites the *Spaniards* ſo eagarly, to poſſeſs themſelves by Conqueſts of theſe *Northern* parts, beſides the Treaſure they find in them, is, out of Miſtruſt or Jealouſie, leaſt the *Engliſh* from *Virginia*, and other Collonies, ſhould be induſtrious in ſubduing and ſteping in before them.

Thus having briefly run over the chief *Mexicon* Provinces, under the *Spaniſh* Dominion, I now proceed to take a Survey of ſome others, and in the firſt place, of *Quivira*, ſeated in the moſt *Weſtern* part of *America*, over againſt *Tartary*, from whence not being much diſtant, many ſuppoſe that this new World was firſt inhabited from thence; for the *Indians* in their Manners, Likeneſs, and many Cuſtoms among them, much accord with the *Tartars*, they make their Cattle their chief Riches, feeding them in the Plains, Valleys and Mountains, the Country affording

Europe, Afia, Africa, *and* America. 215
affording every where ftore of Pafture, and thofe that look after the Cattle, carry Tents with them for fhelter, and drefs their Food in the Fields as the *Tartars*. This, and the *Southern* parts of *America*, appears to be far better Peopled than that towards *Europe*, fo that though it is but a conjecture, yet it is a very probable one, that the firft peopling this Country, was from *Afia*, either accidentally by Ship-wrack, or driven out of their Country by Famine, War, or fuch Calamities; they were conftrained to feek new Habitations, and fo after much wandering at Sea, found out this Country, though the *Indians* have a tradition, which is a received Opinion amongft many of them, that their God with Blazing Fires, lighted and guided them Day and Night, over the *Northern* Rocks and Mountains, covered with Ice and Snow, feeding and cherifhing them by the way with Pulfe and other Food, when they had been oppreffed by Gyant-like Enemies, and driven out of their former Habitations. The Inhabitants of thefe parts take a greater pride in Glafs Beads, and other Trifles, than in Gold and Jewels, and are eafily impofed on for the Exchange of the Hides of their Cattle; they make Coverings for their homely Cottages; of their Bones they make Bodkins and Needles; of their Hair, Thread; of their Sinue, Cordage; of their Blood, Drink; and of their Flefh, Meat; of their Horns, Paunches, and Bladders, Veffels: Some are of Opinion, that there is a Traffick on this Coaft from *China*, or *Cathagina*, from whence *Vafquez de Corovado* made a Progrefs into fome parts of it, with his Army of *Spaniards*, which he faw from the Rocks, and high Mountains, on the Sea Coaft, Ships at Sea, not of common Building, feeming to be well laden, and bearing in their Prows *Pillicans*, which could not be conjectured to come from any Country, but one of the two before named.

In *Quivira*, there are but two Provinces that are well known to the *Europeans*, and thofe are *Cibola* and *Nova Albion Cibola Lys* on the *Eaft*, where a

P 4 City

City gives that Name to the Province; the next to it is called *Tolontua*, a pleasant place in a very temperate Air, Scituated on a River of that Name; the third Town that offers is *Tinguez*, inhabited by *Spaniards*, and in it, the Jesuits have a stately College, and are appointed to Preach to the *Indians* in those parts.

Nova Albion, lies on the *West* side towards *Tartary*, this was discovered in the Reign of Queen *Elizabeth*, by the Renowned *Englishman* Sir *Francis Drake*, who gave it this Name upon the King of the Countries Surrendering his Crown of Network and Feathers, curiously wrought, and submitting himself and people to the Queen's Protection. It is in some parts inhabited by a few *Spaniards*, but not yielding any considerable store of Riches, they have not much coveted to People 'it, though it abounds with Fruit pleasant to the Eye and Taft. The People are very Curteous and Affable to Strangers, but mostly given to their old Idolatry, practising Charms; and some affirm they dance with the Devil on certain mid-night Feasts, and revels, offering him human Sacrifice. The Bounds between this *Quivira* and *Mexico*, is *Marvir Miglio*, or *Californio*.

The next belonging to *Mexico* in the *Northern* Tract, is *Jucalan*, the first that Discovered it by *Francisco Hernandez de Cordovo*, Anno 1517. who asking an *Indian* the name of that Country, and he not understanding the *Spanish*, answer *Jucatan*, which in the *Indian* Language, is, *What do you say*, and from thence they named it, and so it has ever since been called. This Country is at least 900 Miles in Circuit, and a kind of a Peninsula. It is fixed over against the Island of *Cuba*, and divided into three parts; *Jucatan* properly so called, which has in it the Cities of *Campeche*, *Valadolid*, *Merida*, *Semancus*, and one which for its Greatness and Beauty, they call *Caire* the chief; the Commodities here are Honey, Wax, Hides and Sugar, Cana, Fistula, Sarsaparila, &c. As for Food, it produces great
store

Europe, Asia, Africa, *and* America.   217

store of *Indian Maize*, and is well Watered and Wooded in all parts; the Timber is so good, that the *Spaniards* Build Tall-Ships there; they have store of Turkeys, and other Fowl, which with other Commodities, they pay as Tribute to the *Spaniards* for their Possessions, who keep them low and poor, which makes them apt to fall into Mutinies and Rebellions.

Another part of this Track is called, *Guatemala*, where the Cruelty of the *Spaniards* has destroyed near a Million of the Natives; yet this Country is populous, and has many flourishing *Indian* Towns in it. The chief Cities are *Guatemala*, *Caffuca* and *Chiapa*; it is well Watered with Rivers, and has some large Lakes full of Fish, and at Seasons, covered with wild Fowl; it abounds in Fruit, Corn and Cattle.

The third part of *Jucatan* is *Acafamil*, an Island over against *Guatemala*, which the *Spaniards* usually at this day call, *Sta Cruz*; it lies advantageous for a Harbour, and the advantage of Trade.

The fourth Division of the Northern Track under the Government of the *Spaniards*, is *Nicaragua*, standing South East from the City of *Mexico*, about 450 Leagues; yet it agrees with it in the Temperature of the Climate, the People are of good Stature, active and strong, and of Complexion indifferent White. Before they were brought under subjection, they had standing Laws, and many politicks in their Government, particularly, if one robbed an other, he was not put to Death, but became his slave till his service had made Satisfaction for the Damage done; they had no Law for the Murther of a King, as concluding none would be so wicked as to act such Villany. This Country gives a pleasant prospect, and abounds in all things necessary for human support; here grows the famous Tree so much Written of, which if a man touch but one of the Branches with his Finger, it presently whithers: There are great Flocks of Parrots, as of Crows or Pigeons in *England*; also Turkeys, Quailes, Rabbits

bits. The Spanish Cities here have a Bishop's See, and *Granada* standing on a Lake of fresh Water, about 300 miles in compass, which continually Ebbs, and Flows, though it has no intercourse with the Ocean.

And thus much, having thought fit to speak of the *Mexicon* Provinces, and the Dominion of *Spain*, wherein I mostly Travelled, I now come to speak in their Order of the *Peruanian* parts, for richness in Gold and other Mettals.

This principally contains 5 large Countries, as I have already hinted. This Southern part of *India* is held to be Richer than the Northern, for although it wants the conveniency of Traffick by the Northern Sea, which the other has, and is therefore obliged to send its Commodities to *Pannama*, and from thence have them Transported over the Streight, or Isthmus, by the River *Chiagree*, to *Portabel*, upon the North-Sea, yet the great store of Gold, Silver, and other Mettal, make richly amends for their pains and Travel, and such store is found, that a Prohibition or Injunction is laid by the Court of *Spain*, not to open new Mines, till the old ones are sufficiently wrought; the huge Mountains of *Potosi* are thought to consist mostly of Gold-oar, and here grow all such Fruits as are found in *Spain*, beside many others natural to the Country; the Olives are larger than those of *Spain*, the Oyl sweeter and clearer, the Grapes yield Wine stronger than *Spanish* Wine, and here they have more Liberty than in *Mexico* to make it, because it cannot be so well brought from *Spain*; they have store of Wheat and other Grain, the Soil all lying under the high Mineral Mountains, being very Fruitful, the Water that defcends fatning the Valleys, for there is but little Rain, and the Evening and Morning Dews give great refreshment. The Vice-Roy has his Residence in the City of *Lima*, a place much subject to Earthquakes, and of late has been terribly shaken, and almost destroyed by 'em; there

is

is held a Court of Chancery, and it is an Arch-Bishop's See. It is well fortified since the *Bucaniers* have made so many Depradations and Pyracies on the Coast; two Miles from it is a convenient Harbour or Port, called *Callau*, where the Ships lie that convey the Treasure to *Panama*, and other Ships that Trade to divers parts, and beside *Casteella Aura*, or *Golden Casteel*. *Chille* is very Rich in Golden Mines, which has caused an obstinate War between the *Spaniards* and *Indians* that Inhabit it, who are very hardy, and dextrous at Fire-Arms, most part of them being the Sons of *Spanish* Women by *Indians*, so that a great many of the best Soldiers out of the *Neatherlands* and *Italy* have been sent thither under an Experienced Captain, who has the Command, as a Recompence for his Service in *Europe*. The *Spaniards* by their Wars have got strong footing, and are possessed of 3 principal Cities, beside many Towns of Note, as the *Conception*, which is a Bishop's See, *Santjago*, and *Valdivia*, this latter, took its Name from a Governor so called, whose thirst of Gold through Covetousness to grow Rich on a sudden, in using great Oppression, made the *Indians* of *Chille* break out into a Bloody War, and surprizing him in his House, poured melted Gold down his Throat, saying, *Since he had so eargerly coveted it, he should have his fill of it, and so much of it as should last him all his Life-time*; and accordingly it did, for the scalding Mettal presently killed him, but the War ended not with his Death, but has at times continued ever since.

As for *Guiana* and *Brasil*, the latter belonging to the Crown of *Portugal*, and States of *Holland*, by reason of their remoatness I had not an opportunity to Travel there, and since I can speak little of them, than what I have from Report, *viz.* that they are Rich, and Flourishing Provinces; I shall pass them over, and return again to *Castella Aure*, in the Southern or *Peruanian* Track. This containeth the North part of *Peru*, and

part

part of the Isthmus, that runneth between the North and South-Sea, and beside the Gold in it, it is plentifully stored with Silver, Pearl, Spices, Medicinal Herbs, and Drugs; it is divided into 4 Provinces, the first is called *Castella del oro*, the second, *Nova Andaluzia*, the third, *Nova Granada*, the fourth, *Carthagena Castella del oro*; is Situate in the very Isthmus, and not over peopled, by reason of the unhealthful Air, occasioned by the noysom Vapours arising from large standing Lakes, or Pools; the chief places here belonging to the *Spaniards* are *Theomimay*, or *Nombre de Dias*, on the East; the second, which lies 6 Leagues from *Nombre de Dios*, is *Portabel*, chiefly Inhabited by *Spaniards*, *Mulottos*, and *Blackamoors*; this latter, has a very fair and goodly Haven, from whence it seems to derive its Name, well fortified at the Entrance with 3 Castles, where the Guns reach and Command one another; in these places *Drake* braved the *Spaniards*, and did Exploits worthy the Fame of his Countrey. *Nombre de Dios* (so called by *Didacus Niquesa*, who after many crosses at Sea, first Landed here, Founding this and *Portobel*,) is now in a manner forsaken, by reason of the little Commodiousness or Security of the Harbour, lying open to the insults of Pyrates, and more for the unhealthfulness of the Air coming off the Sea, and some Lakes near it, so that it was once removed, by an Order from the Court of *Spain*, in hopes that the Air might become more healthful in placing it some little distance from the Sea, but it little availed.

 In this part of the *Indies* it was, that our Valiant, tho' Unfortunate Country-Man, *John Oxenham*, Arriving with about 60 Companions, drew ashore his Ship, covered it with Boughs, and passing over Land cut down Timber in the Woods, of which, he made a Pinnace, and Navigating the South-Sea, took several *Spanish* Prizes, richly Laden with Gold and Silver, and safely recovered the main Land; but there by the Mutiny of his
Company

Europe, Asia, Africa, *and* America. 221

Company, about sharing the Booty, all miscarried, for they gave the *Spaniards* time to set upon, and cut several of them off, among whom he fell, Courageously Fighting; and so the Riches, to the Value of a Million of Duccats, which might have plentifully satisfied them all, was lost by their division among themselves.

Nova Andeluza, has for its principal City *Tocoio*, by the *Spaniards*, new Named St. *Margrets*, and an other little inferiour to it, called St. *Espiritu*, both Rich in Trade, and the Country throughout gives a good Prospect of Plenty and Pleasure. *Nova Granada*, is Situate on the South-side of *Carthagena*. It contains 6 principal Cities, *viz.* *Tungua*, supposed to be directly under the *Æquator*; *Tochamum Popaian*, a very Rich Trading City; *Sta fee*, or St. *Faiths*, an Arch-Bishop's See, and a Court of Justice and Chancery, Governed by a President, 6 Judges, the King's Attorney, and two High Justices of Court, who have allowed them out of the King's Treasury 6000 Duccats a Year. *Palama* and *Merida*, and through this Country of *Granada*, lieth the Road way to *Lima*, all by Land. It is strong, by reason of its Situation, much among stony Crags or Rocks, which environ it, and through which there are very narrow passages, yet is it full of pleasant Valleys, which yield much Fruit, Corn, and *Indian* Maize; it affords Silver Mines, and many Golden Sand Rivers.

Carthagena, the last Province of *Castella Aurea*, is of a very Fruitful Soyl, but not without some evil quality; for it produces a Tree that grasped by the Hand proves a rank Poyson, and the party hardly escapes without loss of Life, or Member; the Chief City is *Carthagena*, Surprized and Plundered by *Drake*, Anno 1585. who, beside a Rich Booty, carried from thence 230 pieces of Ordinance. It is now reasonably well Fortified, tho' not so strong as *Portobel*; the City is Fair and very Rich, by reason of the great quantity of Pearl brought thither from *Margarita*, and the King's

Revenue,

Revenue, which for all *Nova Granada*, are sent to this place; it is a Bishop's See, and in it are many Stately Churches and Cloysters, adorned with Riches; to this City likewise comes yearly small Vessels, Laden with Indico, Cochinele, and Sugar, made and had in the Country of *Guatemala*; the *Spaniards* thinking it safer to Ship their Goods in those little Vessels on the Lake of *Granada*, in *Nicaragua*, and from thence to send them hither, to be Shipped in the Galeons, that come from *Portobel*, with the Treasure of *Peru*, than to send them by *Honduras*, in which way, they have become a Prey to other Nations. The City next in Rank, is *Abuida*; the next, *Sta Martha*, Inhabited by *Spaniards*, who are very Rich; it is Seated on the River *Abuida*, otherwise named St. *John*; and *Rio di Grand Venezuel*, and New *Cales*, in this Track, are Towns of considerable Note, Rich, and Populous; and these three Provinces, viz. *Andaluzia Nova*, *Nova Grana*, and *Carthagena*, the *Spaniards* term it their *Terafirma*; for that from the North, they are the strength of *Peru*, and the basis of this Reverse *Pyramis*.

There are yet many Rich Islands under the *Spanish* Power, as that of *Margarita*, Situate in the Sea, near *Castella Aurea*, called the *Jewel-Island*, from the great quantity of Pearl and Precious Stones found about it. It is true, it is but poor in Fruit-Trees, Corn, and Herbage, having scarcely any upon it; the Water is likewise scarce, as is any thing good or pleasant, so that the Inhabitants in the hot-seasons will exchange a Tun of Wine for as much curious Cool Spring-Water; but the Jewels got there make large amends, by greatly enriching the People, so that there are many Rich Merchants, who have 30, 40, or 50, *Blackamoor* Slaves, kept purposely to dive for Pearls, and other Precious things. These are let down in Baskets, and feel about the Rocks and places where they suspect they are, and will stay under Water a Quarter of an Hour, and when their

their Breath begins to fail, they give the Sign, by pulling a Rope to those on the surface in their Boats, to draw them up with such things as they have rifled the Ocean of; and their Masters are obliged to Feast and make much of them, least out of a sullen humour they should under Water be careless of so weighty a business, where they cannot see them act, nor give them directions; for the *Spaniards*, though they love the Profit, are themselves averse to the fatigue and hazard in procuring it; for many times these poor Divers are drawn up with a Leg or an Arm off, and sometimes taken quite away by some devouring Sea-Monstrous Fish; at other times when they Dive without a Basket or Rope, they are sucked by the Water under the hollow caveties of the Rock, whence they cannot with all their strugling disentangle themselves, but there unavoidably perish. From this Island, the Pearls are sent to be dressed and bored at *Carthagena*; where is a Fair Street, of no other Shops than Pearl-dressers. Commonly in the Month of *June*, there is a Ship or two ready in this Island to carry the King's Revenue, and Merchant's Pearls thither; and one of their Cargoes is seldom valued at less than three or fourscore Thousand Duccats, which sometimes falls into the Hands of Free-Booters.

Cuba, is an other Island, 300 Miles in length, and 70 broad, found out by *Columbus*, in his second Navigation to these Coasts; it is full of Woods, Lakes, Rivers and Mountains, the Air Temperate, the Soil very Fruitful. It produces Brass of exact perfection, and some Gold, though not so fine as in other parts. It abounds with Ginger, Cassia, Mastick, Aloes, some Cinnamon, Canafistula, Sarsaparilla and Sugar, great store of Fish, Fowls, and other Flesh; so that the ships on their return to *Spain*, take in much Provision here. The chief Cities are St. *Jago* on the Northern Shoar, but *James de Valasco* is a Bishop's See. *Havana*, which is also seated on the Northern Shoar, and is a very commodious Haven for Shiping, so strongly Fortified, that the *Spaniards* term it the Key of *America*, to lock up the Door or Entrance; here usually Rideth the King of *Spain*'s Navy, and in this Port meet all the Merchants Ships from several Ports and Havens in Islands or Continent, and commonly in the Month of *September*, joyn all the Treasure, as I may say, of *America*, all the King of *Spain*'s Revenues, with as much more of Merchants Goods, which is often worth 30 Millions: It has two strong Castles, one at the point of the Haven, where the Enterance lies towards the Sea, and the other on the other side within, almost over against it, and by reason the passage of the Entrance is so narrow, that not above one great Ship at a time can sail in; these Castles admirably defend it, or may well do it against a strong Naval Force. I took a view of these Castles, and found them very strong and regular; there are besides others, 12 pieces of great Brass Ordinance, called by the Names of the 12 Apostles, yet the Dutch, and other Nations, have sometimes insulted them in the Mouth of this Haven, and taken considerable Prizes within sight and reach of the Castle Guns; and in the Year 1629. they took no less than 7 Millions, most of it the King of Spain's Treasure going for *Cales*, and from one Friar, they took a Cabinet of Gold Chains, Pearl, and pretious Stones, worth 40000 Duccats, and forced the Galleons on shoar, in a River near the Port, which Miscarriage being laid to the charge of *Don Juan de Guzman Y Torres*, the Admiral, at his return to *Spain*, he was Imprisoned, and soon after lost his Head.

The next that presented was another Island, much greater than any I have yet mentioned, now called *Hispaniola*, anciently by the Natives *Hatie*. It is in compass 1500 Miles, the Air very Temperate, Soil fertil, and has in it several rich Mines; there is a considerable Town from the Neighbouring Coasts, for this Island produces Amber, Ginger, Sugar, Hides, Wax, and many other Commodities;

ties; the Gold is here very fine, and the Sugar-Canes larger than in other places, so that one of them will fill 20, and sometimes 30 Measures. The Corn usually yields a Hundred Fold, the whole Island being Fertilized by 4 great Rivers proceeding from a huge Mountain standing in the Center, viz. *Juna* running to the East, *Artihinnacus* to the West, *Jacchius* to the North, and *Naibus* to the South. The Woods are vast, and breed abundance of wild Swine, whose Flesh is a great Dainty, yet the Country in many places is but thinly inhabited, because the *Spaniards* on their first possessing it, destroyed about 3 Millions of the Natives.

The chief City is St. *Domingo*, where there is a President and Court of Chancery, with six Judges, and other proper Officers. It is likewise the See of an Archbishop, who, though he possesses not so great a Revenue as the Archbishops of *Mexico* and *Lima*, yet his Honour exceeds them, for he is Primate of all the *Indies*: This Island having been conquered, and settled, it bares Precedency by Antiquity; there are other rich trading Cities and Towns, as St. *Thomas*, St. *Isabella*, St. *John Maragna* and *Porto*, where the Merchants Trade much, and are very Wealthy.

America, is at this time so called from *Americus Vespusius*, who claimed the Honour of naming it, tho' *Columbus* first discovered it, as has been already hinted. There are in all the *Spanish Indies* (for other Nations possess large Territories, as well as they, where at present, my Travels lay not, and therefore I shall not undertake now to describe them) four Archbishops, viz. of *Mexico*, *Lima*, St. *Domingo* and St. *Fee*, and about 30 Bishops subordinate to them; the publick Administration of Justice is Principally committed to the two Vice-Roys of *Peru* and *Mexico*, the former residing at *Lima*, and the latter at the City of *Mexico*, and with subordination to other Presidents, Governours, and chief Justices, except the President of *Guatemala*, and St. *Domingo*, who are accountable only to the Council of *Spain*.

CHAP. XXV.

The Nature, Superstition, Manner, Customs, Labour, Diet and Observations of the Indians *in particular, and in General of the* Spaniards; *shewing the Tyranny of the Latter over the former, and many other things worthy of curious Remarks, with my Return for* England *by the way of* Spain, *and other matters.*

THus having taken a Survey, and discribed the greater Inhabited part of the new World (as many term it, which Nature had so long reserved from our Knowledge, as her private Tireing-room, that being decked in all her Beauties, and Golden Ornaments, she might at length appear more glorious than at first;) pursuing my Method, I now in the close come to speak more particularly of the Inhabitants, and chiefly of the Indians, for the Humour, Customs and Religion of the Spaniards, which vary little in this distant Region, are already sufficiently known to Europeans.

The Indians are Vassals to the Spaniards, and for the most part little better than Slaves, to be at their Beck, and fulfill their imperious desires with
the

the labour of their Bodies, and the little Wealth they can scrape together, for though in the Towns alloted them, where they are in any Number, they are allowed Officers of their own, yet they dare act little without the concurrence of the Spanish Magistrates, even among their own Tribes; and to keep their courage low, they are deprived of offensive Weapons, and great Penalties laid on such, where, upon search, they shall be found. The Friars and other Ecclesiasticks, command their service for nothing, having a certain number allowed at the publick charge of other Indians to do their Drudgery, as fetching Water, Wood, Fishing for them, Tilling and Sowing their Ground, and the Seculars allow them but half a Ryal a day, though they compel them to leave their own Land untilled, leaving their Families to come many Miles to serve their turns; and to this, they are pressed to severe Penalties, being inflicting on the Refuser for a set number of days, as shall be required, and many times these poor Wretches leave their Wives and Children starving at Home in the mean time; and when they have done their Work, they are sent away with little or nothing, except sometimes Threats and Cudggeling, if they dare dispute it, or so much as murmur at what is said to them, or else turned over to an other that will give the Spaniard any allowance for their Labour, according to the first, or standing Agreement, though the work be never so hard, or above their strength; though indeed, they are mostly of very strong Bodies, and well proportioned in their Limbs, and would be far more industrious than they are, had they any tolerable Incouragement. But seeing their Lives and Estates are at the mercy of the Conquerors, few, considering their vast Number, strive to encrease Riches, but content themselves with a supply of ordinary Food and Rayment, going mostly Bare-footed in all Seasons, and any Passenger travelling the Road, may require an Officer to furnish him with an

Indian

Indian or *Moor*, to guide his Mules, and carry heavey Trunks; and after they cavel with them at the Journeys end, for some pretended neglect, and send them back with Blows instead of the promised Reward of their labour. If they refuse to Work when ordered, or run away when Hired, they are sought out by the Officers, and publickly Whipt in the Market place; this, and more severe Usuage, than I think fit to name, least it should not be credited amongst compassionate Christians, makes many of them weary of their Lives; so that coming Home from these Labours and Abuses, they have refused to Eat, and voluntarily pined themselves to Death, notwithstanding the Tears and Perswasion, of their Wives and Friends, to incite them to a patient bareing of the Sufferings, and live.

As for their Religion, some in the remoter parts are still Heathen Idolaters, paying Adorarion as covertly, as they can the imaginary God's of their Ancesters, and lay a great stress on their Protection, as Fire, Air, the Sun, Moon, and other things by several Names; for anciently they Worshiped a great number of Gods, and had stately Temples Erected to them, sacrificing Human Flesh and Blood on their Altars, either of Prisoners taken in War with one another, or such as voluntarily offered themselves, or were chosen by Lot: The Names of their several Idols, and manner of their Antient Worship, not being proper to my Subject, but rather for a History, I shall pass them over: however at present, they have a kind of publick Esteem, or a kind of Veneration for certain Beasts, which they make exceeding much of, and cherish as their Gaurdians or Titulars, though they profess the Romish Religion, as the Priests have incerted it unto them; and one thing I took special Notice off, that they were more Admirers of the Pictures of those Saints, that have Pictures of Beasts painted by them, as St. *Mark*, with a Lyon, St. *Luke*,

Luke, with a Bull, St. *Dominick*, with a Dog, and a flaming Torch in his Mouth, &c. then of those that are without such Emblems, confessing that they like them the better, and comply with the Devotion payed to them, because it agreed with the Worship of their Ancestors. Those that are able, are very careful to buy the Picture of one Saint or other, as their fancy leads them, and give the Priest Money to have a place for it in the Church; and by this a great deal of Money is screwed out of them, for from that time the Priest stiles the Party, the Patron of that Saint, and he is obliged to bring Offerings, and leave before him, especially on his Day, very considerable, which being left, the Priest sweeps away, and Converts it to his own use, selling then the Wax Candles they offer many times over and over, which, with other things, brings a great Income. Where there is a number of these Saints in a Church, and often he stirs them up with Tauntings and Revilings, to mind it as a Duty, or to expect some great punishment from their angry Saint, if they slack in their Offerings, and many times he lays hold of Sickness in their Families, or Death of Cattle, telling them for want of their Offerings, and neglect of their Devotion and Charity, their slighted Saint is Angry, and has thus punished them, which frights them into large Contributions; on which, the Priests lives Fat, and laughs in his Sleave at their Simplicity and Ignorance. Yet for all this, he himself so little fears the Saint, that he will throw his Picture out of the Church, if the party who owned him dies, and none of his Kindred, or others, come at a set time, after Proclamation made, with their Offering, to own and new Patronize him, declaring such Saints as have none to offer to them, are useless and incumber the places in the Church, where others might stand who have Patrons that would bring Offerings; and the Picture being thrown out of the Church, is carried to the Town-House,

House, and then if the Friends of the Owner will have it again, they must pay the price that will be set upon it, which is usually more than it cost at first.

 The Indians are very Ignorant in their Devotion, and undiscerning in matters of Religion; for if they be asked any material point, their usual answer is, *It may be so for ought they know*; and indeed, those that should be their Spiritual Guides, labour to keep them as Ignorant as they can, that they may the better work their Ends on them, though when they come to Church, they outwardly in Jestures appear very Devout, and are careful when at the point of Death, to have a Confessor, and receive the Extream Unction, tho' some of the heads of them that are somewhat more Learned than the rest, are held secretly to practice Magyck, and traffick with the Devil; some affirm they can change their shapes into Beasts and Birds, and in that shape, some of them have been shot, yet as soon as Dead, they were in their own shape again; though this, I believe, may be a tale of some *Spaniards*, who had Murthered them, and forged it upon them to excuse their own Guilt. Yet this is certainly Recorded, that one *Gomez* and *Lopez*, Heads of *Indian* Tribes, and both in years, who had seemed very Devout in the Romish Religion, were justified by several Witnesses, to be seen Fighting on a Mountain; the first, in the shape of a Lyon, and the latter, in that of a Tyger, and when the first came home, he was much Bruised, Bitten and Wounded, and of it soon died; and though he confessed nothing of it to the Priest, who Confessed him, and gave him the Extream Unction, yet the latter by the Spanish Justice, was seized and Tryed, and hang'd as a Magycian, or a Practiser of Charms and Witchcraft. Its true, they had been a long time mortal Enemies, and the one might be guilty of the other's

death;

death; but as for their transforming their shapes, that I leave to be believed, or disbelieved, at your pleasure.

The Indians keep the Festivals of the Romish Church with great Mirth and Jolitry, Singing and Dancing; to conclude them after an Antick fashion, they act the Show of the Wise Mens coming to Christ at his Nativity, with their Offerings, &c. in their Churches or Chappels, and have every thing prepared there suitable to that purpose, making great Mirth and Feasting after it is over; and on such days the Priests fairs well, for there are few that offer not Money, but Fowl, Bacon, Coco-Nuts, Wax, Tapers, and the richest amongst them, are procured to present the Kings of the East, who fail not to provide Gold, Frankincense and Mirrh, and all this falls to the Priest's share who manages the Show.

Their Funerals are after the Romish Fashion, unless upon some Disgust they are refused Christian Burial, but that may be recalled for Money; they Marry, and live very peaceably in their Families, the Women being very Obedient to their Husbands, owning them to be their Lords and Rulers, thinking nothing they can do too much for them; they are very Fruitful in Children, and most commonly Healthy, so that though such multitudes of them have been purposely Destroyed, consumed in the Mines, and put in Lakes and Rivers, yet the Spaniards, who are not by half so Fruitful, are but a handful in Number to them, though these few have so broken their Spirits, and kept them under, that now they are of no Courage comparable to what Historians Report of their Ancesters, who disputed it in many well fought and Bloody Battles with the Spaniards, putting them hard to it before they could bring them under subjection, and settle what is now, by the Pope's Donation,

nation, the King of *Spain*'s claim in Sovereignty, as rightful Inheritance, tho' indeed their Orders are for kind usage to the *Indians*, and that they shall not be made Slaves, but have in a due proportion an equal Foot with the *Spaniards*; but these things are not minded, and their Complaints when made to the *Spanish* Magistrates as little regarded, for they have rarely any redress; but if they put any Abuse or Affront upon a *Spaniard*, they are severely punished, and compelled to make a three-fold restitution for any thing they defraud them of; beside Corporal Punishment, there lies an Appeal of Punishment in ordinary Cases, from their own Magistrates, to the Priest of the Town where they live, who determines the Sentence, whither after given by the Magistrates, the Criminal shall be Punished, or Acquitted; and if he be Punished, then the Priest has the ordering of it in the Church; and this the *Indians* seem to rejoyce at, saying, *their being Whipped by the Church Censure is for the good of their Souls, and cannot any ways redound to their Disgrace*; and whilst the Priest is in the Town, the *Indian* Magistrates dare not inflict Punishments, or lay Fines, without his Leave and Approbation, therefore sometimes they contrive to do it in his Absence; but this often displeases him, and makes him exert his Power, to cause those Magistrates to be whipped in the Church, who dared to do it in Contempt of him; and so Absolute are they over the Towns where they are placed as Curates, that the people dare not repine, but seem willingly to accept of what Stripes or Punishments are laid on them by him, foolishly conceiting that his Wisdom, Sentence, and Punishing Hand, is the Wisdom, Sentence and Hand of God, whom they have been Taught, is above all Princes, Judges, and Worldly Officers, and so that the Priests as his Ministers, are above all secular Power and Worldly Authority.

As

Europe, Asia, Africa, *and* America 233

As for their lying, it is only in Mantles wrapped about them, in their Houses, on the bare Ground, or some Mat or Quilt under it; the better sort have two Rooms on a Floar, without any other Story; the poor have but one; the Chimney is in the middle of the Kitchen, and a hole made for the Smoak to go out at the Top of the House, so that the Soot spreads the Roof, and they live in a continued Smoak, whilst their Fires last; their Meat they sell to the *Spaniards* is course, saving their Fowl, as Shins of Beef, sliced and dried in the Wind, then seasoned with Salt and Water, and rowled up in little hard lumps, which boyled, serves them in their Travels; they make likewise Frixola's of Turkey-Beans and Maize, of which, they have great plenty, and industriously seek for Hedge-Hogs in the Season, which they count a dainty Dish, and the *Spaniards* also Eat them, they Tasting like a Sucking-Pig; but whether this Creature is Flesh or not, or to be Eaten in Lent, there is yet a Dispute among the Priests; some allow the Eating of them, others contradict them; so nice are they in frivolous scruples, when in weightier things their Consciences are not touched. When the *Indians* get Venison in the Woods they Bury it, and cover it with Boughs, until it corrupts or stinks, then they parboyl it with a Herb like our Tansey, then dry it in the Wind, and afterwards in Smoak, and so boyl it well; and indeed it Eats very short, but according to their Dressing not over Savory; they have other sorts of Provisions, yet are but indifferent Cooks.

Their Liquor is chiefly Chochalet, made ordinary, with Coco-Nuts, and some other ingredients, but not Costly, with Spices and Perfumes, as the *Spaniards* make it; when they have a mind to be Drunk, they have another sort of Liquor,

R

quor, made of Coccos Molasses, and the juyce of Tobacco-Roots, which they keep in a Jarr a long time, till it has a strong stinking Scent, and then they get a great many privately together in a House to Drink it; for it is Prohibited them, because when they are Drunk, they are Raving, and in a manner Distracted, committing Outrages on their own Family and others; and for that reason they are Prohibited Wine also, unless as a Cordial, when they are Sick or Faint; yet the *Spaniards* entice them to their Houses, and privately Sell it them at Dear Rates, for their own great Gain; for they know when they are Drunk they will Spend all they have to the last Peney, if they can get Wine for it, not disputing the Score, how much soever they are Cheated; and when they are Drunk they Quarrel with them, their Money being first all Spent, and turn them into the Streets, so that the Stocks are combered with them, and on this particular account many *Spaniards* have got very great Estates.

This Country is often subject to the Plague of Locust, as well as violent Earthquakes, prodigeous Thunders and Lightnings, and in some places great innundations; yet by these Calamities the Priests gain much Money, by carrying the Saints in Procession, and Selling them Bread stamped with the Image of a Saint, to protect their Persons, Fields, and Houses, and much more Money for Masses, to the Saints, when the Calamities is over, by whose Intercession, they make the *Indians* believe, it ceased. Purgatory brings them a vast Income, few *Indians* Dying but leave so many Crowns, for so many Masses to be said for the good of their Souls.

Thus Reader having, as I think, given you a satisfactory Account of this Golden Country and
People,

People, tired with long Travel, I now prepare to return to my Native Country. You may remember I was got as far as *Havan*, and gave you also an Account of *Hispaniola*, &c. being then successfully Embarked with the Gallies, without meeting any opposition from Enemies, though we heard there were several abroad; we weathered two or three Storms, and lost but one Ship in the Gulf or Streights of *Bahama*, of 600 Tun, very Richly Laden; and having at length a prosperous Gale, came to *Cales* in 8 Weeks, from our last loosing Anchor. I had got something of Value in the *Indies*, which I Quilted up in my Cloaths and Bed, it lying in a small room; and after I had viewed the Town, (which is now Fairly Built, and well Fortified, though in the Reign of Queen *Elizabeth*, the *English* made themselves Masters of it, and almost destroyed it,) I went to visit my Merchant, who received me with great kindness, asking many Questions of my Travels, which in brief I resolved him, and made him sensible how desirous I was to return to my own Country; and after so tedious a Travel of almost encompassing the Globe of the Earth, there to repose my self, and keep my Promise with my Friends, who I knew would be overjoyed to see me return; he did not oppose it, but kept me off with delays, in laying before me the danger I was in, of being taken by the *French*, or *Barbary* Corsaries, that infested the Seas, unless I staid for a Convoy; I was ruled by him, and he entertained me with all the Civility imaginably, and no sooner the *English* Ships were to Sail, and such an opportunity offered, but he gave me notice of it, presented me with Rasins, Sugar, Oranges, Lemons, and a Cask of good Canary; sent several Letters by me to his Correspondents in *London*, and so we friendly took leave of each other. I soon agreed for my Passage and Diet, at the Master's Table, and so to be brief,

came

came safe to *London*; where, my Friends after so long absence, my Speech being much altered in Toneing the Languages of divers Nations where I had been, scarce knew me, though before to their great satisfaction I had written to them, from the *Downs*, of my safe Arrival there; but when they saw by evident looking, it was their Prodigal returned in safety. from strange Lands, after so much Toil, Fateigue, and Hardship, the Escaping so many dangers, &c. the Fatted Calf, was instantly Killed, great Feasting and Rejoycing ensued, which being moderated by time, and a little over, to avoid ten Thousand Questions, of where I had been, and the particulars of what I observed, at the Request of those that had done so well for me, and now so Lovingly received me, I took leisure time to Write what you have perused, hoping it will give my Country-Men as an entire satisfaction as I have had, in the undertaking and performing my Travels, and then no doubt but both of us will be well pleased.

www.ingramcontent.com/pod-product-compliance
Lightning Source LLC
Chambersburg PA
CBHW031739230426
43669CB00007B/400